An Orange
Revolution

Askold Krushelnycky

An Orange Revolution

A Personal Journey Through
Ukrainian History

Harvill Secker
LONDON

Published by Harvill Secker 2006

2 4 6 8 10 9 7 5 3

Copyright © Askold Krushelnycky 2006

Askold Krushelnycky has asserted his right under the Copyright, Designs
and Patents Act 1988 to be identified as the author of this work

First published in Great Britain in 2006 by
HARVILL SECKER
Random House, 20 Vauxhall Bridge Road,
London SW1V 2SA

Random House Australia (Pty) Limited
20 Alfred Street, Milsons Point, Sydney,
New South Wales 2061, Australia

Random House New Zealand Limited
18 Poland Road, Glenfield,
Auckland 10, New Zealand

Random House South Africa (Pty) Limited
Isle of Houghton, Corner of Boundary Road & Carse O'Gowrie,
Houghton 2198, South Africa

The Random House Group Limited Reg. No. 954009
www.randomhouse.co.uk

A CIP catalogue record for this book
is available from the British Library

ISBN 978 0436206234 (from January 2007)
ISBN 0436206234

Papers used by Random House are natural,
recyclable products made from wood grown in sustainable forests.
The manufacturing processes conform to the environmental
regulations of the country of origin

Typeset in Rotis Serif by SX Composing DTP, Rayleigh, Essex
Printed and bound in Great Britain by
Bookmarque Ltd, Croydon, Surrey

To my parents and their parents

ACKNOWLEDGMENTS

There are many people – too many to list them all here – who helped me in the writing of this book by sharing their knowledge and providing advice and encouragement. I am grateful to all of them. Particular thanks to my wife, Iryna Chalupa, whose exceptional knowledge of all things Ukrainian was an invaluable resource and whose advice and comments were always wise. Her smiles and support cheered me up and gave me confidence. I also want to thank Ivan Lozowy, Roman Kupchinsky, and Taras Kuzio for their friendly assistance and admirable insights into contemporary Ukraine.

This is the first time I have written a book and fortune dealt me an immensely fine hand in the form of my agent, Kevin Conroy Scott, and editor, Stuart Williams. Kevin's sage knowledge and boundless enthusiasm propelled the project forward. Stuart's astute advice was always given gracefully and the subsequent improvements demonstrated the finesse of his skill. I have learned a great amount from both of these new friends.

During my research for this project I read many books and articles which were informative and thought-provoking. Among the books that I found most helpful were Orest Subtelny's outstanding *Ukraine – A History,* Danylo Yanevsky's Ukrainian-language *Chronicle of the Orange Revolution*, and Jaroslav Koshiw's *Beheaded – The Killing of a Journalist.* Of considerable use have been an English-language Internet publication called *Action Ukraine Report*, edited by E. Morgan Williams, and the Ukrainian and Russian-language *Ukrayinska Prvada* Internet daily newsletter. Both provide comprehensive coverage and analysis of the country's news and the latter has been a brave champion of Ukrainians' fight for democracy.

CONTENTS

Chapter One

MOMENT OF TRUTH

In October 2004, Ukrainians knew that the forthcoming presidential election might determine whether their country finally emerged from centuries of slumber, cocooned in repression and tragedy. They had been talking about little else for a year, and all the omens were that it would be a very dirty election: people feared the regime would not shrink from using violence to prolong its corrupt and increasingly authoritarian rule. The sort of techniques used to usurp elections in Third World tinpot republics were already at work, with secret police intimidating and arresting opposition supporters and planting explosives and weapons on them. There would soon be an assassination attempt against the opposition leader and scares about a possible civil war.

When I returned to Ukraine to cover the first round of the election, the country was at a fever pitch of excitement and apprehension. I had covered most of Ukraine's presidential and parliamentary elections since the country became independent in 1991 when the Soviet Union disintegrated, but the previous elections had not generated a fraction of the emotion that now crackled in the air of the capital, Kyiv. Ukrainians recognised they were at a historic crossroads: these were the most important elections ever held in their country and the vote would determine whether Ukraine charted a path westwards towards democracy, or whether it would be subsumed in a putative new authoritarian Russian empire.

I had expected to be in Ukraine for several weeks. In the end I stayed for more than three months as the election unfolded into a tense and often dangerous drama that became known as the Orange Revolution. It was also a magnificent and exhilarating time. When television screens carry depressing daily news of war and terror, people crave evidence that the corrupt and the wicked are not invulnerable. The protests in Ukraine provided some inspiring proof. Viewers around the world who had never before heard of Ukraine watched avidly the courageous, graceful and good-natured display of people power. They identified with the protestors, the men, women and children, whose attentive, dignified faces were sometimes creased with laughter and at others streaked with tears; determined faces that seemed fearless but not ferocious. It was easy to admire these genial revolutionaries – they were not a mob baying for blood but ordinary, peaceful people from diverse backgrounds who had risked their safety to defend simple ideals of decency and fairness that were readily understood throughout the world.

My entire working life has been spent as a journalist and I have been privileged to cover stories about the hopes, and often savage fates, of people who grasped at ideals so difficult to define, yet instinctively easy to grasp, as 'democracy' and 'freedom'. I have seen civilians standing their ground against ranks of security personnel for these ideas in Kosovo, or enduring prolonged sieges and savage artillery poundings in Croatia and Bosnia. I have witnessed poorly armed and outnumbered fighters under assault from armies with superior weapons in Afghanistan, the Middle East and Nagorno-Karabakh, because they believed freedom and decency were worth making sacrifices for. I have always been captivated by these people of conviction and I have often been sympathetic to them. As events gathered speed in Ukraine in the autumn and winter of 2004 it seemed that violence was almost inevitable and the conflicts I had seen happen in many places elsewhere in the world would happen in Ukraine, the country of my parents.

I was born and raised in Britain but my parents instilled in me a lifelong fascination in, and affection for, Ukraine. Journalists are not supposed to take sides, but in a situation that is loaded with emotions it can be impossible not to, especially if one has come to know a place and its people closely. Objectivity, however, is more than uncritically allowing both sides to have their say, particularly when one of them is a proven liar. But then a journalist can be open to charges of subjectivity if he uses judgment and experience to select facts and comments that he believes accurately reflect, in the space and time available, the essence of what is happening. It is the way the selection is made that distinguishes between propaganda and an attempt at honest reporting. And whilst I have always tried to be an honest reporter, I have frequently been a far from dispassionate observer. The regime that had been in power for a decade in Ukraine was irredeemably bad and getting worse, and my sympathies were firmly with the opposition.

Much of what was playing out at the end of 2004 and the beginning of 2005 was unfinished business from thirteen years earlier when the former Soviet Union fell apart. Every post-Communist country has had to deal with the economic problems and corruption that were the legacy of Soviet rule. Those that had been Soviet 'satellites' like Poland, Hungary, and the Czech Republic rapidly reoriented themselves towards the West and fast addressed these problems. So did, for historical reasons, the three Baltic republics, Lithuania, Estonia and Latvia. For a host of reasons, though, not least economic, many of the former Soviet republics found it difficult to evade Russia's influence. In both Ukraine and Russia the tight Communist networks mutated into powerful oligarchic clans where government, corrupt business and organised crime intersected. Whatever the disputes between the two countries and their ruling clans, they were bound together by their very illegitimacy.

Georgia had been the first to attempt to complete that unfinished business with a popular revolution after a fraudulent election in 2003, which swept away President Eduard Shevardnadze. A year later the Ukrainian authorities were warning that force would be used to prevent a repetition of 'the Georgian scenario'. However, millions of opposition supporters were preparing to challenge the regime's presumption that elections could still be run according to Stalin's precept that it is not important how people vote, but only who counts the vote.

The stakes in this election were, therefore, immensely high. The outcome would determine not only whether Ukraine jettisoned a corrupt and increasingly sinister regime but also if it broke free of its former colonial master, Russia. A truly independent Ukraine would also mean a shift in the traditional balance of power in Europe. Instead of Russia being the undisputed leader in Eastern Europe, a strong Ukraine would alter the political centre of gravity and attract other former Soviet republics tired of Moscow's bullying. And failure for its policies in Ukraine would not just bruise the Kremlin's pride but strike a fatal blow at its ambition to weld together and lead an eastern equivalent of the European Union.

Many people in Western Europe had either never heard of Ukraine or would have been unable to locate it on a map before the Orange Revolution. However, Ukraine is the largest country in Europe after Russia, with a population of some forty-eight million. Millions more Ukrainians now live outside their country. Some ten million have long settled in Russia and other former Soviet republics. An estimated seven million have sought work in Russia or Western Europe since independence but are eager to return if conditions improve. The US and Canada are home to the descendants of millions of Ukrainians who emigrated in an earlier era but still proudly recall their Ukrainian origin. A large community of Ukrainian émigrés, mostly refugees from the fallout of World War Two, settled in Britain. There are other Ukrainian communities scattered throughout Western Europe, Latin America, Australia and New Zealand.

Ukraine was, after Russia, the most important component of the old Soviet Union. Agriculture thrives on its rich black earth, which had for centuries earned the region the label of the 'breadbasket of Europe'. Buried below its fertile soil lies coal, oil, gas, iron ore, precious minerals and metals like titanium, and one of the planet's largest known reserves of uranium. Ukraine was also a huge industrial powerhouse producing steel, aluminium, building materials, aircraft, cars, trucks, trams and household wares such as televisions, radios and refrigerators. These consumer goods, though, were often shoddily made; the televisions, for example, had a disquieting habit of exploding and engulfing viewers in flames. Much more stringent quality-control standards applied to the items manufactured in Ukraine's large slice of the Soviet Union's military-industrial complex, the all-enveloping enterprise to equip its giant war machine. Here things did not usually explode spontaneously, although in 1986 in the closely linked atomic energy sector, Ukraine's Chernobyl power station became the world's biggest nuclear disaster whose tragic aftermath lingers throughout the region.

The military-industrial complex still employs more than three hundred thousand people. At its height millions were employed directly or indirectly in the manufacture of cutting-edge equipment including fighter and bomber aircraft, tanks, missiles, anti-aircraft and aircraft-detection systems, and the electronics, optics and other sophisticated components to make them work. Before he entered politics, Leonid Kuchma, Ukraine's president for a decade and whose corrupt regime was the target of the Orange Revolution, had run Yuzhmash, the ugly acronym for the innocuously named Southern Machine Building Facility. At the heavily guarded, sprawling complex in south-east Ukraine, Kuchma presided over the manufacture of rockets to propel nuclear warheads to targets in Western Europe or the US in the event of war against NATO.

When the Soviet Union broke apart in 1991, nuclear weapons deployed in Ukrainian territory made the newly independent country the world's third largest nuclear power, behind Russia and the US but ahead of China, Britain, France, and newcomers Israel, India and Pakistan. Pressure from the West, and Ukrainians' own repugnance towards all things nuclear after the tragedy of Chernobyl, meant that Ukraine became the first ever country to give up its nuclear arsenal. The missiles were handed over to Russia, thus transferring them from the custody of a people who last launched an invasion more than a millennium ago, to an unstable country whose dwindling superpower status depended solely on its rusting nuclear arsenal, a threat which remains.

Apart from its industrial and agricultural value, Ukraine was an enormous reserve of human resources for the Soviet Union. Her people, with their reputation for hard work and intelligence, were deployed all over the USSR, often without much choice. Ukrainians furnished a high proportion of the

Soviet Union's intellectual elite, scientists to design and manufacture the Soviet war machine, and much of the human material to man it. The Soviet forces had a disproportionately high number of Ukrainian warrant officers, the mainstay of any army. It had long been clear that the Kremlin needed Ukrainians as fodder for any serious war against the West.

Russia found it hard to accept the loss of empire and many dreamed of reviving it. Many also found it difficult to reconcile themselves to the notion of an independent Ukraine, not only because she was an important economic asset, but also because she was a vital component of Russia's myths about herself. The enormous psychological wrench of Ukraine's departure and the prospect of her drifting still further from Moscow's sphere of influence were painful. Russia's president, Vladimir Putin, a former KGB colonel who had won a second term of office in 2004, months before the Ukrainian election, often harked back publicly to the days of Soviet glory. His political support grew whenever he hinted at a resurgence of Russian power and his emerging ambition was to reconstitute a new multinational union led by Moscow.

Russia's role – whether as master or equal – in Ukraine's future came to be one of the dominant election themes and each option had its champion. The Ukrainian prime minister, Viktor Yanukovych, the regime's anointed candidate, was for a closer relationship with Russia. Putin backed him and committed huge resources to try to ensure his victory. The opposition leader, Viktor Yushchenko, was a hate figure for the Kremlin, being openly in favour of membership of the European Union and NATO. Yushchenko also wanted to purge his country of a regime which enriched its leading supporters while using increasingly ruthless means to suppress anyone challenging it. Opinion polls and informal conversations with Ukrainians both showed that the over-whelming majority of voters, regardless of who they supported, expected the government to use intimidation, dirty tricks, lies, fraud, and possibly violence, to try to ensure Yanukovych would win.

The predictions turned out to be accurate. Everyone knew that the government was capable of violence, yet most were still shocked when Yushchenko was poisoned in a clear attempt by his political enemies either to kill him or render him incapable of fighting the election.

There was widespread rigging during the first round of the election on 31 October, which whittled down the twenty-four presidential hopefuls to two. In the three weeks before the second round, the level of intimidation rose exponentially as the regime prepared to steal the presidency for its candidate. Sure enough, as the run-off on 21 November proceeded, there were reports from across the country that Ukrainian and foreign election monitors had been denied access to polling stations and other observers had been threatened or beaten up. Some of the incidents were captured by television cameras. There were many reports of thousands of paid Yanukovych supporters using special documents to vote repeatedly as they were bussed to different polling stations. Independent exit polls showed that Yushchenko had won, but as the official results began to be announced they told an entirely different story; it was obvious the government was preparing to declare Yanukovych the winner.

I waited to see how people would react. In past Ukrainian elections the electorate had been eerily indifferent about their vote being manipulated. Election rigging was accepted as an immutable part of their reality in much the same way that the poverty that enveloped most people, in contrast to the fabulous wealth of those associated with the corrupt government, was grudgingly accepted as a part of life. But during the long months of this election campaign a different and defiant atmosphere had emerged. People were exasperated, they wanted a change and did not seem afraid to say so. In the critical hours when it became clear the government was willing to impose a fraudulent result on its people, however, I wondered whether the new mood would generate sufficient resistance to overcome the government successfully.

On the day following the election, people started gathering early in Kyiv's Independence Square. They listened to opposition speakers and watched as election results were flashed up on a giant television screen.

An opposition organisation with a predominantly youthful membership, Pora, named after the Ukrainian word *pora*, meaning 'it's time' or 'the time has come', had vowed that it would fill the streets with protestors if there was electoral fraud. Now they began to make good on their promise and by the time Yushchenko arrived to address the crowd, Independence Square was crowded and more people were pouring in.

Yushchenko did not have to convince anyone to come out on to the streets – people were already committed to a fight. As the evening of 22 November wore on, with rumours of an imminent government crackdown, the mood of defiance hardened and before the night was out hundreds of thousands of opposition supporters filled the streets. Something extraordinary had begun: the outcome of the contest was so important that the election had already taken on some of the characteristics of a liberation struggle.

Over the previous decade, the government of President Leonid Kuchma had become accustomed to periodic protest by Ukrainians. The regime had never before felt seriously threatened and fended off these outbursts with barely concealed contempt. Demonstrators demanding the removal of a corrupt leader or an explanation for the murder of an opposition figure were routinely fobbed off with transparent lies or, more often, simply ignored. On the few occasions demonstrations became too irritating, the paramilitaries were sent in to show who was in charge.

The government did not expect the demonstrations of 22 November 2004 to be any different from previous ones. While they felt that thousands of opposition supporters might turn out to protest against its massive fraud operation in the previous day's election, they also clearly believed the protestors could be dispersed within a matter of days.

They were wrong, and the crowd, decked out in the opposition's orange campaign colour, kept growing. More people defied the freezing temperature, swelling the rally and listening attentively to politicians and opposition activists speak from the stage. The protestors sang along and danced to music played by Ukraine's best-known rock artists who showed their solidarity through performances that raised morale and took away the chill. Entire families turned out with parents clasping babies and younger members looking after older relatives on the slippery pavements. A young man in a wheelchair, a long orange ribbon fastened to its armrests, skilfully tipped his front wheels skywards and rocked his chair in time to the beat of the music.

Adding to the swirl of colour and the noises of impassioned voices and musical instruments were columns of cars winding through the streets with passengers perched precariously out of the windows, waving orange or national flags as the drivers blared their horns in the triple cadence signifying three syllables: YUSH-CHEN-KO.

More opposition supporters arrived in the following days

from other parts of the country by train, by car, by plane. Some coming by road were turned away at police road-blocks. Others used cunning to get through; one simple ruse was to display the blue and white campaign colours of Yanukovych, whose emblems were otherwise almost completely absent in the capital.

Within hours of the start of the protest, tents were pitched on the wide main boulevard. Within days several hundred tents had sprung up, supervised by the well-organised Pora, who had stores of tents standing by and thick polystyrene mats to keep the cold at bay. Tented enclaves of anti-government protestors had become a tradition in Ukraine over the preceding years. Some had been violently dismantled by the paramilitaries who had clubbed the inhabitants indiscriminately. The Pora leaders vowed that this time they would fight back against any attack.

The thousands of inhabitants of the swiftly expanding tented city were mostly young people in their teens and twenties, much the same age as many of the heavily armed special police detachments deployed around and inside the capital. But there were also plenty of older men. Nearly everyone in Ukraine and the former Soviet Union had served in the military as conscripts. Some of the new campers wore camouflage uniforms and army boots. Some were veterans of the savage Soviet war in Afghanistan and had seen action amidst its rugged, mountainous, unrelenting terrain. They had been forced to fight a war for an empire that few had loved. Now they were ready to fight for their own country.

At times the orange sea of people was several hundred thousand strong, sometimes half a million, at others more than a million. By some mysterious social alchemy, the rally gradually evolved into something more powerful than a long-running protest. The mood changed from one of outrage and indignation into a commitment to resist and overcome. Apprehension about how the authorities might react remained, but fear faded. There was a realisation that a momentous psychological barrier had been breached; the return to rule of a mendacious and sinister regime became unimaginable.

Opposition supporters were pleasantly surprised to discover how many others shared their euphoric feelings. That sense of common purpose and readiness to support one another, the pleasure of speaking freely and from the heart, was seductive and binding. It lifted the spirit and provided an impassioned determination. The mass protests that had begun in the capital of one of Europe's largest but lesser known countries had now transformed into something that was called 'revolution'.

As the regime's traditional underhand tactics to control opposition failed, there were calls for using force to crush the demonstrations under the pretext of avoiding bloodshed, terrorism, anarchy or civil war. The paramilitary police blocking off both ends of the street containing the Ukrainian presidential administration building were tense and braced themselves for trouble. They were mostly young conscripts, clad in black uniforms with riot shields and batons. Snowflakes melted on the holsters containing their automatic pistols. Their equipment glistened in the glare of the television camera lights.

Facing them were some of the opposition supporters who had surrounded key government buildings. The young policemen had been told that among these protestors were people of violence and even terrorists.

Among the protestors was Ihor Tokarivsky, a twenty-three-year-old lawyer from the West Ukrainian city of Lviv. He was one of thousands from the city who responded to calls from the opposition to come to the capital. Tall, slim, with a big grin, Ihor was there because he thought every person who joined the protests contributed to transforming their country. He came from a family which over the generations had struggled and suffered to make life better. His grandfather had been a member of a Ukrainian guerrilla army which fought the Germans during World War Two and the Communists after the war. Ihor looked into the faces of the police, many his age, many even younger, and wondered if they would really attack him and the other protestors. 'We'll see,' he said. 'Anyway, we can't step back now.'

In Kyiv and throughout the country there were millions of people who had decided they would not step back. Their courageous actions over the tense days that followed proved a turning point in Ukrainian history, one with a potentially profound effect on Europe and beyond.

Chapter Two

ACCIDENTS OF HISTORY

Ukrainian history and my own history converged at Independence Square in the centre of Kyiv, and there was nowhere else in the world I would rather have been that winter.

Most of the crowd were actually on Kyiv's main boulevard, Khreschatyk, which adjoins Independence Square, whose name was soon clipped affectionately to 'the Square', *maidan* in Ukrainian. The Maidan very swiftly acquired symbolic meaning. It became the locus for the hopes and prayers of millions, a code that brimmed with emotion and a determination to change the country. To go to the Maidan was to answer a moral call to arms, and meant you were no longer prepared to remain silent; you had taken your place at the barricades and were willing to stand up for freedom, however perilous that might be.

I had been raised in another country and in another culture but Ukraine and its culture were precious to me. I was born in London, the first generation of Britons with this tongue-twisting surname. My parents were forced out of Ukraine by World War Two, which littered their country with millions of corpses. They met in Britain where they both arrived after the war as penniless refugees in a strange land, unable to speak English. I am proud of Britain because it offered my parents – and tens of thousands of others – safety and an opportunity to make of their lives what they would. Most, like my parents, did well. They worked diligently, learned English, and within ten or fifteen years had good jobs and had bought their own homes.

Hundreds of thousands of Ukrainians, like many other peoples from Central and Eastern Europe, had been forced out of their homes by the war. Most Ukrainians who stayed in the West chose to go to the US and Canada where substantial Ukrainian communities already existed. These were people who had emigrated in the late nineteenth and early twentieth centuries tempted by the cheap, sometimes free, land being offered to those who were willing to clear the virgin territory and farm it. They were tough pioneers who struggled against the climate, terrain and, sometimes, prejudice. They zealously embraced their new countries but did not forget their homeland. Immigrants often transported little bags of seed grain, worn around their necks like the crosses hanging there, so that the first crop they harvested would have something of Ukraine in it.

Other Ukrainians had settled in the US after World War One, the Bolshevik Revolution of 1917, and a failed war of Ukrainian independence in the years that followed. The immigrants built meeting places for their communities, and Ukrainian schools and churches to preserve their culture. As they prospered they gained influence and learned to play the political system. Canada's policy – originally prompted by the need for compromise between British and French colonisers – of allowing a diversity of languages to flourish, meant that Ukrainian was, and still is, offered at state schools in regions inhabited by people of Ukrainian background, many now fourth- or fifth-generation Canadians.

There were no organised Ukrainian communities to speak of in Britain before the war and those who chose to go there demonstrated a great talent for constructing them from scratch. Using funds they collected among themselves, they bought buildings in the towns and cities where they lived to use as social and cultural centres. They also bought churches, as religious faith – Ukrainian Orthodox and Ukrainian Catholic – was a mainstay of their identity. They were highly politicised émigrés, unwilling exiles from their native land, and most yearned to return. They wanted to preserve their Ukrainian identity and pass it on to their children. I was the eldest of my parents' three children, and we were all taught Ukrainian before English. All my little friends were, like me, of Ukrainian origin and spoke only Ukrainian. It was a great shock on my first day at school to learn the rest of the country spoke an entirely different language that I knew nothing of. On Saturdays we attended a Ukrainian school at the social centre, and on weekday evenings we sang in Ukrainian choirs, practised often fiendishly atheltic Ukrainian traditional dancing, and played in Ukrainian orchestras. We led parallel lives. I played a violin in the orchestra at my English grammar school and a mandolin in the Ukrainian orchestra. Both are strung identically – G, D, A, E – except the violin has one set of strings, played with a bow, while the mandolin has two strings of each, plucked with a plectrum. The transition from one instrument to another is easy and I played both with an equally hideous lack of skill.

My parents' story was fairly typical of the Ukrainian refugees who settled in Britain. They were both born at a time when Ukrainian lands were divided between several masters after the Treaty of Versailles following World War One settled an uneasy peace upon Europe. My father, Ivan, and his sister, Leonida, were born Soviet citizens near the Black Sea port city of Odessa in the largest of the ethnic Ukrainian territories, the Ukrainian Soviet Socialist Republic, part of the Soviet Union then ruled by Joseph Stalin. My mother was born a Polish citizen near the city that is now called Ivano-Frankivsk, in West Ukraine, but what was then Stanyslaviv in East Poland. Another fragment of ethnic Ukrainian territory lay in Czechoslovakia, which like Poland had emerged as an independent country from the collapse of the Austro-Hungarian Empire. Ukrainian-populated lands were also incorporated into Romania.

This awkward and doomed arrangement of peoples arose from the destruction of two empires, the Austro-Hungarian in Central Europe and the Russian in Eastern Europe. The Ukrainians in Austro-Hungary had, like Poland and Czechoslovakia, made plans to declare independence on the eve of the empire's collapse as its defeat, and that of its ally, Germany, loomed in the autumn of 1918. On the night of 31 October, Ukrainian soldiers from the disintegrating imperial army occupied key buildings and hoisted Ukrainian flags in the predominantly ethnic Ukrainian region called Galicia by the Poles and Halychyna by Ukrainians. The region's most important city, Lviv, was, on 1 November, declared the capital of the newly formed West Ukrainian National Republic. Unfortunately, Halychyna was also claimed by Poles preparing to re-establish their state.

My mother's father, Volodymyr Zolotnycky, thirteen years old at the time, described how he rode the train to school that morning as an Austrian citizen and soldiers, unaware of the previous night's momentous events, still wore the insignia of empire on their uniforms. However, returning later that day he said there was a mood of both apprehension and elation as people learned about the independence declaration and the Ukrainians among them, my grandfather included, proudly called themselves Ukrainian citizens. To his astonishment, most of the soldiers in his carriage had already replaced their Austrian insignia with an ancient Ukrainian national symbol, the trident.

Meanwhile, Ukrainians in what had been the Russian Tsarist Empire declared various degrees of independence from Russia following the overthrow of the tsars in February 1917. That initial uprising, prompted by the slaughter and economic ruin brought about by World War One, spawned a ramshackle, ineffective government which was itself blown away by the whirlwind savagery of Lenin's Bolshevik Revolution. It was only after the Communist forces unleashed a reign of terror and demonstrated they had no time for any notions of real Ukrainian autonomy that the Ukrainian National Republic was proclaimed in January 1918. Composed mainly of idealistic but inept young Leftists, the new Ukrainian government was riven by internal dispute. Many of the government members were so eager to build a new world, free from war, that they opposed the principle of a standing army despite being surrounded by enemies. Around three hundred thousand former Tsarist soldiers of Ukrainian origin had sworn allegiance to the new government, but the politicians prevaricated for so long about what to do that the soldiers mostly drifted off to their homes. The government was therefore helpless to defend itself against assaults by 'Red' Russian Communist and 'White' Russian anti-Communist forces, who both opposed Ukrainian independence. Havoc reigned as the Reds and Whites used Ukraine as a battleground for their own civil war.

Appeals to the outside world for help yielded little sympathy. Britain and France were more interested in a victory for the Whites, which would restore the Russian Empire and remove the Bolshevik threat, than independence for Ukraine. As the young, floundering government faced destruction by the Red Army, it made a deal with Germany to provide millions of tons of food in exchange for protection. Soon, though, Berlin became dismayed at the Ukrainian government's incompetence, and installed a dashing Tsarist general from an aristocratic Ukrainian family, Pavlo Skoropadsky, as their puppet dictator. Skoropadsky was relatively benign as military dictators go, and was responsible for a number of reforms that set about solidifying a distinct Ukrainian identity for the new republic, but he quickly grew unpopular and was swept away at the end of 1918 when Germany lost the war, and was replaced by another patriotic Ukrainian former Tsarist officer, Symon Petliura, a Socialist.

Petliura was more popular than Skoropadsky and, as a soldier, appreciated that ideas were empty words without the muscle to back them up. But his idealistic predecessors had squandered the opportunity to build a formidable army while Skoropadsky had relied on German arms, and there was no time in which to build forces that could withstand those now ranged against Ukraine. Petliura, the Ukrainian National Republic and its enfeebled army stood no chance as the country descended into terror. The government lost control of communications and the railways, and had no bureaucratic system in the towns and villages to carry out its instructions even if there had been some way of transmitting them. It could not provide its citizens with food, security, fuel, electricity, or water. Most of the Ukrainian population simply tried to survive by remaining inconspicuous. The unpredictability of the violence added an extra layer of horror. Without any of the modern means that make the transmission of news almost instantaneous, people in the countryside did not even know much of the time who was in control of their country. As in the days of Mongol invasions from the east, hordes of heavily armed men on horse and foot would descend on largely defenceless communities without warning or provocation, leaving a trail of killing, pillaging and devastation. The fighting was particularly barbaric: execution of military and civilian prisoners was frequent, often accompanied by torture.

It was not only the Reds and Whites that clashed against each other and fought against the Ukrainian army on the republic's territory. The victorious British and French allies sent troops to Ukrainian territory to bolster the Whites against the Communist forces. For good measure, two large (and dozens of tiny) anarchist armies, many with cavalry formations, prowled around the country.

In January 1919 the two Ukrainian republics merged and the well-disciplined and battle-hardened West Ukrainian troops transformed the less efficient and smaller numbers of the East Ukrainian army into a more promising force. By autumn of 1919 they were fending off attacks by the Whites and the Poles and facing an invasion by a Soviet Russian army of one and a half million men. Then another enemy struck, one that could not be defeated by guns or courage. Typhoid killed or disabled most of them. Fewer than ten per cent of the fifty thousand who had left their homes the previous year remained fit to fight. Many of those who survived had no chance to flee to West Ukraine, now under Polish control, before the invading Soviet army, which grew to an estimated three and a half million men, drove out the last of the Ukrainian and White military formations. Amongst those still lying in makeshift hospital beds when the Communists seized most of Ukraine was my father's father, Teofil.

Grandfather Teofil's family was from an area called Ternopilschyna in West Ukraine, adjoining the region where my mother's family came from. Both families were from the middle class that in the mid nineteenth century had helped transform Ukrainian national consciousness into a modern movement for greater autonomy and, ultimately, independence. Among them were teachers, priests, artists, soldiers, junior civil servants, journalists, and a world-class opera singer, Solomiya Krushelnycka.

Teofil had been a teenage recruit in the Austro-Hungarian army during World War One. His father was also a soldier but in a different Austro-Hungarian regiment. I have a photograph of them when they met by chance on what is now the Croatian coast. The photograph fascinates me because more than seventy years later I was to travel along that same dramatically beautiful coastline many times while reporting the Balkans conflict in the nineties. When the West Ukrainian army travelled east, Teofil and two of his brothers went with it. One, Pavlo, was killed in battle, one was unscathed and managed to return home, but Teofil fell ill with typhoid and was still in a hospital near Odessa when the independent Ukrainian state was defeated by the Communists. Soon afterwards the Soviet and Polish authorities signed a peace deal that left him on the wrong side of a heavily patrolled river border to his homeland in the ethnic Ukrainian lands assigned to Poland.

Grandfather Teofil was not to see his home again until after the outbreak of World War Two. He concealed his past as a Ukrainian soldier, found a job at a state farm and later married Vera, a Belarusian. My father and his sister, my aunt Leonida, who was three years older, were born and grew up in a country where Stalin was tightening his grip and transforming fear into terror. At school they were taught the Communist version of history and a fearsome new morality which placed unquestioning loyalty to the system above everything else. Every schoolchild knew about fourteen-year-old Pavlik Morozov whose behaviour was held up as a model throughout the USSR. Little Pavlik was such a devoted young Communist that he denounced his father to the authorities for criticising Stalin. Morozov senior was shot while his son became a Soviet martyr after his own relatives killed him. Statues of the spunky lad wearing one of those stern, gazing-into-the-future countenances beloved of Soviet and Nazi monuments were erected all over the USSR. But at home, in whispered conversations to prevent them being overheard by informants for Stalin's secret police, my father and aunt learned a patriotic and truer version of their country's history.

The infamous German-Soviet non-aggression pact of August 1939 between Stalin and Hitler made it possible for Teofil and his family to return to his home town of Buchach in Ternopilschyna, which between the wars had been a part of East Poland. The deal, also called the Molotov–Ribbentrop Pact after Stalin's and Hitler's foreign ministers, consisted of a promise not to attack each other for at least ten years and a trade agreement, but also secret protocols to divide Central and Eastern Europe between the two dictators. Germany was to march into Poland and take most of that country while Stalin's forces grabbed East Poland and took control of Latvia, Estonia, Lithuania, Finland and part of Romania. Britain and France had vowed to declare war against Germany if Hitler invaded Poland. Hitler was confident he could win against Poland, France and Britain, but even he was sceptical of victory if he had to fight the Soviet Union at the same time. The agreement precluded that risk, and a week later, on 1 September 1939, the Nazis launched their *Blitzkrieg* against Poland and World War Two began. The Poles fought back bravely but help from Britain and France did not arrive, and when Soviet forces invaded from the east on 17 September it was all over.

The Soviet Union stood aside from the war that now

engulfed Europe. After victory in Poland, Germany swiftly defeated France and effectively gained control of all mainland Western Europe. For nearly two years Britain battled alone against the Nazis whilst, under the trade agreements between Moscow and Berlin, Stalin supplied Germany's war machine with oil, raw metals, and other essential goods. This is one of the many awkward episodes that were omitted or glossed over in Communist versions of history, and continued to be so even in more recent Russian versions. It is one of the reasons that the Kremlin and diehard Communists do not use the term 'World War Two' but prefer to talk about 'The Great Patriotic War' which only began in June 1941 when the Germans broke the pact and launched a surprise attack on the Soviet Union. On the eve of commemorations to mark the sixtieth anniversary of the end of World War Two in 2005, President Putin still refused to apologise to countries that had suffered because of the agreement between Stalin and Hitler.

In German-occupied Poland, the Nazis ruthlessly crushed any resistance and set about executing Polish intellectuals and patriots. The Soviet occupation forces did the same to Ukrainians and Poles in the areas they now controlled. One of Stalin's justifications for invading East Poland was to unite its considerable Ukrainian and Belarusian populations with their compatriots in the Ukrainian and Belarusian Soviet Socialist Republics. A month after the invasion, the new Communist authorities swiftly organised sham elections showing people had voted overwhelmingly to join the Soviet Union. Most of East Poland was incorporated into an expanded Ukrainian Soviet Socialist Republic and the old borders disappeared.

So as one war had taken my grandfather Teofil away from Buchach, the beginning of another allowed him to return to his home. His enforced stay of nearly two decades in Odessa meant he missed the era of Polish rule, but it was a much-changed land he came back to.

Buchach is a small town in a hilly landscape. It was certainly a settlement in the fourteenth century but may have been inhabited from as early as the twelfth century. From one of the hill crests the crumbled remains of an ancient fortress peer down at the town like a weary old soldier. Pretty and ornate buildings, dating from the days of the Austro-Hungarian Empire, survive among the cobbled streets, including an impressive church, monastery and a town hall designed by Italian architects imported by the Habsburg rulers.

The splendid buildings reflected the town's prosperity founded on a variety of crafts. The foremost trade was shoe and boot making, the leather produced at the town's own tannery. There was a thriving meat industry which exported goods to Vienna, there were furriers and tailors, and the town enjoyed a reputation for its skilled craftsmen. Buchach was the only place in West Ukraine which manufactured richly woven carpets of oriental silks, sometimes embroidered with gold thread. Most of the exotic product was exported to Western Europe and the US; few locals could afford to buy the carpets, which cost more for a few square metres than the price of a modest car.

Although the population of Halychyna was predominantly Ukrainian, most Ukrainians lived outside the big towns and cities where the majority of the inhabitants were Poles and Jews. The official Polish statistics for 1939 show that of the population of Buchach, nearly half, 5,150 people, were Jews, 3,550 were Poles, and 2,400 were Ukrainians. My father's family returned in 1940. They arrived in a region where relations between the three communities had always been far from harmonious, each harbouring resentments and prejudices against the others. During the interwar years, the relationship between Ukrainians and Poles had become more bitter and dangerous.

Poland was supposed to give its Ukrainian population a measure of autonomy when the Treaty of Versailles awarded it control over Halychyna. However, Warsaw soon gave up any pretence of doing that and introduced a harsh policy to stamp out Ukrainian identity by suppressing political and cultural organisations. In the same way Russian governments worked to 'Russify' Ukrainians and belittled or denied the existence of a separate Ukrainian culture, so the new Polish government tried to 'Polonise' Ukrainians on its territory. Ukrainians who agreed to this process found life easier in terms of receiving higher education, government employment, or getting ahead in business. Sometimes the attempt at Polonisation was conducted more harshly: there were raids by mounted forces who rode into Ukrainian villages, smashed up community meeting halls and disrupted church services. It was a surprising and shortsighted way to behave for a Poland only recently restored after having been dismembered in 1795 by Russia, Germany and Austro-Hungary. With such a proud history of courageous patriotic struggle themselves, Poles should have known that oppression seldom produces the desired results and would only arouse indignation and determined resistance among Ukrainians.

As antipathy towards the Polish authorities developed, nationalist organisations sprang up to keep the fight for independence alive in both the Soviet Union and what was now East Poland where, as Moscow's methods of repression were incomparably more ruthless than Warsaw's, it was easier for them to take root and spread.

The most important of these was the Organisation of Ukrainian Nationalists, which traced its beginnings to groups formed by exiled officers from the armies of the briefly independent Ukrainian republic who were determined to fight another day. The OUN split in two, the most significant part led by a young firebrand called Stepan Bandera. Organised in secret cells, members underwent ideological training, acquired the practical skills needed for the national uprising they planned during a European conflict they believed was inevitable after Hitler's accession to power in 1933, and carried out terrorist attacks against Polish government officials and politicians.

Elsewhere the first organised armed opposition to Fascist expansion came from Ukrainian nationalist groups in the Carpathian easternmost part of Czechoslovakia. When, in March 1939, German troops moved in to devour all the Czech lands, Hitler's Hungarian allies entered Carpatho-Ukraine which, in a hopeless act of courage, declared full independence. Hundreds of Ukrainians died in bitter fighting against overwhelming numbers of Hungarian troops. The conflict received scant attention in the West but struck a powerful chord for Ukrainians elsewhere, who saw it as heralding the beginning of a new phase in the fight for Ukrainian independence.

When World War Two began, many of the Polish units fell back eastwards, not suspecting that on 17 September Stalin would send his army to stab them in the back and crush any chance of continued resistance. In the chaos, the OUN scooped up many of the weapons abandoned by the Polish army and hid them in secret stores. The organisation had around twenty thousand members in 1939 and continued to grow.

Amidst the turmoil and uncertainty, Teofil and his family

moved into a small house with a garden stretching down to the river Strypa which bisects the town. My father and his sister enrolled in a local school while their father worked at a factory producing household goods.

They had all experienced life under Stalin with its succession of denunciations, repressions and murderous purges, but the inhabitants of the freshly annexed territories now received a savage introduction to Soviet rule. Immediately after the unification of Ukraine, Soviet authorities began mass executions and deportations of any possible sources of opposition, whether from Ukrainians or Poles. One of the most notorious and extensively chronicled Soviet atrocities was the execution at Katyn Forest, in what is now Belarus, of some fifteen thousand Polish army officers who surrendered to the Soviets. Many other Ukrainians and Poles met similarly cruel deaths. Hundreds of thousands were deported to camps in Siberia and Central Asia over the next twenty-one months. Aside from military officers, prime targets were the prominent members of the middle class who foster ideas of patriotism and occupy key jobs that enable a state to function: teachers, lecturers, doctors, writers, artists, clergy, local government officials, landowners and farmers, shopkeepers and businessmen. These were the backgrounds of many on both sides of my family, and like thousands of other Ukrainian families, both my mother and my father lost relatives who were deported to camps in Siberia. A few returned many years later but most were never heard of again.

Others were killed nearer home by the NKVD Soviet secret police. Throughout the first Soviet occupation, thousands of Ukrainians were taken for interrogation to prisons in the biggest city, Lviv, and to smaller prisons elsewhere. Many never emerged and were killed and buried in mass graves.

One of Grandfather Teofil's brothers, Andriy, was arrested at the end of May 1941 on suspicion of being a Ukrainian nationalist. On a burning hot day, he and other prisoners were marched along dusty roads towards a prison thirty miles from Buchach. An eyewitness in a village they passed through said the prisoners were forbidden to drink water from a well there, but Andriy, parched with thirst, moved to take a drink and was shot along with two others. The bodies, with nothing to identify them, were left where they fell and the villagers buried them. Years later my aunt pieced together what happened to her uncle but has not been able to locate the graves.

When the Germans launched their surprise invasion of the Soviet Union on 2 June 1942, the NKVD slaughtered its prisoners before retreating. They were still being murdered in dungeons and courtyards in Lviv and other locations only hours before the first German military vehicles rolled in. Distraught relatives rushed into the prisons as soon as the NKVD left and discovered the corpses of their loved ones, men and women, old and young. The most recently killed were still in their cells but hundreds of others were found crammed into basements or burial pits. Most had been executed in the NKVD's favoured manner, a shot in the back of the head, but others had been tortured, their skulls smashed in with hammers or clubs, or they had been hacked about by meat cleavers. Other burial sites could not be located or excavated for almost another half a century until Ukraine became independent in 1991.

In November 1990 I went to the town of Drohobych, seventy miles south-west of Lviv, where a mass killing ground had been discovered in what had been the area's NKVD headquarters from 1939 to 1941 and again after the Soviets returned in 1944. In the last years of the Soviet era the building had been a teacher-training college, its students unaware of the horror that lay just beneath them. The excavation was led by Yaroslav Lukych, then sixty years old and whose older brother had been killed in 1945 after the resumption of massacres with the return of Soviet rule. Lukych and his assistants, all volunteers, had unearthed more than 450 sets of remains and the results of this archaeology of terror were laid out in the courtyard in neat rows of skulls and bones on long shelves, of the kind a keen gardener would have in his potting shed.

It had been possible, said Lukych, to identify only a handful of the victims because their clothes had disintegrated and few had any personal belongings that might have provided clues. Many of the skulls, though, still contained the bullet that killed them. Lukych explained to me that the .455 calibre lead bullets without a metal cladding had been developed specially by the NKVD for efficient short-range execution. The bullet made a small entry hole and the lead then expanded inside causing a massive wound and making death near certain. The bullet was supposed not to exit from the skull, thus avoiding messy blood splashback.

I wondered what the last thoughts of the doomed were as they were forced to kneel and stare at a pit filled with the corpses of those murdered minutes before. Fear, panic, resignation, anger, frustration, sadness? I have also puzzled over what kind of people – scientists, engineers, and perhaps doctors – designed a bullet with optimum specifications for efficient and stress-free mass executions.

The arrests, deportations, and killings during the first occupation continued incessantly in a climate of fear. Beyond this, the oafishness and arrogance of the occupying forces seemed crude to the West Ukrainians. It became obvious that the workers' paradise from which the 'liberators' had arrived was a much poorer place than the 'liberated' territories, because at every opportunity things were stolen by the soldiers and carted away eastwards: private farms and businesses were turned into collective enterprises, which from the outset went into decline; the stocks of silk carpets in Buchach were hauled off by Communist officials, and the proud little factory ended up producing shabby towels; houses whose owners had been denounced and killed or deported were stripped of furniture, carpets, kitchen and bathroom fittings, and even doors, windows, and the frames around them. Although some of the political officials and soldiers were ethnic Ukrainians, they were in a minority. The most important politican in Ukraine, and the man supervising the harsh occupation, was a Russian, the future Soviet leader Nikita Khrushchev. The language they spoke was Russian and, like their manners and behaviour, it was alien to the West Ukrainians who did not buy the Soviet propaganda line about the equality of nations. West Ukrainians knew their country did not have parity with Russia, and they knew that it was not their compatriots in the capital, Kyiv, who were calling the shots, but the top Soviet officials in Moscow. They associated the murder and misery not only with Communism, but also with Russia. Communism was believed to be just a fig leaf for Russian imperialism during and after the war, and on until Ukrainian independence.

After the horrors of their first experience under a Soviet regime, many, perhaps most, West Ukrainians were relieved when, on 22 June 1941, the Germans launched Operation Barbarossa, the invasion of the Soviet Union, and sent the Red Army into headlong retreat.

German propagandist film-makers did not have to stage shots of welcoming crowds. Astonished German commanders were greeted by men and women in embroidered Ukrainian national costumes offering them the traditional signs of Ukrainian hospitality, bread and salt. Others threw flowers under the tracks of German tanks as they trundled through their towns and villages. The welcome was not limited to the recently annexed territories in the west but continued as the German forces pushed eastwards. The gestures were repeated almost everywhere the Germans swept away Soviet rule – Crimea, Belarus, the Caucasus, and even in Russia itself. Few believed that anyone else could match Stalin and the Communist regime for the suffering and inhumanity they inflicted.

It did not take long, however, for the Germans to dispel any notions that they had come to Ukraine with benign intentions. Hitler and other senior Nazis, steeped in racism, believed that all Slavs were subhumans, *Untermenschen,* and would not countenance the formation of a Ukrainian army. He made some exceptions. The Don Cossacks were treated as honorary Aryans and allowed to serve with the German forces. Puppet states swearing allegiance to Hitler were formed in Croatia and Slovakia, both Slavic, and they were also allowed to raise military formations. Other *Untermenschen* were only reclassified by the *Übermenschen* after the German army's turning point defeat at Stalingrad in 1943.

Hitler in fact saw Ukraine only as a geographical entity and violently overrode any Nazi officials who suggested that giving Ukrainians a tiny measure of self-rule, a completely ersatz independence, might prove useful for Germany in the long run. For Hitler, Ukraine's only destiny was to furnish the *Lebensraum,* new territory for German colonists, and for its subhuman inhabitants to provide the labour to extract the agricultural and mineral resources the Third Reich required.

To this end Ukrainians were to receive only enough rudimentary education to enable them to read, and obey, instructions issued them by their German masters.

On the heels of the ordinary German soldiers came the units with the task of eliminating all opposition and establishing absolute control over the conquered territories. Among these were the SS, the Gestapo and the *Einsatzgruppen*, Special Action Groups. Their largest target group was the Jewish population, who were executed in their tens of thousands in towns and villages or herded into ghettos for subsequent transportation to the death camps where they were murdered in their millions. But they were also after similar categories of people that their Soviet counterparts in the NKVD rounded up for extermination: anyone who posed a threat to the new order, particularly potential leaders and the intelligentsia.

When I was at school in Britain most of my classmates had heard nothing of Ukraine, but if they had it was often, as they would tell me, that Ukrainians had been German collaborators during World War Two and they were involved in killing Jews. Some of the people in the Nazi extermination units were indeed Ukrainian collaborators, just as there were collaborators in France, the Netherlands and Norway. But they were a minority in Ukraine, as they were in each of the nations where they sprang up like a symptom of the Nazi disease. I have never heard any Ukrainians, either in public or private, defend them or the atrocities they committed. I do wish, though, I had known the following statistics at school: during World War Two more Ukrainians died fighting the Nazis than all the Western allies' casualties put together. Ukraine lost up to nine million people, including about two and a half million military casualties, according to Ukrainian, Soviet and Western estimates. During the same period, according to the *Encyclopedia Britannica,* the total military and civilian losses among the Western allies (the British Commonwealth, the US, France, Greece, Belgium) were some 1.8 million people dead of whom about 1.2 million were military. Should pity for a nation multiply accordingly? Are mass executions by shooting, hanging, or gassing more lamentable than mass killings by bombs falling from the air or nuclear explosions? I'm not sure. But I wish I had known those figures.

When Hitler's plans for Ukraine became obvious, nationalists from the OUN seized the main radio station in Lviv on 30 June 1941, proclaimed independence and announced the formation of a government with the young OUN activist, Yaroslav Stetsko, as prime minister. The declaration was enthusiastically read out by patriots in towns and villages across West Ukraine, but the OUN knew that, without a force that could complement the heady words, their position was hopeless. The leaders were arrested and sent to German concentration camps where they remained for the rest of the war, or died. Although for the moment snuffed out, the declaration of independence was not merely a pipe dream; it once more demonstrated that Ukrainians were not prepared to live under subjugation.

As German brutality and racial arrogance turned Ukrainians against them, two main resistance movements developed – one spearheaded by the nationalists of the OUN and the other directed by the Communist authorities in Moscow. The fiercest resistance was in West Ukraine where the mountains, hills and forests afforded perfect terrain for guerrilla fighters unlike the exposed, flat steppes further east. The OUN's activites were at first carried out by small groups of resistance fighters who led outwardly normal existences, going to work and living at home, but by 1943 the number of volunteers had grown to such formidable numbers that a full-time, uniformed guerrilla formation emerged called the Ukrainian Insurgent Army, UPA. Armed intially with weapons abandoned by the defeated Polish and Soviet armies, and even old guns hidden after the liberation struggle at the end of World War One, those joining were committed to fighting any foreign force, German or Soviet, which aimed to control Ukraine.

All these events drew in relatives from my mother's and my father's families. There had always been women members of the OUN, and the newly formed UPA also had plenty of women both in support roles and as fighters. My mother's older sister, Halya, and their mother helped the UPA in support roles, relaying messages, while living in what had been a pension for holidaymakers who came to enjoy the scenery and fresh air in the foothills of the Carpathian mountains. Sometimes my mother, Bohdana, who was eleven years old when the Germans invaded, also carried messages written on small, tightly rolled scraps of paper which she plaited into her long braided hair.

Her father, Volodymyr, was the only one of my relatives of his age I know of who managed to avoid service in any army. He had a small metal engineering business, was fond of drink, had a great store of anecdotes, played the banjo, and massively discredited himself by carrying on a series of affairs. He was great fun to be with but his rakish behaviour fell far below the rectitude required by the UPA, though there is no evidence he ever wanted to join their ranks. He knew that his wife and elder daughter had close contacts with the guerrillas but he did not know what they did or that his young daughter, Bohdana, also performed tasks for the organisation.

Some German officers were billetted at the pension and on

one occasion several of them returned while two UPA fighters were in the kitchen talking to his wife, my grandmother Paraskevia. The two UPA men quickly gathered up their weapons and hid in another part of the house, but somehow in the rush the distinctive circular drum magazine of one of their PPD Soviet sub-machine guns had become detached and lay in a corner of the kitchen where the officers were waiting to be served tea and to chat with my grandmother. My grandfather walked into the kitchen and a chill ran down his spine as he immediately spotted the magazine, which his wife had also seen. Contact with the UPA meant interrogation, torture and probable death, and both knew their lives depended on the Germans not noticing it. They tried to appear as cheerful as possible and sat on the opposite side of the table to where it lay. To their immense relief, after some time the Germans departed. The two UPA fighters crept back in to retrieve the magazine and noticed that my grandfather's nerves were extremely frayed. The next day, unknown to him, my grandmother was summoned to a meeting with local UPA officers to discuss whether my grandfather, who had been very obviously scared by the incident, could be trusted not to betray them. The guerrillas thought it would be prudent to shoot him. My grandmother, who had been greatly pained by her husband's infidelity, never revealed whether she was tempted to take up an opportunity of which many a betrayed wife could only dream. Instead she successfully argued that whatever Volodymyr was, he was not a traitor. No action was taken against him and he never learned how close he came to death.

As the war progressed the Germans took more people to Germany as forced labour. In 1944 it was the turn of my mother and her parents. The elder daughter, Halya, was in love with a doctor in the UPA and slipped away to stay with the guerrillas. Bohdana and her parents were squeezed into cattle wagons for a train journey that before the war would have taken a couple of days but now took two weeks. Food and water were provided irregularly, but the captives were allowed out in some places to relieve themselves and get some fresh air. For several days they remained somewhere in the Czech lands and she never forgot the kindness of local people who came up to the train and brought water and gave them food. A young Czech girl befriended my mother during those few days and fifty years later my mother could still recite the Czech poem her friend taught her.

Halya remained with the UPA, which mounted attacks on the Nazis during the war and disrupted transporation of slave labour to Germany. The UPA fighters then waged war against the Soviets when they returned to Ukraine, in a little known but vicious guerrilla conflict which lasted until the early fifties. Around two hundred thousand people joined the UPA, operating in well-disciplined detachments from bases hidden in the forests and an elaborate network of bunkers which housed barracks and hospitals. The UPA's support network numbered many more hundreds of thousands, and to have a relative among the guerrillas was considered an honour. They held out against huge odds and relied on their own abilities for replenishment of their supplies, particularly weapons. As with the Poles routed in 1939, and the retreating Soviets in 1941, the Ukrainians grabbed weapons from the Germans fleeing the Soviet advance in 1944. Fresh supplies were captured in the following years from the Soviet NKVD troops who spearheaded the fight against them and carried out savage reprisals against the civilian population.

The UPA mounted large-scale raids on NKVD forces, sabotaged Soviet enterprises and assassinated senior

Communist officers and officials. Its operations petered out in the mid-fifties after its commander, Roman Shukhevych, who had become a legend under his *nom de guerre*, Taras Chuprynka, died in battle in March 1950. Some UPA guerrillas surrendered after the Soviet authorities offered an amnesty to those who turned themselves in, others tried to conceal their past and resume their lives at home, but that was difficult to pull off successfully. Most of those who surrendered or were subsequently discovered were sent to serve long sentences in Soviet prison camps in Siberia. Others were executed. But many did manage to blend back into life under the Soviet regime after first burying their weapons in caches to be unearthed for a future battle. Their stories told to families and trusted friends kept the embers of Ukraine's independence dream glowing.

The UPA was a valiant force which repeatedly proved its courage and fighting prowess during years of vastly unequal battles. It was probably the most effective resistance force to emerge during the war, and subsequently received a compliment from a strange quarter – the leaders of the Cuban Revolution, Fidel Castro and Che Guevara, who although Communists, admired and copied many of its techniques.

My mother's sister died, aged twenty-one, in 1945, from an illness that required the sort of hospital treatment unavailable in partisan forest bunkers. While the graves of thousands of UPA members gradually fused into the landscape, Halya's was tracked down years after her death by relatives who reburied her in a cemetery. I found her grave during my first visit to Ukraine. It is near a graceful old wooden church on a rise above a village in breathtakingly beautiful scenery with views of the Carpathian mountains. In 1999 I and my wife, Iryna, interred my mother's ashes in the grave of the sister she last saw in 1944 but never ceased to love until her own death in 1998.

The Soviet Army was in 1943 again heading towards West Ukraine and everyone believed the terror of 1939–41 would return with it. Most Ukrainians detested the Nazis but many still believed the Germans were the lesser of two evils. As the Nazis suffered more defeats and their racial prejudices slackened, they started recruiting Slavs and in 1943 formed a division made up of Ukrainians. For their part, Ukrainian leaders expected that a similar sort of chaos would reign over their territory at the end of this war as it had after the previous one, and believed a strong military force was essential if Ukraine stood any chance of gaining independence. Some thought that Germany's new eagerness to recruit, train and equip Ukrainians provided an opportunity to create just that.

My grandfather Teofil, who had fought the Bolsheviks a generation before, was determined the Soviet army, which was pressing into service men from the 'liberated' areas, would not conscript his son and he enlisted Ivan into the German forces. The Halychyna Division was one of nineteen non-German divisions among the thirty-eight in the SS. Most of the half million men who served in these foreign divisions came from Eastern Europe: Albanians, Belarusians, Bosnian Muslims, Bulgarians, Croatians, Estonians, Hungarians, Latvians, Romanians, Russians, Ukrainians and some ethnic Germans born in Eastern Europe; there were also SS divisions from Western Europe, including France and the Netherlands.

Explaining how the volunteers of any unit in the German army, let alone one with the damning 'SS' designation, were not necessarily evil is difficult, especially as the SS committed some of the vilest deeds in military history.

Few in eastern Europe, however, had the luxury of a

simple choice between good and bad as people had in, say, Britain and the US. The non-Russians in the Soviet Union felt their countries to be Russian colonies whose plight or desire for independence was of no concern to the Western democracies. One of the largest foreign formations in the German army, far larger than the Ukrainians, was composed of Russians who hated Stalin and Communism. For their part, Ukrainians, without a sovereign country of their own, had not shaped the events that launched Europe into another war. They were caught between modern history's two most powerful and bloodiest tyrants and they tried their best to help their country in a situation where they had little control over its destiny. Those who joined the SS Halychyna were not supporters of Hitler, and were certainly not interested in propping up or expanding a Nazi empire: they were people who believed they would be able to give Ukraine some bargaining chips in a move for independence. At a more basic level, they believed they could protect their compatriots from the approaching Red Army. They joined on the explicit understanding they would only fight Soviet forces and they never fought against the Western allies.

In the final stages of the war the division ditched the hated 'SS' designation, renamed itself the 1st Division of the Ukrainian National Army and came under the command of a Ukrainian general who was a veteran of the independent Ukrainian army formed after 1917. As Germany crumbled, the division gained recruits from smaller Ukrainian units in the German forces and from among the slave labourers. Many thought that after the German surrender war would erupt between the Western allies and the Soviet Union, and the new Ukrainian division hoped it would play a pivotal part in defending Ukraine's people and interests. But it became obvious there was not going to be an immediate conflict, and the Ukrainians' top priority became their own survival. They knew that if they were captured by Soviet forces they would be executed or sent to Siberia. With Soviet forces attacking them all the way, they fought their way into Austria to surrender to British forces there.

My father, like most of the Ukrainian division, was transferred to a prisoner-of-war camp near Rimini on Italy's Adriatic coast – on the other side of the sea from where his father and grandfather had briefly crossed paths during a conflict in a previous generation. The Soviet authorities demanded the Ukrainians should be handed over and accused them of war crimes and atrocities. The Ukrainians strenuously denied the accusations. British and US authorities carried out investigations into the division's history and deployments, vetted the prisoners and found there was no evidence of war crimes. In 1947 around eight thousand Ukrainian soldiers were allowed to go to Britain where there was an acute labour shortage. The majority took up the offer of jobs that were mainly three varieties of manual labour: in coal mines, on farms and in textile mills.

That is how my father came to arrive, still wearing parts of his old German uniform, in Bradford, where he was assigned work at a textile mill. He seldom spoke about his time in the division. My father was only sixteen when he joined the army, but he had a talent for languages and had learned German from his father and at school, and worked as an interpreter between German officers and Ukrainian soldiers. But he also took part in combat and during one battle he was wounded in his leg by shrapnel from a tank shell. He told me how, when in the final days the division became Ukrainian, the troops were overjoyed as they swapped their old insignia for the Ukrainian trident emblem. I have his old army belt where the swastika on the buckle has been knocked out and a motto in German has been roughly scratched away. For a fleetingly short time, Ivan and his comrades thought they may be heading back towards their homes to fight for their country and protect their families, but that was not to be. If they could have, they might have joined the UPA guerrillas, as many of their comrades had managed to do the previous year, but that proved impossible too.

He was never to see his native land again, but Ukraine was always in his thoughts and he dreamed of and worked for Ukrainian independence until the end of his life. He knew that he and his comrades had not been involved in war crimes or committed atrocities, and was saddened that they had not been able to fight under a Ukrainian banner. They fought well and bravely. Many of them shed their blood and many of them died. But, in the final analysis, their sacrifice did not significantly help their cause, and their courage – in the service of Ukraine, not Germany – is obscured by the lightning bolt SS symbol.

At the time that my father enlisted in the German army, his sister was already a battle-hardened member of the Red Army. Leonida, three years older than him, had fled Buchach with a Jewish girlfriend of hers when the Germans attacked the Soviets in the summer of 1941. They went to her aunt's home in Odessa thinking that the fighting was a border quarrel and would soon be over, but as the Germans continued to advance, she decided, at the age of sixteen, to join the Red Army as a nurse. The army was driven back across the river Dnipro, then further east out of Ukraine altogether, into the North Caucasus where Leonida found herself in the 3rd Squadron of the 75th Cavalry Regiment. She said her mounted unit looked magnificent, but soldiers on horses were no match for German planes and tanks, and the unit was almost wiped out. They were reorganised as an infantry unit and spent much of their time fighting in mountainous terrain.

Leonida remembers her unit winding its way in bitter winter cold, hauling their equipment along narrow, precipitous trails made yet more treacherous by snow. As men fell wounded during the battles she risked her life amidst bullets and shells to help carry them to safety. In February 1943 shrapnel from an artillery shell blew out a fist-sized chunk of her right leg and she was lucky it was not amputated. Leonida spent nearly six months in hospital and convalescence in the Soviet-held Georgian capital, Tbilisi.

She recovered and returned to duty with the advancing Soviet army and in 1944 arrived in West Ukraine. Leonida had lost touch with her family, but as her detachment neared Buchach, she learned that her brother was in the German army. She feared her unit would clash with the division and she would find her brother's body among the dead. But they were not to meet on the battlefield or anywhere else for more than twenty years.

Leonida was awarded many medals for her war service and courage. During the Soviet era she received the perks awarded to other Red Army heroes, including subsidised vacations in Crimea, access to better accommodation, medical care and food. Even in post-Communist Ukraine, she continued to receive recognition and greetings on 9 May, the day the Soviets commemorated victory over Hitler. President Leonid Kuchma presented her with another medal for heroic war veterans, she received a free cruise down the Dnipro to the Black Sea in 2003, and her pension is a little less meagre than the pitiful sums on which other elderly people have to survive. Most of the anti-Communist and pro-independence UPA guerrilla fighters were executed or condemned to long sentences in hard-labour prison camps if captured. Those who survived were excluded from war veterans' perks even after Ukrainian independence, although some received help from charitable groups. It is not the perks they crave, but the recognition that they and their fallen comrades also fought bravely for a freedom they hope has now finally arrived.

My mother and her parents spent the last year of the war in South Germany. She and her father worked in munitions factories while my grandmother worked as a cook at a camp for Soviet prisoners of war. The allied air raids became more intense as the number of remaining targets decreased, so that often hundreds of bombers, sometimes a thousand, would be concentrated in attacks which my mother said felt as if they heralded the end of the world. Foreign labourers were not allowed into the air-raid shelters which were reserved for Germans, and had to find protection as best they could. Their guards knew the slave workers had nowhere to run and left the *Untermenschen* to fend for themselves.

Soviet prisoners of war were not entitled to the relatively humane treatment that Western captives received because Moscow had not signed the Geneva Convention. On top of that the German authorities did not see a need to provide tolerable conditions for subhuman Slavs and consequently conditions in the camps were hideous. Millions died of disease, hunger and mistreatment. My grandmother felt pity for the tragic lot of these doomed, skeletal men. There was little she could do to help, but occasionally she managed to pass a few potatoes or pieces of bread surreptitiously through the barbed wire fences, and muttered any encouraging news she might have heard. She was at the camp when it was suddenly liberated by American soldiers. Those prisoners who could rushed towards the camp commandant's offices and the kitchen and tore apart or beat to death any of the camp guards they caught. As these men who had suffered so much approached her, my grandmother thought that in their fury they would also kill her. But they surrounded her and, some of them weeping, others kissing her hands, thanked her in Russian and Ukrainian for the scraps of food she had smuggled to them, slivers of kindness amidst relentless cruelty and death.

My mother and her parents remained, along with hundreds of thousands of other former slave labourers, in the US-occupied zone of Germany, at a camp near Regensburg for displaced people and those who did not want to go home to live under Stalin. Many of the returning slave labourers and Soviet soldiers who had been prisoners went directly from German captivity to Communist prison camps as punishment for allowing themselves to fall into Nazi hands, and because they were tainted by exposure to the West. Most refugees chose to go to the US or Canada. However, my grandmother failed the health inspection for North America and the three of them joined others invited to settle in Britain which needed to rebuild its shattered cities and economy. In 1948 they also arrived in Bradford, where my father was already working in a mill. My parents met through the growing Ukrainian community and married in 1952.

Most of the Ukrainians in Britain had come from similar patriotic backgrounds and the yearning for independence bound them together. They followed as closely as they could what was happening in Ukraine and the fight being waged by the UPA guerrillas. They organised themselves to provide what support they could, mostly by informing the Western world about the struggle and lobbying for international pressure and aid. My father threw himself into helping to organise the Ukrainian community in Britain and his talent for languages meant he quickly learned English. He became the editor of a Ukrainian émigré newspaper and a prominent member of Ukraine's pro-independence diaspora, sworn enemies of the Communist regime. He was denounced in Soviet newspapers as a traitor and killer.

One day, some time after the Soviet return, a Communist functionary in Buchach told my father's mother that my father had been captured and hanged with other 'traitors' in a field on the outskirts of the town. She described how she rushed to the spot, convinced as she approached the makeshift scaffold that one of the grotesque figures swaying there was indeed her son. She said she collapsed and crawled through the muddy field to the foot of the gallows where she saw that the corpses were those of strangers. It transpired that the person who had told her had done so out of deliberate malice. In 1953 my grandmother and aunt returned home after being out for the day. They found Grandfather Teofil hanging from a rafter with his throat and wrists slashed. The authorities called it suicide. My father believed his father had been killed by the Communists as revenge for his son's activities in Britain. This guilt haunted my father for the rest of his life.

The next time my father and his sister faced each other was when she and her mother were allowed to visit Britain in 1965. My sister, adored by our father and named Leonida after his own sister, my mother, father and I went to the airport to meet our relatives from Ukraine. My father and his sister and mother embraced each other and all wept in the crowded arrivals hall. I had never seen my father cry before and never saw him do so again. I remember that one of the first things he told his mother was: 'I have never killed anyone. There is no blood on these hands.'

There followed many days of emotional conversations and catching up on twenty years of news that could not be communicated in letters examined by KGB censors. After a while my sister and I sensed a certain uneasiness in the relationship between our mother and our aunt. The cause emerged only many years later: our aunt was suggesting our father should return to Ukraine. My grandmother revealed what lay behind this when she took my father aside during a country walk. She told her son that for a couple of years before they were allowed to make the trip, my aunt, Leonida, had been ordered in for interviews with the KGB; her standing as a war hero gave her and the family a measure of protection, but the KGB told her there could still be unpleasant consequences of the family's well-known record of antipathy towards Soviet rule. The KGB intimated her children's education and work prospects would suffer if she did not fall in with their request for her to persuade my father to return to Ukraine, and said there was no question of her going on the visit if she did not agree to do as they asked. My aunt's children and husband naturally had to remain in Ukraine while they were visiting Britain and it was understood they would suffer if Leonida and my grandmother failed to return. The KGB convinced them that Soviet intelligence would watch them wherever they were and could listen to all their conversations within our family home. That was why my grandmother chose to draw my father aside during a rambling walk along a beautiful Berkshire countryside path, lined with bluebells, to communicate her painful information.

If my father returned to Ukraine, she warned, he would be tortured and probably forced, in television appearances or published statements, to confess that he and the rest of the Ukrainian émigré community were Fascists and murderers working for the CIA and the British intelligence services. After that he would be executed or, at best, face a long prison term.

My grandmother's revelations did not alter my father's love toward his sister. He had never seriously countenanced returning or leaving his wife and children and knew very well the fate that would befall him if he did go back. That his sister had been forced to cooperate with the KGB he accepted as just another horrible facet of the system he was fighting.

I know that she also loved him. My father died long before Ukrainian independence and they never met again. Whenever I visit her at her one-bedroom apartment in a crumbling sixties Buchach housing block, the conversation inevitably revolves around my father and is conducted in a tone of reverence. Aunt Leonida, it is obvious, told tender stories about him to her own children, even during the Communist era. One of her children, my cousin, Bohdan, so hero-worshipped him that he practised his handwriting to mimic my father's exactly.

My parents moved to London in the fifties and that is where I, and two years later my sister, were born. My brother Victor was born ten years after that. Our parents both worked hard to build up the Ukrainian community and my father edited the only Ukrainian newspaper published in Britain. I used to go to his office when I was very young. I loved expeditions to the basement where the paper was printed amidst an exciting, seemingly chaotic bustle; a mechanical clatter assailed the ears and the smells of printer's ink and melting lead mingled. The heart of the process was a marvellous 'hot metal' press machine which looked like an ancient typewriter keyboard embedded in a church organ. The lines of reverse type were created from the hot lead and these were locked into wooden frames the size of the page, which were in turn placed into a primitive machine, which seemed as if it dated from the time of Caxton, called a flatbed printer, to produce the newspaper. This newspaper, *Ukrayinska Dumka,* or *Ukrainian Thought,* was the last publication in Britain to use the flatbed process

When I was eight my father decided that to support his family he needed a job that paid more money, and he joined the BBC to work for them in their Caversham monitoring station, some forty miles west of London. The facilty had been created during World War Two to listen to broadcasts in German-occupied Europe. It got a new lease of life during the Cold War and was jointly financed by the British and American governments to listen into and translate broadcasts from the Communist countries of Europe. My father monitored Russian and Ukrainian broadcasts and, like his colleagues, not only translated them but had to assess their significance and try to garner information about the impenetrable world of the Kremlin from nuances and shades of meaning. A change of policy might be detected by a miniscule shift in emphasis or the selection of a particular word, while the outcome of a power struggle might be indicated by the order in which dignitaries made speeches, or by their absence. Caversham still operates at its home in a beautiful, secluded eighteenth-century country house set in extensive grounds. The skills of the 'Kremlinologists', once imperilled by the end of the Cold War, are again sought after as Moscow's government returns to its traditional opaque style.

At home my sister, my brother and I talked in Ukrainian with our parents even though they by this time spoke fluent English. Their friends and visitors were mostly like-minded folk for whom Ukraine was the focus of passionate hopes and plans. Many of them had been involved one way or another in the fight for Ukraine, and for us children these extraordinary persons were the norm. We got to know people who had risked their lives in battle as guerrillas or soldiers, parachuted into Ukraine on secret missions, suffered the loss of their parents, brothers and sisters through deportation or execution, or had themselves been imprisoned in Nazi and Soviet camps. One of my father's friends was Yaroslav Stetsko, the man who had for a few days been hailed as prime minister after Ukraine's declaration of independence in 1941. Another visitor to our home in London was Stepan Bandera, leader of the OUN until he was assassinated in Munich by a KGB agent in 1959.

I always tried to stay informed about what was happening in the Soviet Union and particularly Ukraine. During my student years I edited a magazine about events in the Soviet Union, helped organise demonstrations and took part in hunger strikes outside the Soviet consulate in London, wrote leaflets, disrupted Soviet-organised propaganda events, and smashed the windows of Soviet offices in London.

Eventually I fell into journalism. Although most of my professional life was spent reporting in places a long way from Ukraine, my thoughts were never far from there. When the world's worst civilian nuclear disaster happened at Chernobyl in 1986 I was surprised at how keenly I thought about the pain and horror of the victims.

Sometimes my work linked my life closely to Ukraine. About a year after I began working as a journalist in London, the Soviet army invaded Afghanistan in Christmas 1979. Six months later I was in Afghanistan as a freelance reporter accompanying a mujahidin group on a raid against Soviet forces. It was the first time I had ever left the Western world; it was my first time in the Muslim world, it was the first time in battle, it was the first time I saw people killed, it was the first time people tried to kill me. I went there many times and I was, of course, always happy to survive. But I was also always conscious that, except for an accident of history, I could have been one of the Soviet soldiers that were the targets for my guerrilla companions' attacks.

I have met some of these veterans since Ukraine's independence, including one who told me he was part of a group that was detailed to 'liquidate' me in Afghanistan. In a remarkable coincidence, the driver of a taxi my mother hailed in Kyiv said he was part of a detachment of hundreds of Soviet and Afghan soldiers that in 1988 spent several days hunting for me in Afghanistan to kill me as a Western 'agent'. I made numerous visits to Afghanistan to report on the conflict, always accompanying a group of mujahidin crossing into their homeland from bases in Pakistan's North-West Frontier Province. Most of the journeys lasted several gruelling weeks because travel was mostly by foot, sometimes by horse, and, it seemed, almost always up a mountain that was as unyielding as the spectacular scenery was beautiful. The guerrillas only started to use vehicles for part of the journeys after US-supplied Stinger surface-to-air missiles largely eliminated the threat from Soviet helicopters. Usually the group of fighters I was with would raid a Communist base or armoured column and withdraw, but sometimes they joined up with other units to launch an attack on a wider front. I was on one of these trips at the time my putative killer, Serhiy Smirny, a repairman moonlighting as a taxi driver, said he and his companions tried to track me down. But the Soviets' information was wrong and I was in a different part of the country, completely unaware that there was a hunt for me. On that particular trip things went wrong, the Afghan guerrillas took a lot of casualties and the group I was with ended up retreating towards the Pakistani border.

I was suspicious that my mother was being deceived for

some reason, so I looked up the taxi driver in Kyiv. We met and he took me to meet his wife and children in their high-rise apartment block. Food was swiftly laid on the table and the first of a number of bottles of vodka came out. He showed me photographs of himself in Afghanistan with his comrades from the 357th Battalion of the 40th Army, where as a senior warrant officer he commanded thirty men. He described where he had been during his term of service for a year and it was quickly obvious that Serhiy, a friendly and intelligent man, was telling the truth and he really had been in Afghanistan. He said: 'There were six hundred people involved in the operation. We were transported in helicopters and dropped along the routes that we thought you might be travelling. The operation lasted about four days.'

Serhiy said they were told that I was armed and working for Western intelligence to help the Afghan guerrillas kill Soviet troops and their instructions were to 'liquidate' me. I thought that Serhiy was mistaken about the term 'liquidate' and suggested they had really been told to apprehend me as I was just a journalist. 'No,' he said, 'we were not supposed to take you back. The orders were to liquidate you and I would have done it. There was a KGB officer with us at all times so we would have shot you.'

He saw that I was mulling that piece of information over in my mind and wanted to assure me it was nothing personal: 'I didn't know what I know now,' said Serhiy, 'we just believed what we were told. You were just the enemy. I would have killed you. Thank God we didn't meet in Afghanistan because we wouldn't be here together now. But I'm glad we didn't get you.' I said I shared his sentiment and we filled the glasses for a toast of mutual affection and downed them.

Chapter Three

BAD NEIGHBOURS

Ukraine's geographic location, its agricultural value and its natural resources have made it a magnet for invaders and a crossroads for others passing to and from every point of the compass. In the hilly West, wooded country and the Carpathian mountains have afforded some protection from invaders and cover from which to fight them. However, the flat, mostly featureless steppes that make up much of the country and stretch thousands of miles eastwards skirting the Ural mountains deep into Asia left the territory vulnerable. They have proved inviting to both the twelfth-century mounted warriors of Genghis Khan's Golden Horde sweeping in from the east and the World War Two tanks of Hitler's panzer columns grinding in from the west.

Pinning down the origins of the East Slavs and how they emerged as three distinct peoples – Ukrainians, Belarusians and Russians – is complicated due to a lack of reliable records. For centuries, with the exception of one brief interlude, Ukrainians did not govern themselves and, therefore, Ukraine was largely invisible. If the world knew anything at all about Ukraine, it knew the versions of history that were most convenient to her foreign rulers at any particular time. These were moulded like plasticine and their only consistent aspect was that they belittled, and frequently reviled, the role of Ukraine and its people in European history. Interpretation of Ukraine's turbulent, bloodily busy past has itself often turned into a battlefield as powerful neighbours tried to annex its history along with the territory.

The idea that the victor writes history has been attributed to, among others, Winston Churchill, Walter Benjamin, Oliver Wendell Holmes Jr and Pliny the Younger. For most Ukrainians, in the last few centuries, that victor has been Russia – either in the form of the Tsarist empire or the Soviet Union. And Russia's version of history, which attributed the leading and most compelling roles to Russians, percolated through to the rest of the world. The subject peoples of the Tsarist or Communist Russian empires had few opportunities to state their own cases: access to the records and archives was controlled by Russian officials who decided what to release to their own people or to foreign researchers; there were periods when printing books in Ukrainian was illegal and even using the language laid one open to persecution. There was little opportunity and no incentive for Ukrainian scholars living in the Tsarist or Communist empires to present a 'Ukrainian' version of history. Exiled Ukrainian historians who attempted to refute the distortions rarely had the resources to challenge seriously the dissembling, state-backed Russian versions. Even those who were sceptical or hostile to Communism were forced into a Moscow-centric perspective because they were unable to visit, without great effort, the other fourteen republics that, with Russia, made up the USSR. Willingness to propagate the Kremlin's inter-pretation of events was rewarded with greater access to information or important personages.

Russian historians, whether Tsarist or Soviet, usually portrayed the three East Slavic peoples as essentially all Russians with differences in nuance just as the discrete identities of the Baltic peoples or those of the Caucasus were smothered under the cloak of Russian chauvinism.

Some scholars have suggested that as the name 'Ukraine' means on the borders or on the edge, the place is merely a shifting area, peripheral to a real country but not one itself. Ukrainians have also often been dismissed as the junior or peasant branch of another people – Poles or Russians – who have been duped into daring to think they can call themselves a separate nation. Their language has been mocked as a peasant dialect of a superior Polish or Russian tongue. There are still many in Ukraine who know only the distorted history taught during Communist times which gave the heroic lead to Russia and a minor part to Ukraine, whose very existence seemed impossible without Moscow. That counterfeit version of history not only does injustice to all the millions who perished struggling for independence but it is also a threat to contemporary Ukraine and in 2004 was used to sow division and raise the spectre of civil war.

The area that is now modern Ukraine has been inhabited, according to some authorities, for around 150,000 years. The northern forested areas were more isolated from the invaders and nomads who made the open steppe regions to the south look like a Piccadilly Circus of newcomers, some of whom settled while others passed on westwards. The earliest agricultural communities in Eastern Europe took root between 5000 and 4000 BC of which the most highly evolved was the Trypillian Civilisation which flourished between 3500 and 2700 BC in the south-west, between the Carpathian mountains and the river Dnipro and in areas that are modern Romania and Moldova.

Evidence of the Neolithic Trypillian culture, named after the region where it was detected by an archaeologist in the 1890s, caused a great stir at the time but the political upheavals of the twentieth century, the Communists' prohibition on foreign archaeologists visiting the USSR and ideological curbs imposed on their own, meant that further research was fitful. After Ukrainian independence, interest was revived. The leader of Ukraine's Orange Revolution, Viktor Yushchenko, is himself passionate about Trypillian culture and has encouraged more investigation. Many archaeologists believe they will lead to exciting new discoveries and could prompt an important overhaul in the way Europe's early history is viewed.

Investigations so far have revealed an advanced society of farmers and craftsmen living in well-built timbered houses arranged in a circle around a central open space. Aerial photography has shown that in the later stages of Trypillian culture, settlements consisted of hundreds, or thousands, of dwellings. These towns covered hundreds of acres and in one case more than a thousand – larger for their time than the civilisations that existed in Mesopotamia or Egypt.

The Trypillians had discovered the wheel and there is also evidence that they were developing a method of recording information using symbols. They were skilled at working copper and produced superb, elegantly decorated, coloured pottery made on potter's wheels and baked in special ovens.

The Trypillian culture was displaced by a combination of climate change and arrivals from the east. Over the centuries a procession of warrior peoples swept in to establish themselves for a time in the area, each leaving traces of their distinct cultures. They included the Cimmerian people, who settled between 1500 and 700 BC and who were mentioned by Homer in *The Odyssey*. They in turn were driven out or absorbed by other nomadic warriors, notably the Scythians who ruled the steppes down to the shores of the Black Sea. The Scythians had a fierce reputation as fighters but were farmers and traders conducting commerce with the Greeks, from whom they learned new ideas and skills such as the manufacture of intricately beautiful jewellery found in their large burial mounds scattered throughout Ukraine. The Scythians were overwhelmed by the Sarmatians who themselves were overrun in the second century AD by the Huns and Goths.

Whilst much has been pieced together about the ancient inhabitants of Central and South Ukraine, little is known about the early history of the Slav farming communities of related tribes in the northerly and north-western areas, but what is certain is that by the ninth century they were well on the way to creating a militarily powerful and cohesive society called Kyivan Rus, which took its name from its principal city, Kyiv, founded by Prince Kyi in the sixth century, capital of today's Ukraine.

Precisely how the previously passive and scattered Slav communities managed to form the sophisticated Kyivan Rus civilisation relatively quickly has been a subject of dispute for centuries. Viking traders seeking to open up a trade route from the Baltic Sea to Constantinople, then the world's biggest and richest conurbation, via the river Dnipro and across the Black Sea, undoubtedly played a key role in the new state's development, but exactly what is still debated.

The Vikings, also called Norsemen or Normans, and Varangians by the Slavs, established trading posts in what is now North-West Russia. Some historians hold that the Slavs were too quarrelsome to agree upon a ruler from among themselves and asked the Varangians to become their over-lords. Others argue that the bellicose Vikings were used as mercenaries or allies by some Slav leaders to gain supremacy over their rivals. Gradually the Viking warrior elite and traders mingled with the local population and adopted their language. Theories abound about the origin of the name

'Rus', one being that it is derived from the Scandinavian for 'Swedish people', *Ruotsi*, another from rowers of Viking longboats, *rodr*.

Both Ukrainians and Russians claim Kyivan Rus as the inception of their national identities. However, what became Kyivan Rus probably began as an ambitious commercial enterprise with greed as its engine and only later evolved into state-building. Kyivan Rus developed its military initially to protect its trade interests and to force tribute payments to its dominant Slav tribe, the Polianians, from the other inhabitants. Later its invading armies expanded the territory under Kyiv's control and in 911 took on the most formidable regional force, Byzantium, inflicting a defeat on the Byzantine army and looting Constantinople. The people of Kyivan Rus were pagans until their rulers decided that a monotheistic faith would bring greater stability as well as valuable political allegiances with other Christian states. In 988 Kyiv's population was baptised en masse after Prince Volodymyr the Great embraced Christianity and later, when the Christian Church split into Catholic and Orthodox, Kyiv chose the Orthodox confession of Constantinople. In the following years Kyivan Rus became one of the most powerful political conglomerates in Europe, boasting impressive civil and military establishments. It had alliances and matrimonial links with the Byzantine emperors and many European royal families including those of France, Poland and England. With Christianity came splendid churches, cathedrals and monasteries, and the introduction of an alphabet which together saw Kyivan Rus grow into an important centre for culture and learning; a codified system of laws was produced in the eleventh century. Invasions gained territory in the Balkans and to the north-east, where Muscovy later emerged. By the eleventh century, Kyivan Rus was Europe's largest state and stretched from the Carpathian mountains in the west to the Volga in the east, and from the Baltic Sea in the north to the Black Sea in the south.

But Kyivan Rus's glory was to be short-lived and destined to be destroyed by weaknesses of its own making, and finally by the scourge of Mongol invasions. Militarily the Kyivan princes overextended themselves and bloody succession struggles debilitated the society from within: every such conflict left Kyiv's authority and prestige diminished. Kyiv's power and wealth continued to decline after merchants from Western Europe found more convenient routes to Constantinople and beyond and in the thirteenth century the Kyivan Rus empire faced a threat that, even united, would have been difficult to withstand – invasion by huge hordes of Mongol cavalry which thundered in from Central Asia. The warriors were equally skilled with bow and sword, on mounts or on foot, and their ferocious reputation for annihilating those who did not surrender instilled terror. But even that fear failed to unite the quarrelsome principalities and the Mongols picked them off one by one. In 1240, after a long, fierce siege, the grandson of Genghis Khan, Batyi, captured Kyiv and then destroyed it.

Kyivan Rus was shattered as a political entity by the Mongols but the two western principalities, Halychyna and Volyhnia, struggled for almost a century to resist the Mongols and succeeded for a short period in restoring their rule over much of former Kyivan Rus. A king of Halych, Danylo, was crowned by a papal envoy in 1253. Many Ukrainians regard this period, framed by the ruin of Kyivan Rus as it was, as the cradling of a Ukrainian identity.

Kyiv, which had been the core of the Kyivan Rus state, came under Mongol rule but was not restored to its leading role and continued to diminish in importance. Other powers were arising and these competed for slices of the land of Kyivan Rus.

In the West, from the thirteenth century onwards, the Lithuanian Grand Duchy grew with remarkable speed into a powerful force, and by the middle of the fourteenth century had incorporated areas of Kyivan Rus that are today Belarus and much of what is modern Ukraine. The Lithuanian acquisition was largely peaceful because local inhabitants preferred them as rulers to the Mongols and because Lithuania, with a relatively small population, coopted the Rus aristocracy into the ruling elite. The language used in official documents was the Church Slavonic of the Rus people, similar to modern Ukrainian, although most of the nobility spoke Polish at court. The Lithuanians – Europe's last pagans – did not interfere with the population's Christian religion. Polish encroachment on former Rus territory, by contrast, intruded on both language and religion. Its declared aim of converting the population to the Catholic faith was strongly resented by the Ukrainian Orthodox.

For a time Lithuania and Poland clashed for supremacy in the region, but in 1386 concluded a pact which made the reigning Lithuanian grand duke, Jogaila, Polish king after he converted to Catholicism and married the Polish queen. Thus began four hundred years of close association between the two countries which were bound more tightly by formal unification in 1569. From the fourteenth to sixteenth centuries this dual empire, led by Lithuanians, dominated much of Eastern Europe and stretched from the Baltic to the Black Sea. Under the union terms Lithuania formally remained an equal and distinct state but, in practice, slipped into a subordinate role. Poland also annexed large areas of present-day Ukraine that until then had been considered part of the Grand Duchy.

Some of the old Rus, Orthodox Ukrainian nobles became Polonised and converted to Catholicism in order to retain their privileges but this caused friction with those Ukrainians who remained true to their Orthodox faith. In 1596 the Catholic Church and some Orthodox bishops in the Polish-Lithuanian empire believed a solution to the religious divisions, and a way to avoid the Moscow Orthodox Patriarchate's claims to be their superior, was to submit to the Pope's authority while keeping most of the eastern-rite customs and rituals. Thus the Greek Catholic Church of the Byzantine Rite, also known as the Uniate Church, came into existence.

To the north-east Moscow, which had only started to grow when the Mongol invasions overran Kyivan Rus, quickly adapted to rule by their Mongol conquerors. By displaying loyalty to their masters, Moscow's rulers received preferential treatment and were able to start building the Muscovite empire while themselves formally still a component of the Mongol empire. Some believe that the Kremlin's harsh methods throughout history can be traced to Moscow's experience of the Mongols' oppressive and ruthless rule. In any case, Moscow was able to rule over or to destroy neighbouring older city states like Novgorod and Vladimir which had flourished during the Kyivan Rus era. As Muscovy's appetite for expansion grew it looked southwards and westwards to the Ukrainian lands that the Polish-Lithuanian empire also coveted.

Ukraine's fate depended on the complex interplay and clash of the powers around her who sought control of the strategically important and agriculturally rich land. Muscovy – the name Russia was not yet used – attracted support among sections of the Ukrainian elite because of their common Orthodox Christian faith. Muscovy's emergence as a regional power and the attention it was paying Ukraine brought it into confrontation with its Polish-Lithuanian imperial rivals. Descendants of the original Mongol hordes had settled in the Volga region and Crimea. Known as Tatars, they had converted to Islam and this added another jagged dimension to prevailing ethnic and religious antagonisms.

Large tracts of East and South Ukraine were sparsely occupied since the destruction of Kyivan Rus and were prey to marauding Tatar raiding parties, who killed those they did not take to be sold into slavery. But in the late fifteenth century these lands began to be settled by an exotic mixture of bold men who were to become known as Cossacks, a word of Turkic origin meaning free men. Many were serfs who ran away from their Polish-Lithuanian oppressors, or adventurers determined to gain land and fortunes. The hardy farmer-pioneers developed a prowess as mounted fighters to defend their homesteads against the Tatar raiders. The settlers banded together and within a few generations the Cossacks had developed into a formidable society founding and protecting hundreds of small towns.

They practised an early type of democracy where every Cossack had the right to vote in elections for their supreme leader, the *hetman,* and for their officers. The Cossack organisation took on many of the attributes of state government, with the appointment of officials responsible for civil as well as military functions. The Cossacks came into conflict with the Polish state, which tried to buy off the Cossacks by giving some of them privileges and incorporating some of them into its forces to fight against Muscovy and the Crimean Tatars. But the Cossacks frequently operated independently of the Polish authorities, giving rise to bitter quarrels, and before the end of the sixteenth century there were outbreaks of rebellion leading to armed clashes between Polish forces and Cossacks backed by ordinary Ukrainian peasants. Cossack prestige rose among the other inhabitants as they mounted raids which freed thousands of Ukrainian slaves in the Crimean khanate and launched naval expeditions against the Ottoman Sultan's capital in Constantinople.

The Cossacks' victories, courage and fierce loyalty to one another made them legendary figures with elements of knightly chivalry and Robin Hood benevolent banditry. They were certainly colourful: sporting scalplock hairstyles, they had adapted some of the garb and weaponry of their Ottoman and Tatar enemies, such as billowing trousers that were cool and convenient for riding, and curved swords. Membership of their brotherhood was open to any Christian man and their devotion to Christianity was matched only by their love of adventure and reputation for bawdiness. Their exploits have been a source of inspiration for Ukrainians ever since.

Friction with the Polish government increased and culminated in 1648 in a large-scale Ukrainian rebellion, spearheaded by the Cossacks, who inflicted a series of crippling defeats against the Poles. For a while the Cossacks and Ukrainians were masters of much of their land. But the Poles, with the Tatars now as their allies, threatened to overwhelm the Cossacks whose leader, Bohdan Khmelnytsky, entered into a treaty in 1654 with the tsar of Muscovy, who was an enemy of the Poles. The treaty has remained a point of intense controversy ever since. The original documents disappeared centuries ago and only unreliable copies exist. Russian historians and the Kremlin insist that by the treaty Khmelnytsky united the Ukrainian lands and people with Russia; Ukrainians argue that it was merely a temporary military alliance with Moscow.

Khmelnytsky himself soon became disturbed by the implications of the treaty and dismayed at the behaviour of Russia which immediately began tampering with the Cossack forms of government and the privileges of its ruling class, building up a permanent Russian military presence on Ukrainian territory. His successors tried to prevent their land becoming a Russian province. However – displaying a trait that bedevilled the rulers of Kyivan Rus and has continued throughout Ukrainian history to this day – the Cossacks argued amongst themselves about how to preserve their liberties. Some fought against the Russians and urged alliance with the Poles. Other Cossacks, despite disillusionment with the Russians, were more suspicious of the Poles. There were even clashes between opposing groups of Cossacks. Eventually, in 1667, Poland and Russia concluded a peace in which they agreed to split Ukraine between them. The land west of the Dnipro came under Polish rule while that east of the river went to Russia which also took Kyiv. In both halves the rights and powers of the Cossacks were severely diminished and the basis of what, only shortly before, had seemed destined to become a Ukrainian Cossack state was dismantled.

Many pragmatic Cossacks and Ukrainian nobles, though, became faithful servants of their new Russian masters. One of the seemingly most faithful was Ivan Mazepa, the eponymous hero of an epic Byron poem. Of noble birth, well educated, and acquainted with the West, Mazepa became *hetman* of the Cossacks in East Ukraine in 1687 and one of the closest confidants of Russia's modernising Tsar Peter I. Dissatisfaction with Russian encroachment on Cossack rights had long festered, but the tsar's use of Ukrainian Cossacks and soldiers in wars that had nothing to do with Ukrainian interests increased anger against Moscow. When King

Charles XII of Sweden marched on Russia, Mazepa became his ally in return for guarantees of Ukrainian independence. In June 1709 the forces of Mazepa and the Swedes faced the Russian army near the city of Polatava. The battle ended with a great victory for the Russians, and Charles XII and Mazepa were forced to flee to avoid being captured. Mazepa died later that year and although his successor tried launching a revolt against Moscow some years later, Russia's hold over much of Ukraine was further consolidated. Before the end of the century the last remnants of Cossack power were dismantled and its most potent symbol, a large fortress called the Zaporizhyan Sich on an island in the Dnipro, was destroyed.

When the Polish Commonwealth was partitioned at the end of the eighteenth century, most of Ukraine was incorporated into the Russian Empire while West Ukraine went to the Austrian Empire and Ukraine remained thus split until the upheavals caused by World War One. While neither the Russian nor the Austrian empires had any interest in encouraging the development of a separate identity for Ukrainians, the two autocracies differed in vital aspects that made the Austrians more sympathetic towards Ukrainian aspirations than the Russians.

The rulers of the Austrian Empire were the Habsburg family who treated their lands, populated by people of various nationalities and religions, as a grand landowner might look after his vast estates, adding to his properties and developing them to optimise their yield. Although everyone was a citizen of the Empire and most business was conducted in German, there was little attempt to turn all the inhabitants into Austrians. Indeed part of the mechanism by which the Habsburgs remained in control was by fomenting jealousies and tension between the disparate nationalities, binding some by allotting privileges and using them to balance the power of recalcitrant groups. Ukrainians, referred to as Ruthenians in the Austro-Hungarian Empire, frequently suffered under Polish officials appointed by the government in Vienna, but were eventually given representation in parliament, probably in part to keep the Poles in check. Under Viennese rule, Ukrainians were allowed not only to preserve their national identity but to embark on cultural, educational and political projects that breathed fresh life into ambitions for autonomy or even independence.

Things were far different for Ukrainians in the Russian Empire which from its earliest days suffered from an identity crisis. Moscow had been of little importance when the Mongols destroyed Kyiv and established a cruel hold over the region, whose rulers abased themselves before their new masters and were used to solidify Mongol control. But when Moscow threw off Mongol rule and its tsars pursued a ruthless expansion, it needed a subtler rationalisation for its aggression than greed, and invented a grandiose mission: to lead the Slav world. To bolster its pre-eminent position Moscow not only expropriated the prestige of Kyivan Rus but also proclaimed itself 'The Third Rome'. Constantinople, 'The Second Rome', had been captured by the Muslim Ottomans in 1453 while Rome itself was the headquarters of Orthodoxy's bitter schismatic enemy, the Catholic Church. Moscow's dual purpose was thus to lead the Slav world and the Orthodox Christians.

Russia can certainly trace connections to Kyivan Rus but has never been content with merely doing that, and Russian scholars have used astonishing distortions to claim monopoly over its history. Their version held that the people of Kyivan Rus decamped to Moscow after Kyiv was destroyed by the Mongols and continued developing their society there. Ukrainian historians contend, however, that if there was a population shift, it was not north to Moscow, occupied by the Mongols, but westwards where the Rus principalities of Halych and Volyhnia continued to resist Mongol rule and were the direct successors to Kyivan Rus. During Stalin's rule the official view was that there was originally one prototype Rus people who developed Ukrainian and Russian peculiarities only in the thirteenth and fourteenth centuries, but that Ukraine then returned to the fold when its Cossack leader, Khmelnytsky, signed the controversial treaty with Russia in 1654.

The name 'Russia', meanwhile, did not emerge until centuries after the fall of Kyivan Rus. Russian scholars, however, stood history on its head and the term was applied retrospectively to make it seem that Kyivan Rus and Russia were synonymous. To the unfamiliar the words are sufficiently similar to assume equivalence. Russians seldom hastened to correct confusion between Rus and Russia or, in a later era, the common error that Soviet Union and Russia were interchangeable terms.

Using the same chimerical logic, Russian academics deduced that all East Slavs were variations of Russians, and Ukrainians were called 'Little Russians'. They were 'little' because there were also 'Great Russians', descended from Muscovites. Some historians say the names were assigned by the Byzantines and Little Russia originally referred to the core area of Rus around Kyiv and was meant to denote the senior or more important part of the old Rus empire. Whatever its origin, the term Little Russian, for most people, came to imply that Ukrainians had a junior or inferior national standing. For the adherents of imperial Russia, the debate boiled down to whether the Little Russians were actually a sapling of the Great Russian tree or merely suffering from a delusion they were Great Russians. The term Malorossiya – Little Russia – was the official designation for Ukraine until the downfall of Tsarist rule in 1917. Belarusians – meaning White Russians – were also regarded as a chip off the Great Russian block.

As Russian scholars had demonstrated, by historical legerdemain, that the Great, Little, and White Russians were all really one people then it followed there was only one language and Ukrainian was classified as a dialect of the Great Russian tongue. In the late nineteenth century the Tsarist government banned the printing of Ukrainian-language books or publications.

During the chaotic closing stages of World War One and after the 1917 Bolshevik Revolution, Ukrainians snatched at the opportunity to proclaim independence, an attempt which, as we have seen, proved unsuccessful. But it did draw tens of thousands of young people into the struggle and nurtured their patriotic ideals despite the defeat in battle. The new Communist leaders in Moscow, anxious to avoid fresh conflict, jettisoned the specious history that labelled Ukrainians as Little Russians, and acknowledged their separate nationality. The Ukrainian Soviet Socialist Republic entered the USSR as an equal, in theory at least, and a programme of Ukrainianisation was initiated in the twenties to make the system attractive to the local population. It promoted the Ukrainian culture, including the language, and huge numbers of Ukrainians at all levels of society enthusiastically took advantage of the new opportunities. It came at a time when the Communists had also launched a literacy drive, and millions of Ukrainians learned to read and write in Ukrainian. There was an explosion of newspapers, books and plays in Ukrainian, much of the material innovative and straying from the Communist line. The

Ukrainian Orthodox Church was revived, independent of the Russian one, using the Ukrainian language, and modernised some of its rules.

But what worried the leaders of the Soviet Communist Party most was that leading members of the Ukrainian Communist Party were also seized by the passion for Ukrainianisation. They behaved increasingly independently and criticised the Soviet leadership for reverting to what was in all but name a Russian-dominated system. The Soviet crackdown came at the end of 1929 and was aimed first at non-Communist Party members of the Ukrainian elite, intellectuals, scientists, teachers. Many were executed or exiled after being condemned at show trials for terrorism, spying and seeking to secede from the USSR. Hundreds of the Ukrainian Orthodox Church clergy suffered the same fate.

The following years saw the beginning of Stalin's efforts to smash the peasant farmers who stubbornly clung to their private smallholdings and opposed Communist attempts to introduce collective farms. There were millions of these peasant farmers, disparagingly called *kulaks*, who Stalin hated for their traditional self-reliance which smacked to him of capitalism and challenged the entire Communist system. The vast majority of them also happened to be Ukrainians. Although they spoke in Ukrainian, and Ukrainian traditions and customs were woven into their everyday lives, most would have been surprised to discover they were deemed to be secretly harbouring dangerous nationalist tendencies.

In 1932 and 1933 Stalin imposed crippling demands upon peasants for grain and other foodstuffs which were extracted by special armed units. Anyone resisting was executed, many of them shot on the spot as their family looked on. Nothing was left for the peasants to feed their families and the inevitable outcome was starvation. By the spring of 1933 millions of people in Ukraine were reduced to eating grass, tree bark and earthworms. There were hundreds of cases of cannibalism in a country with some of the world's most fertile farmland, and at the famine's climax an estimated twenty-five thousand people were starving to death each day.

British historian Robert Conquest, an expert on the period, calculated that at least seven million died, mainly in Ukraine, in the early thirties – most in 1933. Other sources calculate up to ten million died as the result of this savage human engineering. Millions of others were deported to hard-labour camps in Siberia and the Arctic where great numbers perished.

Next it was the turn of the Ukrainian Communists who were accused of being nationalists and of planning to break away from the Soviet Union. Around a hundred thousand were put before firing squads or sent to the camps. Some of them had actually gone mad or committed suicide earlier when they saw that the party they had served with such devotion had littered the Ukrainian countryside with emaciated corpses and had driven desperate mothers to cook the bodies of their dead children. The Ukrainian leadership was thoroughly purged and then, in 1937, just for good measure, the entire new Ukrainian government was executed, along with thousands of other 'enemies of the people'.

There is plenty of evidence that many of the victims of Stalin's purges in Ukraine were slaughtered principally because they were Ukrainians helping to keep alive their country's spirit. One of the most poignant examples of this involved exponents of Ukraine's folkloric tradition of travelling balladeers, called *kobzari*, *lirnyky* or *bandurysty*. For centuries the *kobzari* were living depositories of

Ukrainian history, passing epic tales of past glories from one generation to the next, especially the exploits of Cossacks in battle and in love. They sang the stirring ballads while accompanying themselves with a musical instrument native to Ukraine, the *bandura*, shaped like the progeny of a lute and an outsize guitar and, in its various forms, using sometimes more than thirty strings. The players were often blind men who made a living wandering over the land to perform at concerts, weddings and other festivals. They were venerated as guardians of their nation's history and so identified with its traditions and legends that they in turn became a part of those legends.

These living history books came to the baleful attention of the Soviet commissars who saw in them an offensive enemy to be eradicated. Perhaps they considered the balladeers treacherous because they sang of times when their people had arisen to strike back at oppression. The authorities announced, as part of a cultural programme, a conference in Kyiv for balladeers. Hundreds arrived because they believed it was a rare opportunity to discuss the future of their art and to exchange the words of ancient songs that only they or a few others might still know. Those who were sighted must have been taken aback when armed men wearing the uniforms of the NKVD burst in. Their captors roughly bundled the *bandurysty* into trucks and drove to a forest where they were led to freshly dug pits and shot.

The killings made a deep impression on the Russian composer Dmitry Shostakovich, who wrote this in his memoirs: 'When they shoot a folk singer or a wandering storyteller, hundreds of great musical works die with him. Works that have never been written down. They die for ever, irrevocably, because each singer represents certain songs. I am not a historian. I could tell many tragic tales and cite many examples, but I won't do that. I will tell about one incident, only one. It's a horrible story and every time I think of it I grow frightened and I don't want to remember it. Since time immemorial, folk singers have wondered along the roads of Ukraine . . . And then in the mid-thirties the First All-Ukrainian Congress of *lirnyky* and *bandurysty* was announced, and all the folk singers had to gather and discuss what to do in the future. "Life is better, life is merrier," Stalin had said. The blind men believed it. They came to the congress from all over Ukraine, from tiny, forgotten villages. There were several hundred of them at the congress, they say. It was a living museum, the country's living history. All its songs, all its music and poetry. And they were almost all shot, almost all of those pathetic blind men killed.

'Why was it done? Why the sadism – killing the blind? Just like that, so that they wouldn't get underfoot. Mighty deeds were being done there, complete collectivisation was under way, they had destroyed *kulaks* as a class, and here were these blind men, walking around singing songs of dubious content. The songs weren't approved by the censors. And what kind of censorship can you have with blind men? You can't hand a blind man a corrected and approved text and you can't write him an order, either. You have to communicate everything in speech to a blind man. That takes too long. Collectivisation. Mechanisation. It was easier to shoot them. And so they did.'

The terror continued after the war. There were more executions and the Soviet concentration camps were packed with millions of political prisoners. The Ukrainians always formed the disproportionately largest group of inmates. Industrialisation also continued apace in the post-war period, as did Russification of the people who swelled the rapidly growing towns and cities. Under both Tsarism and

Communism, the Russian language was associated with modernity and prosperity, while the Ukrainian language was demeaned as the tongue of peasants.

Ukraine's history was, therefore, ethnically, religiously and linguistically diverse, and various sections of the country have experienced long stretches of rule under very different forms of government. When Ukraine became independent in 1991, there were many warnings that these different experiences represented faultlines along which the country would fracture. A CIA report in 1993 predicted Ukraine could suffer the type of cataclysmic upheavals that shattered the former Yugoslavia. During the Orange Revolution many journalists and commentators referred to 'the mainly Ukrainian-speaking and Catholic west of the country and the Russian-speaking, Orthodox east' and warned that there could be a civil war.

The real state of affairs is of course more complicated. The majority of pro-Yushchenko demonstrators in the Maidan routinely used Russian as their first language; they were also mostly Orthodox Christians, and they were from all over the country. They were, however, *Russian-speaking Ukrainians*. For them there was no confusion between the language they used and their nationality.

A 2001 census showed that Ukraine's population was 48.5 million and that seventy-eight per cent of the population regard themselves as Ukrainian, while seventeen per cent declared themselves ethnic Russians. The only region where ethnic Russians outnumber Ukrainians is Crimea, presented in 1954 to the Ukrainian Soviet Socialist Republic as a 'gift' to commemorate three hundred years of close association between Ukraine and Russia by the then Soviet leader Nikita Khrushchev. At the time Moscow believed the USSR would last for ever. Russian forces had conquered the Muslim khanate on the Crimean peninsula at the end of the eighteenth century, and there was a large influx of Russian colonisers and military.

The 2001 census shows a population of three million fewer than the previous survey in 1989. Political uncertainty and miserably low wages mean many young couples have postponed having children or are having fewer than their parents' generation. Since independence, perhaps seven million people have left the country either permanently or to find work, the vast majority from West Ukraine where the population is almost entirely ethnic Ukrainian.

Being a good Communist meant using the Russian language; even after the death of Stalin, using Ukrainian was frowned upon and imprudent if one wanted to get on in one's career or in the Party. There were incentives to use Russian, and the best educational facilities worked in Russian. In West Ukraine the native language remained prevalent, and although Russian was used by town dwellers elsewhere, even in the east Ukrainian was widespread among the rural community.

When I first visited Kyiv in 1990, the last complete year of Soviet rule, hardly anyone seemed to speak Ukrainian. Some were still fearful that speaking their native language in public, especially with a foreigner from the West, could lay them open to accusations of bourgeois nationalism. Others were simply unused to using Ukrainian and embarrassed that they had forgotten the vocabulary and grammar. In fact many Ukrainians speak a strange blend of Ukrainian and Russian called *surzhyk* which mangles both languages. The Ukrainian language had not been forgotten, though, and very quickly after independence people showed they knew how to speak it. In Kyiv and other cities they may still not routinely use Ukrainian, and in shops and restaurants in much of Central and East Ukraine people rarely initiate a conversation in Ukrainian, but most will respond in Ukrainian if addressed in it. Many in the crowds that turned out in the centre of Kyiv to support the opposition spoke to each other in Russian, but they had no difficulty understanding the speeches which were almost entirely in Ukrainian. They sang Ukrainian songs and shouted slogans in Ukrainian. There were also impassioned speeches by Ukrainians in Russian and patriotic songs about Ukraine sung in Russian. Using the Russian language in Ukraine has never necessarily implied the speaker is pro-Russian, and over the years I have been treated to many colourful tirades by Ukrainians railing against Russia – all vehemently delivered in Russian.

An aphorism attributed to Yiddish linguist Max Weinreich pinpoints the difference between a dialect and a language as, 'a language is a dialect with an army and a navy'. Ukraine's army and navy have never threatened Russia, but it is true that after Ukrainian independence, Russians suddenly found that, contrary to what they had been maintaining for centuries, the Ukrainian language was quite different from their own and difficult to understand. Since then political groups in Ukraine advocating integration with Russia, like the Communists and ethnic Russian political parties, have accused the Ukrainian government of infringing human rights by requiring everyone, including Russian ethnics, to show a minimum proficiency in the Ukrainian language to get state employment. They have stoked fears that ethnic Russian children will not be able to receive education in Russian and have demanded Russian be made a second state language.

Most Ukrainians do not want to exclude the Russian language and there are plenty of Russian-language schools,

TV and radio programmes, newspapers, books, theatres and cinemas. But Ukrainians trying to protect their language know that making Russian an official language could fatally obstruct the reversal of centuries of forced Russification. Mainly it is a question of perception: more people will want to speak Ukrainian when their country becomes one of which they can be proud.

Religious differences are another potentially dangerous source of strife in Ukraine. Those who were bent on mischief during the 2004 presidential election tried to open that Pandora's box. While there are substantial Muslim and Jewish communities, the vast majority of the population is Orthodox Christian of various denominations. Catholicism, overwhelmingly the Byzantine rite variety, is followed by around sixteen per cent of the population and is concentrated in the west of the country. Although the Catholic Church, which has strong traditional links to Ukrainian nationalism, was outlawed by Stalin after the war and many of its clergy and faithful were executed or sent to prison camps, it continued to function underground, holding masses secretly in homes or forests, until restrictions were lifted in the last years of the USSR's existence.

Orthodox believers belong to two distinctly Ukrainian churches and a third that takes its orders from the Russian Orthodox Church, known as the Ukrainian Orthodox Church of the Moscow Patriarchate (UOCMP). The two independent Ukrainian Orthodox churches will eventually probably merge and both have amicable relations with Ukrainian Catholics. However, the Russian Orthodox Church is equally vociferous in its criticism of its Ukrainian Orthodox rivals and Catholics. When the Ukrainian Orthodox and Catholic churches were restored as legal entities after independence, the Russian Orthodox Church was livid because it had to return property confiscated from its rivals during Stalinism.

Although the Ukrainian Orthodox Church is historically the mother-church of the Russian Orthodox Church, celebrating divine services in Ukrainian at the beginning of the twenty-first century is still regarded as heresy by Moscow. The leaders of the pro-Moscow Church in Ukraine refused to greet Pope John Paul II when he visited the country in 2001 and many of its faithful demonstrated against his visit. Some, oblivious to the decidedly un-Christian nature of their supplication, even prayed in the streets of Kyiv for the Pope's plane to crash as it headed for Ukraine. By contrast both Ukrainian Orthodox churches gave the Pope a friendly welcome and, after he died in 2005, the Ukrainians became the first Orthodox Church ever to say prayers for a pope.

During the 2004 presidential elections the UOCMP was the only church openly to back any of the candidates; its blessing went to, of course, the pro-Russian candidate, Viktor Yanukovych. Its priests delivered panegyrics from the altar that characterised Yanukovych as a living saint while Yushchenko grew horns and cloven feet. When it looked as though Yushchenko was going to win, small daily processions of UOCMP faithful trudged mournfully around the capital bearing giant crucifixes and portraits of Yanukovych. Led by priests who looked as if they were clones of Rasputin, the congregation resembled members of an apocalyptic cult. Some of these faithful, trembling with righteousness, listed for journalists Yushchenko's most unconscionable traits, the vilest one being, they fumed – incorrectly – that he was a Catholic. He is in fact Ukrainian Orthodox.

So there are serious divisive issues in Ukrainian society. They are not insuperable but there is considerable evidence that they are being deliberately exacerbated for political gain. Most distressingly, in some areas there is potential for stirring up ethnic conflict. The most volatile area is Crimea where the Russian ethnic population is in the majority. What makes it an ethnic tinderbox is the presence of Muslim Crimean Tatars, expelled en masse by Stalin in 1944 to Central Asia, but who have returned since Ukrainian independence to reclaim their ancestral homes. Ukraine has encouraged their return to dilute Russian ethnic domination, but antagonisms between the Russians and Tatars have sometimes led to brawls and murders. Islamic fundamentalists have tried to establish a foothold in Crimea, and young Crimean Tatars, resentful at being denied land and employment by the ethnic Russian-dominated local authorities, could yet prove a fertile recruiting ground. Russian chauvinist politicians such as the Moscow mayor, Yuriy Luzhkov, and the racist leader of Russia's powerful, ultra right-wing Liberal Democratic Party, Vladimir Zhirinovsky, advocated Crimea's annexation by Russia. The Russian Black Sea fleet is based at Sevastopol on the peninsula and could be used by Moscow to exert military pressure.

Since independence one of Ukraine's undeniable successes has been the absence of ethnic, religious or political conflicts. This comes in marked contrast to the bloody eruptions in Russia and some of the other former Soviet republics which have cost tens of thousands of lives. In previous Ukrainian elections no serious candidates tried to stir up the kind of ethnic or religious hatreds that inflamed the former Yugoslavia and brought a decade of conflict to the Balkans. But that changed in the 2004 presidential elections when Yanukovych's supporters deliberately played on fears of ethnic tension or even civil war and encouraged steps to prise away parts of East and South Ukraine. Prominent Russian politicians like Luzhkov and Zhirinovsky openly backed those fomenting strife and secession in Ukraine, and President Putin neither chastised them nor apologised for their actions.

Chapter Four

THE LONGEST FIGHT

Ukraine, wedged between the European Union and an increasingly autocratic Russia, has learned over the years how to walk political tightropes and, left to its own devices, would likely be able to continue its ethnic balancing act. However, it has not been left alone and Moscow has manipulated and interfered in Ukraine, as it has in other former Soviet republics, since the break-up of the USSR.

Russia gives itself licence to intrude in its neighbours' affairs for a cluster of reasons which straddle conventional power politics, irredentist dreams of empire, and wounded pride. In Ukraine's case there is the added dimension that Russia's myths about its own origins and claims to the leading role in the Slav world are strongly bound up with Kyivan Rus and Ukraine. It is discomfiting that what lies at the centre of those myths is not and does not want to be part of Russia's spiritual landscape. Rancour at Ukraine's impertinence in not conforming to Moscow's historical vision has fostered resentment towards Ukrainian independence from the Russian government, church, right-wing extremists, the Communist Party and some otherwise liberal politicians and intellectuals.

Putin has lamented the disintegration of the USSR, which he described as the greatest disaster to befall the twentieth century. In a speech to parliament two weeks before the sixtieth anniversary of the end of World War Two in Europe, he said: 'First and foremost it is worth acknowledging that the demise of the Soviet Union was the greatest geopolitical catastrophe of the century. As for the Russian people, it became a genuine tragedy. Tens of millions of our fellow citizens and countrymen found themselves beyond the fringes of Russian territory. The epidemic of collapse has spilled over to Russia itself.'

Putin voiced the sentiments of many of his countrymen. The psychological reluctance to accept that the days of Soviet empire have gone is evident even in the Russian term for the independent countries of the former USSR – *Blizkoe Zarubizhia* – which means 'the near abroad' and hints at possession as well as geographical proximity. Russian ideas of 'greatness' are associated with territorial control and military might. There is widespread dismay that as a Soviet superpower, Russia inspired fear and respect, whereas now its ramshackle military and debilitated economy provoke sniggers.

When the USSR broke up there were hopes that democracy would at last take root in Russia; instead the rampant corruption, criminality and conflict that accompanied the fall of Communism everywhere became apparent. Its opponents, most vociferously the Communists and ultra-nationalists, explained that these were the inevitable consequences of democracy, and disillusionment paved the way for a nostalgic pining for Soviet-era discipline and stability. Putin, an authoritarian by instinct and by training, has taken advantage of that mood to start turning back the clock. The former KGB colonel has packed the upper echelons of government with other ex-KGB colleagues, while the police and courts do the bidding of the Kremlin. Pro-democracy support is on the wane and membership of it is increasingly dangerous. Press freedom has receded dramatically with most television and radio channels parroting the government line and fewer newspapers daring to offer honest or independent reports. Such extensive control over the media meant that Putin hardly bothered to campaign in presidential elections in 2004 and breezed in with no real opponents.

Putin has also become confident that there will be little Western censure if he pursues such aggressive policies. Russia's oil and gas, much more so than her rusting nuclear arsenal, give him immense political leverage in a Western Europe increasingly anxious about securing energy supplies to replace its own rapidly diminishing sources. When Putin has used the Russian courts to suppress political opposition, or the Russian army has massacred civilians in Chechnya, the West has usually turned a blind eye or issued an indulgently mild reproach. Such a climate has inevitably emboldened Putin to believe that he is free to behave as he likes in Russia's backyard.

It is natural that Moscow should keep a close watch on events in Ukraine, where it has many legitimate interests. Among these is the well-being of Ukraine's substantial ethnic Russian minority. Another is the pipelines which pump Russian oil and gas across Ukraine to Western markets and provide the income that underpins the entire Russian economy. During Soviet times the biggest chunk of the budget was sunk into the military, including weapons development and production, and Ukraine was, after Russia, the largest centre of the Soviet Union's military-industrial complex. Its defence industry remains one of the biggest and most lucrative manufacturers. But its survival depends on cooperation with Russia because, in a standard Soviet-era technique to lock the industries of different republics into mutual dependency, many of the products cannot be manufactured without components from Russia. Russia is also the main market for most of the products. Ukraine cannot just shut down or radically scale back its arms industry because the political repercussions of making hundreds of thousands of people jobless would be disastrous. Neither does it want to be the only peacenik on the block and rid itself of a sophisticated and lucrative industry that brings massive earnings to so many of its economic competitors. But it does want to reduce its dependency on Russia. Moscow, meanwhile, wants continued access to Ukraine's weapons industry and to maintain Ukraine's dependency on Russia.

Russia has other disquieting interests in Ukraine that are redolent of the old dark dreams of military power. Russia's pride was dented when the Soviet Union's Central European satellites – East Germany, Poland, Hungary, the former Czechoslovakia, Bulgaria and Romania – threw off Communism and insisted on the removal of Soviet forces from their countries. When the USSR disintegrated, Moscow, claiming a threat from NATO, was determined to retain military footholds in the newly independent republics and to some extent succeeded. Ukraine's Crimean city of Sevastopol is headquarters to the Russian Black Sea fleet and Russia has a number of other smaller bases on the peninsula secured by strong-arming Ukraine's first independent government into agreeing to lease the bases until 2017. At the same time, the fleet itself was divided, with Russia gaining the most powerful and serviceable vessels and Ukraine allotted the rustbuckets. Ukraine's sole submarine could not venture out until 2004 because it did not have the batteries essential to run the diesel engine under water.

In Georgia and Moldova Russian troops remain in their old garrisons in the guise of peacekeepers, covertly prop up rebel forces, and destabilise the legitimate governments. Their continuing presence in Ukraine and elsewhere provides a blunt warning about the potential consequences of displeasing Moscow.

The Kremlin has floated a variety of schemes since the demise of the USSR to increase Russian control over the 'near abroad' and Putin vigorously pursued his own version to create a powerful Moscow-led multinational body called the Single Economic Zone (SEZ), considered by many as the first step to raise a new empire from the ashes of the USSR. This political entity was supposed to include former Soviet republics Ukraine, Kazakhstan and Belarus as well as Russia, with each of the four countries receiving voting powers proportional to its economic strength. Russia's vote in any supra-government body would be worth more than the combined votes of the other three so it would call all the shots. Ukraine, though, was the essential component without which Putin's ambition was doomed.

Ukraine's foreign minister in governments before and after the Orange Revolution, Borys Tarasiuk, one of the country's most erudite and principled politicans, said: 'I remember different projects originated from the Kremlin at different times. The first, in 1991, was the Commonwealth of Independent States – that was to re-create domination over the former Soviet republics. Then there was a project named "the economic union", then there was another project named "the customs union", and after that "the Eurasian Economic Community". All these projects were designed with just one purpose – to bind in Ukraine. The Single Economic Zone is nothing new. It is the same package to re-create the geo-political space of the former Soviet Union with the domination of Moscow but in a different wrapping.'

Putin knew that Ukraine's 2004 presidential election would be fought for very high stakes, its outcome determining whether Ukraine entrenched democracy and moved closer towards the West or whether it remained anchored in Russia's increasingly malevolent sphere of influence. On this depended his ambitious plans to claw back Russia's super-power status. Other important concerns included the implications for Russia's continued military presence on Ukrainian soil and the example a truly democratic government might set to other former Soviet republics weary of Moscow's bullying. Putin ordered that everything be done to ensure Ukraine should remain firmly within Moscow's orbit and so the Ukrainian elections saw Russian interference taken to outrageous levels.

One of the reasons underlying the awkward relationship between Russia and its former colonies lies in the manner they achieved independence. The Soviet Union collapsed in 1991 not because of armed rebellion by its subject peoples or in a test of military strength against its Cold War enemy, the West, but from deathblows struck from within as the culmination of a power struggle between Russian leaders. However, real independence had not been envisaged for the republics and the corpse of the USSR was supposed to be exhumed in the form of a Moscow-led bloc of nations, the Commonwealth of Independent States (CIS). Ukraine bucked against incorporation into any new kind of union and refused to sign the CIS charter, but since 1991 has faced a series of fierce challenges to its decision to proclaim independence.

After Stalin's death in 1953 the extent of the terror decreased but the Soviet system remained a brutal police state until its end. Ukrainians were always at the forefront of movements for independence from, or at least liberalisation of, the Soviet Union. After the Ukrainian Insurgent Army, UPA, abandoned armed resistance in the early fifties, Ukrainians turned to other means of registering opposition. The scope for any kind of legal opposition was severely restricted and Ukrainian students, writers, artists, scientists, clergymen, poets, union leaders, workers, and even some disillusioned Communist Party members, met mostly in secret to discuss calls for human rights or for independence. They disseminated their ideas in underground literature called *samvydav* in Ukrainian, or *samizdat* in Russian – the term for self-produced publications. Often these were hand-written and handcopied pamphlets, because access to typewriters and photocopiers was strictly regulated. These brave, principled people were hunted and persecuted by the KGB with the psychopathic zeal of every secret police service in a totalitarian society. After sham trials they were sent for long years of imprisonment in the hard-labour camps that were scattered throughout some of the most inhospitable regions in the world, which proved to be death sentences for tens of thousands of prisoners. Many who survived were immediately arrested on completion of their original prison sentence and, after a brisk retrial, sent back to the camps.

In the seventies the Soviet authorities and KGB 'psychiatrists' invented a barbarous new punishment: many political dissidents were diagnosed as schizophrenic and condemned to years of 'treatment' in mental hospitals where they were injected with drugs that caused extremely painful side effects. If the diagnosis of mental illness had been false at the start of such treatment, there was a good chance the nightmarish cure eventually made it real.

Sometimes it was too awkward even for the bogus Soviet justice system to convict someone on flimsy charges, so the KGB murdered them. In the seventies the music of a young composer, Volodymyr Ivasiuk, who blended traditional Ukrainian folk styles with a modern format, became immensely popular in Ukraine. There was nothing overtly political about the tender lyrics, yet Ukrainians recognised in them metaphors that spoke of their country and the dreams of its people. Soon Ivasiuk and his songs came to be seen by the KGB as a defiant rallying point for those who cared deeply about Ukraine. The KGB, which was also fond of tradition, perhaps took inspiration from its predecessor organisation, the NKVD, and how it had dealt with the troublesome Ukrainian balladeers in the thirties. Ivasiuk disappeared in the spring of 1979 and twenty-four days later his body was discovered hanging from a tree in a forest near Lviv. Few believed the official verdict of suicide. Thousands attended his funeral, defying Communist warnings not to do so. The KGB had turned Ivasiuk into a martyr and one of his songs, 'Chervona Ruta', was to haunt them as the unofficial anthem of a growing movement in Ukraine for freedom.

While Russian dissidents in Moscow were sometimes able to make contact with Western journalists and diplomats based there to publicise their causes, Western visitors to Ukraine – and other Soviet republics – were rare. Ukrainian political activists, although always composing a dispro-portionately large part of both the opposition movements in the USSR and the Gulag population, were not usually as well known outside the Soviet Union as their Russian counter-parts like Andrei Sakharov and Alexander Solzhenitsyn. It is difficult to imagine now that not so long ago in Eastern Europe, criticism of the authorities could lead to ten or fifteen years imprisonment in a remote slice of the planet that was bitterly cold during winter and stiflingly hot during the summer. Prisoners were worked mercilessly and survived on sparse rations of bread and cabbage so that illness was omnipresent while medicines and doctors were rare. Visits by relatives were very infrequent.

Yet these people continued to protest, write essays, songs, articles and poems knowing full well what awaited them. In

1985 a hugely talented poet called Vasyl Stus was halfway through his second sentence under Article 62 of the USSR Penal Code, concerning slandering the state. Stus had completed one such sentence in late 1979 and in 1980 was sentenced to ten years' forced labour plus five years' 'internal exile' – a form of house arrest in Gulag territory. 1985 was also the first year of the rule of Mikhail Gorbachev, who had vowed to make the Soviet Union more humane and free through perestroika. Stus had been jailed for protesting against human rights violations. Appeals by Amnesty International for his release went unheeded despite the fact that forty-seven-year-old Stus was severely ill with heart and kidney ailments and not receiving medical aid. The poet had been nominated for the following year's Nobel Prize for Literature and if he had received the award it would have been acutely embarrassing for Gorbachev's government. Stus, however, never became a Nobel Laureate because he was literally worked to death in Hard Labour Camp 36-1 near Perm in Russia where he died without hospital treatment on 4 September 1985. With him perished the danger of a Nobel scandal because the prize is not awarded posthumously.

When he became the Soviet leader, Gorbachev was much younger than his predecessors, who traditionally ruled until they dropped dead. Although a committed Communist, Gorbachev permitted himself to think in a less dogmatic and rigid way than his forerunners and recognised that the USSR's economy could not keep up with that of the West. To save the Soviet Union he offered to scale down its nuclear arsenal and introduce more human rights in return for economic help from the West. He also allowed some criticism of the system and a limited amount of press freedom. But while he was certainly different from previous Soviet leaders, Gorbachev had not grasped that most of the USSR's inhabitants loathed Communism and the bleak, repressive, society it produced. The trickle of freedom he allowed ultimately turned into a deluge.

During the Gorbachev period Ukrainian demands for independence were revived on a mass scale. One of the catalysts for Ukraine's restiveness was the world's biggest civil nuclear disaster, which happened at the Chernobyl nuclear power plant on 26 April 1986. It was the result of an ill-judged experiment deliberately to withdraw safety measures that went catastrophically wrong and caused the core of one of the reactors to explode. Eight tons of radioactive material, more than that from the atomic bombs dropped on Hiroshima and Nagasaki combined, was released into the atmosphere.

From ingrained habit, the Soviet authorities lied to the entire world and for days denied that anything serious had happened at the Chernobyl complex until a spy-satellite photograph showed a terrifying image of the wrecked and blazing Number Four reactor. While firemen and soldiers fighting the blaze were dying of massive radiation exposure, the Soviet authorities ordered that the annual May Day parades to glorify Soviet achievements should go ahead as usual. So hundreds of thousands of people in the capital Kyiv and other towns were told to turn out on the streets to celebrate whilst the deadly, invisible particles swirled about them. Ordinary people did not have access to Geiger counters, but the Communist Party officials did, and many of them secretly evacuated their families from Kyiv and some found excuses to leave the capital themselves. Fortunately for Kyiv, the prevailing wind carried most of the radio-activity north-west of Chernobyl, cutting a devastating swathe through Belarus, but changing wind patterns gradually dispersed radioactive debris over a huge area, penetrating as far as Italy and Britain. If the wind had moved in the opposite direction, Kyiv today would be a ghost city like the modern high-rise settlement at Pripyat, close to the reactors, which housed thirty thousand people – the plant's technicians and their families. Pripyat looks like the set for an end-of-the-world science-fiction movie with its deserted apartment blocks, shops, cinema, hospital and local-government buildings engulfed by weeds and foliage which are breaking up the roads and reclaiming the city for a nature that has proved resilient but, in some instances, has been oddly mutated by the disaster. Perhaps the eeriest scene is provided by a funfair of rusting carousels and overturned bumper cars that had been set up in readiness for the May Day holiday.

Although Chernobyl has since been shut down, technicians still keep an eye on the crumbling makeshift sarcophagus around the wrecked reactor. All the inhabitants within a radius of twenty miles were evacuated in 1986 and, officially, it will not be safe for anyone to live in 'the Zone' for around three hundred years. Hundreds of residents, mostly elderly, in fact returned to their homes in the forbidden zone, preferring to live in familiar surroundings rather than the strange cities and cramped apartments they were moved to after the accident. In 2003 Ukraine's intelligence agency made public previously secret files that revealed some five thousand people had died as a result of the disaster and the Ukrainian government estimates that up to five million of their citizens suffer directly attributable health problems.

In 2005 a team of United Nations researchers said that fear of the health dangers was exaggerated and only fifty-nine victims could be shown to have died directly because of the accident, although the UN report predicted some four thousand would eventually die of radiation-related cancers.

Many in Ukraine dispute the report, but if nobody could say with precision what the accident's effects were nineteen years later, it was certainly impossible to predict the consequences while the disaster was still happening. But the Soviet authorities did not sound the alarm for days and it was that callous disregard for the populace more than the accident itself that produced a powerful backlash of disgust. Officials said that only a few dozen firemen and army conscripts had died, but people in the affected areas believed that the premature deaths of thousands more were fraudulently being attributed to common causes. Parents were terrified – and still are – that their children would be affected by radiation-related diseases like thyroid cancer, which soared after the predicted interval of several years following the accident. A feeling of helplessness accompanied the panic because leaving the Soviet Union was forbidden for most people and even moving to another part of the USSR was difficult. People desperately searched for medicines that they had been told could prevent radiation sickness, trading their most precious possessions for supplies of iodine tablets for their children. The absence of any trusted guidance from the authorities turned many to seek comfort in quack medicines and superstition. Some paid for 'special' stones which, they were assured, if placed under their child's bed would shield him or her from the harmful effects of radiation.

Chernobyl became one of the powerful ingredients driving calls among Ukrainians for democracy and independence. The most vibrant political activity began in West Ukraine in the indomitable nationalist redoubt of Lviv, but the movement for democracy, Rukh, embracing a variety of civic and political groups, spread across the country. By the end of the eighties there were huge demonstrations including one in which a million Ukrainians formed a human chain across their country.

Gorbachev certainly diminished the scale of repression and opened up the USSR for an unprecedented debate about democratic and economic liberalisation. But he was out of tune with the majority: while he wanted to retain the Soviet Union and the Party in a more lenient form, it became clear most people hoped the reforms would lead to the death of Communism. One of the prickliest questions was what to do about the republics, many of which were pressing for more control over their affairs while the three tiny Baltic Soviet republics of Lithuania, Latvia and Estonia were demanding outright independence. In January 1991 Soviet interior ministry troops killed freedom protestors in Lithuania and Latvia. Gorbachev offered a 'Union Treaty' that most suspected would change little and retain Moscow at its centre. Yet the Baltic countries refused to dilute their demands and in late July 1991 Soviet special forces murdered six Lithuanian customs officers with execution-style shots to the head as a warning to those seeking independence.

Enraged Communist hardliners, who did not want to yield their immense privileges and thought Gorbachev was conceding too much, tried to remove him in a coup that summer. A group of Gorbachev's top Party colleagues, including the KGB chief, ordered that he be seized at his Crimean holiday home where they tried to force him to go on extended leave on the pretext of ill health. Their poorly prepared plan depended on government security structures – especially troops from the army and the powerful interior ministry forces – blindly following commands from the Kremlin. But the Gorbachev years had already produced an effect and some of the important players delayed obeying commands and waited to see what happened. The confused plotters had no contingency plan and dithered while Gorbachev's anti-Communist rival, Boris Yeltsin, organised mass demonstrations in Moscow against them. Military support for the conspirators rapidly ebbed and the plot collapsed.

Gorbachev flew back to Moscow to what could have been a hero's welcome if he had not misjudged the prevailing mood so badly. The country demanded condemnation of the Communist Party and KGB which had staged the attempt to restore dictatorship, and the public wanted promises that the bad old days would never return. Instead Gorbachev lamely chastised the black sheep responsible for the bungled coup and tried to exculpate the Communist Party. A sigh of disappointment heaved across the country and Gorbachev achieved what the coup had failed – he toppled himself. Inspiring images of Yeltsin atop a tank addressing pro-democracy demonstrators were still fresh in the public's mind. Yeltsin seized the political initiative and pinned the blame squarely on the Communist Party, declaring that the way to real reforms and a more just society was to strip the Communists of their power and ban the party. Yeltsin's words resonated with the hopes of ordinary people and there was a dramatic shift of support towards him.

Lithuania, Latvia and Estonia, which had been conducting themselves as independent states even before the coup attempt, now declared a final break with the Soviet Union.

I had arrived in a tense Tallinn, capital of Estonia, on the second day of the coup. Western journalists were being refused visas to the USSR in embassies, such as London, where the senior staff were sympathetic to the hardliners. The consul in the Finnish capital, Helsinki, though, was a reformist and gladly issued visas; Tallinn was just a few hours' journey by boat. The atmosphere in the Estonian capital was extremely tense and bloodshed was expected if the hardliners' coup succeeded. Young people had prepared barricades of breeze blocks, concrete, girders and wood in case the Soviet troops (in tanks and armoured personnel carriers stationed around a television tower on the outskirts of the capital) advanced. However, by the end of the second day it was obvious the coup was beset with problems. The Soviet troops were themselves nervous because many of their senior officers had disappeared and nobody responded to their radio enquiries when they tried to have orders clarified. Eventually they moved out and headed for their barracks in neighbouring Latvia.

The happiness was infectious as overjoyed Estonians, many in national costume, paraded through the old town where some of the pastel-coloured buildings hinted at the city's proud medieval history as one of the most precious jewels in the chain of prosperous Hanseatic League ports. People waved black, blue and white national flags, sang traditional songs and listened to speeches about their country's bold future. Tallinn's main statue of Lenin was swiftly uprooted and transported away on a flatbed truck while members of the watching crowd laughed, cried, or looked on pensively.

It was the second time within two years I had witnessed a turning point in the history of Eastern Europe. In November 1989 I managed to get to East Germany on the day people began to pour across the Berlin Wall. In the middle of that night I crossed at the famous Checkpoint Charlie border post into West Berlin in the midst of a stream of thousands of ecstatic people. Over the next days I watched as East and West Germans used sledgehammers, crowbars and their bare hands to start dismantling the hated Wall and with it the myth of monolithic Soviet power. On 24 August 1991, as I stood amongst a crowd of jubilant Estonians who had surrounded the KGB headquarters in their capital, I wondered if Ukrainians too would experience those sweeping changes and uplifting emotions. Occasionally, terrified KGB staff inside the building peeped out from behind drawn curtains. They were frightened that the crowd taunting them might break in and take revenge for the crimes inflicted over the years by people working in that building.

I had visited Ukraine for the first time the previous year, in 1990. In earlier years my parents had asked me not to go because they feared I would be arrested. When I finally went it was in one of two trucks laden with medicines for victims of the Chernobyl nuclear disaster and organised by my mother in her capacity as the head of the Ukrainian women's organisation in Britain. After being delayed for several days at the frontier by obstructive Soviet officials, we drove across the Polish border eastwards into the almost deserted roads of West Ukraine. We were trailed by police cars as we travelled first to Lviv and then on to the capital, Kyiv.

In both cities there was an excitement that changes were both possible and imminent but this was tempered by apprehension that the hardliners might suddenly and violently reassert their power. Ukraine's Communist Party was regarded as more rigid than its counterparts in other republics and moved slowly in instigating even the reforms approved by the Politburo in Moscow. While most in Ukraine's reform movement, Rukh, wanted independence, they spoke in more guarded terms publicly, declaring an agenda for greater democracy and increased autonomy. There were skirmishes between protestors and police at some of the rallies in Kyiv which called for independence.

In Tallinn I was tuning in to BBC World Service broadcasts to find out what was happening elsewhere and it was in the crowd outside the Estonian KGB building that I heard the news that Ukraine had declared independence. I listened carefully to make sure I had not misheard the bulletin and then I cried.

I made arrangements to get to Kyiv as quickly as possible. When I arrived there was a celebratory mood but the atmosphere was restrained compared to that in Tallinn and Riga where people had immediately set about tearing down statues of Lenin and other Communist emblems. In Kyiv there was more a feeling of relief that there had been no violence. People knew important changes were afoot and for a few days the Communists were worried they would be flung in jail or receive some more condign retribution. However, the democratic opposition acted with sluggish caution and limited itself to congratulatory patriotic speeches without grabbing the real levers of power. Perhaps Ukrainians, who had seen so many million of their countrymen die in political purges, in war or by starvation, had had the fight bled out of them and were too timid to seize the historic opportunity. Power remained with the same Communists who had ruled before. Indeed it was the Communists who had declared independence because they saw it as a way of defusing Rukh demands and retaining control; strikingly, the man who had been the Ukrainian Communist Party's chief ideologist, Leonid Kravchuk, became Ukraine's leader. The new government decided to test the will for independence in a referendum on 1 December that year, in which more than ninety per cent of Ukraine's population voted for independence. An election held concurrently elected Kravchuk president.

But there were fundamental matters yet to be settled. A peculiar legal situation obtained because the USSR still existed. Moreover, Gorbachev, who was the darling of Western leaders who much preferred a democratised Soviet

Union to a plethora of new states, was still the president of the Soviet Union. Yeltsin's plan was to make Gorbachev redundant by dismantling the Soviet Union.

On 7 December 1991, President Kravchuk, President Yeltsin and Belarus's Supreme Soviet Chairman Stanislau Shushkevich met at a country house for government guests in the tranquil surroundings of Belarus's Belavezha Forest, believed to be Europe's last woodland undisturbed since primeval times. The three were ostensibly meeting to discuss economic issues but the real agenda was to write the USSR out of existence. The atmosphere was tense and all three men knew that if things went wrong they could face execution as traitors to the system that had nurtured and propelled them to the top. That evening vodka flowed at the dinner table as the leaders calmed their jangling nerves. Some sources say that all of them, or at least Yeltsin, notorious for his drinking, became completely drunk. Many of the details of those two days are hazy and the accounts given by the three men vary. One recurring element is that Kravchuk, who enjoyed his reputation as a wily political operator, took advantage of Yeltsin's insobriety. Yeltsin may not have been ready to agree to full independence for Ukraine but Kravchuk is credited with extracting such a settlement. Whatever was said, it is clear that Ukraine's behaviour was critical. The pioneering secession of the Baltic states was courageous but a far from fatal blow for the empire; small Belarus had symbolic importance because it was one of the three 'core' Slav nations in the USSR, but the USSR minus Ukraine would spell the end of the Soviet Union.

From the various accounts it is possible to assemble a sequence of events. Before everyone retired to bed, Yeltsin asked his aides to formulate a declaration to be signed the next day. The only secretary had already gone home and her office was locked, so Yeltsin's aides slid the document under her door with instructions to type it up first thing in the morning. The next morning the secretary was in her office but claimed she had not seen the document. The horrified aides feared Gorbachev's people or the KGB had somehow got hold of it and were relieved to discover that the cleaning lady had come in early, opened the secretary's office and found what looked like litter on the floor and thrown it out. The document was retrieved and typed up. Kravchuk admitted there was drinking at the dinner but is adamant alcohol was not a factor in the proceedings. 'When we met to work on the document, Yeltsin was as sober as a judge. I'm not exaggerating. He was in good form, vigorous, he had ideas. All of us saw him and everybody can confirm that Yeltsin and all of us were fully aware of what we were doing,' he said.

In his memoirs, Kravchuk claims that he told the Russian leader that Ukrainians had proved their desire for independence only the previous week via the referendum, and as their president he had to insist the agreement they were negotiating must reflect that wish. So amidst drink, secrecy, fear and an element of farce, the three men signed a document of momentous consequences which stated 'The Soviet Union as a geopolitical reality and a subject of international law has ceased to exist'. Independence was confirmed and Ukraine's share of Soviet weapons made it the world's third largest nuclear power after the US and Russia. But the implications of the declaration were mixed. Possession of nuclear weapons soon turned out not to be a boon and the document also contained the seeds of future problems for Ukraine. It indicated that Russia had far from given up its ambition to be the regional boss and the agreement announced the creation of a new entity to be composed of the former Soviet republics – the Commonwealth of Independent States, the CIS.

After they signed the document the three decided to call President George Bush to announce their move before letting a furious Gorbachev know that he no longer had a country of which to be president. Kravchuk said Gorbachev continued to badger him in phone calls offering permutations of the Union Treaty until 25 December, when the Soviet parliament held its last meeting to hand powers over to the newly independent republics and the last Soviet leader finally resigned.

The Communist Party was initially banned in Russia, Ukraine and elsewhere after the attempted coup, but was reinstated by the end of 1992. The Communists could not quite believe their good fortune at surviving and crept out of their hiding places and resumed their arrogant poses. The Communist parties, although no longer in power, exist in all the former Soviet colonies and, as in Ukraine, still have a significant presence in the parliaments of many of the independent states.

The Communists have never apologised for the murder and suffering their party caused, and furiously continue to deny responsibility for the horror their ideology inflicted. Whereas Nazism is condemned for what it propagated as well as its actions, many still applaud what Communism advocates while excusing its realities.

One of the reasons the Ukrainian famine and other mass murders have not gouged out a scar on the world's consciousness is that there has been no equivalent for Soviet politicians of the Nuremberg war crimes trials after World War Two. In Germany pro-Nazi rallies are illegal while in Moscow, Kyiv and other cities in the former Soviet Union, parades of mostly elderly people holding aloft banners of Stalin are tolerated. The hearts of the protestors who hold Stalin so dear are doubtlessly warmed as they watch Putin restore Stalinist touches to Russian society. The Russian president has uttered kind words about Stalin and the bloodthirsty founder of the Soviet secret police, Feliks Dzerzhinsky, whose statue outside KGB headquarters in Moscow was torn down in 1991. New statues of Stalin were erected in Russia in 2004 and 2005 and Putin put Dzerzhinsky back on his pedestal in 2005.

The evidence of Communist crimes is there in miles of shelves creaking under the weight of fastidious state and secret police files in Moscow. The Communists destroyed some of these records when they saw that the Soviet Union was imploding and there were fears people would seek revenge or at least demand the truth. However, it soon became clear there would be no attempt to acknowledge their history by opening the files to the public. There would be no truth commissions, and the NKVD and KGB executioners, by now pensioners, adorned with medals for mass murders efficiently conducted, would never be forced to apologise for their crimes, let alone face justice. Many Communists slid effortlessly into key posts in the new regimes.

Soon after the dissolution of the USSR, Moscow once more made clear the determination to anchor Ukraine within her sphere of influence or to incorporate it in some new union. Kravchuk said that Yeltsin quickly began to take the same haughty attitude to Ukraine as Gorbachev had. 'Undoubtedly, Yeltsin reckoned that Moscow would continue to dominate one sixth of the globe. Wherever we subsequently met, at numerous CIS events, he always considered himself fully in charge,' said Kravchuk.

If the new Russia had developed relations with Ukraine

and the other republics on a basis of equality, then Europe and much of the rest of the world might have entered the twenty-first century with more optimistic expectations. But the Kremlin proved that it was unable to shed the habit of centuries and conduct its relations, especially with its former colonies, along civilised and amicable lines. Perhaps Russia had used threats, bullying and force for so long to get its way, and its paranoia about being beset by enemies is so ingrained, that any compromise is regarded as a sign of weakness. Whatever the reasons, Russia has habitually used its still considerable economic and military clout to try to bend Kyiv to its will.

Russia's principal instrument for securing Ukraine's compliance has been energy. Ukraine has been dependent on Russian gas and oil supplies because its own energy resources – massively exploited during Soviet times – are depleted, and attempts to develop new ones have been patchy. Russia has used that dependency and the resultant huge energy debt to dictate terms to Ukraine on many issues including the right to naval bases in Crimea and as part payment for wholesale purchases of Ukrainian industry.

Although Russia sought to constrain Ukraine's independence, it was the Ukrainians who came to power that were most responsible for curbing the freedoms of its people as they set about plundering their country and plunged it into a vortex of corruption and lawlessness.

Chapter Five

ROTTEN GUYS

Ukrainians in Ukraine and all over the world tried hard to be proud of Leonid Kravchuk and attempted to spin around him a pleasing myth as a venerable father of the country; the hero who had won independence. Delight at independence meant that they were ready to overlook many less than heroic qualities in Kravchuk. Anyway, he convincingly looked the part of a statesman with a pleasant patrician face that could project gravity or light up with an engaging grin.

There is no doubt that when Kravchuk, at the age of fifty-seven, became president in December 1991 he was confronted with a myriad economic and social problems and his room for manoeuvre was severely restricted. When the USSR broke up, Ukraine was supposed to receive a proportion of the former Soviet assets but ended up receiving mostly a share of the debt. Much of Ukraine's industry was out of date, uncompetitive and overmanned. Just before Ukraine declared independence, George Bush arrived in Kyiv to be greeted by Ukrainians overjoyed that the 'Leader of the Free World' was visiting their country. They expected at least some moral encouragement for their moves towards freedom and independence. Instead, in a notorious address nick-named the 'Chicken Kyiv' speech, Bush astonished and dismayed his eager listeners by advising them to steer away from independence and to buckle under to Gorbachev's plan for a new Moscow-led union. The West ploughed cash and aid into Russia while Ukraine's economy went into a tailspin.

The Western leaders' chief interest in Ukraine was to cajole it into transferring all the nuclear missiles on its territory to Russia, it being made clear there would be no significant aid until that was done. Margaret Thatcher referred to Ukraine as a 'state similar to California' in relation to the USSR and regarded its move towards independence as somewhat treacherous.

Born in 1934 in what became West Ukraine after the war, Kravchuk studied economics at Kyiv and Moscow universities at a time when 'economics' meant Marxism, and joined the Communist Party in 1958. He swiftly rose up through the ranks and worked in the Party's Orwellian 'agitprop' section refining the lies that underpinned Soviet society. After that he spent many years as the chief Communist Party ideologue in Ukraine. In 1989 he entered the top raft and became a member of the Ukrainian Politburo, the only West Ukrainian to achieve such a senior position, and then, in 1990, chairman of Ukraine's Supreme Soviet, its parliament. All the time he was a fierce opponent of the Ukrainian 'nationalists' who wanted independence.

Kravchuk, like so many of his senior colleagues in the nomenklatura who had been showered with privileges, displayed a remarkable talent for effortlessly ditching the Party when it became clear its days were numbered.

As the political drama that would decide the Soviet Union's future was being played out, Kravchuk sat on the fence. During the coup attempt in August 1991 he was non-committal until it was clear the hardliner Communists had failed. Had they not, his friends in the Ukrainian KGB were ready to act and had prepared lists of democratic activists to be arrested and, reportedly, had even acquired hundreds of extra pairs of handcuffs. When the coup did fail, he rapidly switched sides in favour of independence and resigned from the Party becoming at a stroke the sort of bourgeois Ukrainian nationalist he had spent his career vilifying. A few months later he was elected president of Ukraine by around two thirds of the electorate and the transformation from Soviet internationalist to Ukrainian patriot was complete.

President Kravchuk shrugged off accusations of hypocrisy. Indeed some said that his pragmatism was just what Ukraine needed. There were jokes about how he did not need a raincoat because he could dodge the raindrops and remain dry. His speeches, delivered in the dull monotone that Communist oratory held to signify substance, were vapid, convoluted, and non-committal. Kravchuk is known to enjoy chess and his political technique eschews aggression for carefully avoiding being cornered and waiting for the opponent to make a mistake. One could listen to him for hours and fail to detect anything of consequence. This is his answer to a question about a looming parliamentary crisis: 'Truly, the situation in the parliament has become acute. But I would not like to see it end in a crisis. The deputies should understand that today, in the political climate that exists, any step in this or that direction will divide both the deputies themselves and the nation.'

So the president acquired the reputation of being a sly fox. On the plus side, this canniness allowed him to keep Ukraine's relationship with the CIS ambiguous. Ukraine attended CIS meetings but never subscribed to the organisation's charter and the body remained a toothless talking shop with its conference resolutions promptly forgotten after the vodka toasts.

The president also won praise for making Ukraine the first ever country to give up its nuclear arsenal. He gained a lot of international cachet for handing over to Russia Ukraine's 176 intercontinental ballistic missiles with 1,240 nuclear warheads and forty-one long-range bombers armed with 328 warheads, but he failed to parlay the deal into adequate economic recompense or serious Western guarantees to assist Ukraine against potential aggressors. In other respects too, Kravchuk turned out to be a rather puny defender of his country's interests. Russia got its way on the division of industrial and military resources, the division of the former Soviet Union's vast assets abroad (including valuable embassy and trade legation buildings), on drawing up borders between the two countries and arranging advantageous trade terms for Moscow between the two countries. Deputies in the Russian parliament who tore up the Ukrainian flag and decried Ukraine's independence worked with ethnic Russian separatists in Crimea to call for the peninsula's annexation by Moscow. Kravchuk managed to keep Crimea, but had to concede a large measure of autonomy to the ethnic-Russian-dominated local authorities, and allow Russian naval forces to remain.

But his biggest failures were economic. Crucially, Kravchuk failed to muster the necessary courage to embark on fundamental political and economic reforms to wrench the country from its outdated Communist quagmire. Such reforms would have been initially painful but could have spared Ukraine the prolonged economic misery that in 2006 still gripped the country. Instead of taking decisive action, Kravchuk allowed the economic situation to deteriorate around him and Ukraine was plunged into runaway inflation, which reached ten thousand per cent between 1993 and 1995. There were shortages of everything, including basic foods. People queued for hours to get a loaf of bread and then had to line up elsewhere to get vegetables or a scrap of meat. They had to search for days and pay bribes to obtain vital medicines and were forced to barter or sell anything of value for a pittance. Women sometimes traded their bodies so they could feed their families. At the time, I was reporting on the conflicts in the former Yugoslavia, and Kyiv seemed to be sliding into the same pitiable and ravaged conditions as the Bosnian capital Sarajevo, only without undergoing war and siege.

Soviet bureaucracy had always been corrupt and it was customary to pay a little bribe – perhaps in the form of Western cigarettes or alcohol – to get anything done. But with the economy in turmoil, the opportunities for corruption, and the demands for bribes to make up for salaries made worthless by inflation, mushroomed. Most people were state employees and the government either gave up paying wages or paid paltry amounts at irregular and long intervals. Doctors, bureaucrats, policemen, teachers, pensioners, miners and farmers sometimes received nothing for six or twelve months. Desperate people worked for one dollar a day. The authorities, including the police, shook down the new small businessmen who sold their goods in street kiosks or market stalls. The law enforcers learned that cooperation with the protection racketeers who extorted money was much more rewarding than challenging the gangsters. The relationship became a template for deals between criminals and the authorities at every level.

Those with government connections received the equivalent of millions of dollars in loans from banks dispensing state funds. Fortunes could be made on currency deals or buying valuable raw materials. Many borrowers defaulted on the loans but inflation meant that a few dollars could pay off what had seemed a massive sum in Ukrainian currency only weeks before. Precious metals and other raw materials could be bought at cheap Soviet prices and sold for dollars, pounds, marks or yen, which Ukrainians called *valuta* to distinguish it from their own almost worthless currency. Kravchuk's years in power saw the birth of large-scale government corruption. In the privatisation of Ukraine's industry, favoured individuals who paid kickbacks had the chance to buy enterprises cheaply. Other friends of the government were simply given licence to steal state assets; ships of the state-owned Black Sea Steamship Company, for example, which had been the world's largest merchant fleet, were sold to foreign companies with the Ukrainian state receiving nothing. Ukraine's first big corruption scandal gripped the nation when it was alleged by members of parliament that a minister had authorised inflated payments for bulls' sperm imported from South America to inseminate Ukrainian cows. The allegations were not proved but Ukraine at least received a short respite of laughter.

Less amusingly, illegal arms sales began during Kravchuk's presidency – to Croatia, which could not otherwise have resisted an onslaught by Serbia, and also to the fighters in African civil wars. While he was cautioned by his security service that he might be called to answer for this, Kravchuk ignored the warnings, thus helping to give Ukraine its reputation of being a supplier of illegal arms to the world's butcher regimes.

The sale of weapons to countries under sanctions, participants in civil wars, and, as suspected by some Western intelligence agencies, to potential terrorists, can only have been managed with the active involvement of important government officials. It is conceivable that some of Ukraine's huge stockpiles of ammunition or small arms, including the ubiquitous AK-47 automatic rifle, the favourite Third World firearm, could be spirited out of arsenals by relatively junior officers. However, selling and transporting tanks, heli-copters, missiles and sophisticated defence systems required the cooperation of the highest echelons of the military, intelligence and political structures. Some Western countries turned a blind eye or even secretly encouraged Ukraine's supply of tanks, small arms, ammunition and other equipment to Croatia in contravention of a UN arms embargo during the conflict in the former Yugoslavia.

It emerged that in 1999 and 2000 Ukraine sold twelve long-range cruise missiles to Iran and six to China. The profits made from illicit weapons deals since independence have been estimated at billions of dollars but an exact figure is impossible to calculate.

In the summer of 1994 the parlous state of the economy and growing corruption forced Kravchuk to call an early presidential election. He was unexpectedly beaten by his former prime minister, Leonid Kuchma, who began a ten-year reign over two terms. Despite the many serious flaws in his presidency, Kravchuk's tenure might have looked like a golden era compared to that of his successor, who presided over a period of rampant corruption and lawlessness that affected everyone in Ukraine. But Kravchuk's ill-judged behaviour after his presidency was to leave his reputation in tatters. Perhaps too young to be content with the role of elder statesman, he threw in his lot with one of Ukraine's largest oligarchic business clans who amassed huge wealth for themselves and their friends by forging opaque links between business and politics. Their histories are often accompanied by tales of intimidation and are littered with a trail of corpses, although the oligarchs maintain they have no criminal links. Most Ukrainians view the oligarchs as their country's scourge and supported the Orange Revolution in large part because opposition leaders promised to fight the corruption and criminality associated with these groups.

Kravchuk became inseparable from the business and

political activities of the oligarchs known as the Kyiv Clan. The two leaders of this clan, Viktor Medvedchuk and Hryhoriy Surkis, made fortunes certainly worth hundreds of millions of dollars, according to some estimates billions, by exploiting political connections. In 2004 Washington put both on a list of people banned from entering the US. The two set up their political party, the Social Democratic Party of Ukraine (United), the SDPU(U) led by Viktor Medvedchuk who was the head of Kuchma's presidential administration during his second, murkiest term in office. Kravchuk led the SDPU(U) in parliament and the party formed the core of support for the Kuchma government. Medvedchuk, loathed as the sinister puppet master behind Kuchma, and the SDPU(U) were implicated in some of the dirtiest political scandals, including organising violent thugs to intimidate voters in elections. The party, including Kravchuk, whole-heartedly endorsed the Kuchma regime's candidate in the presidential election, Prime Minister Viktor Yanukovych. Kravchuk said that one of the biggest achievements of his term in office was the prevention of ethnic conflict, but during the 2004 election he sided with the camp that toyed with the dangerous separatist genie and murmured darkly about the possibility of civil war. After the election he continued to throw his residual authority behind Medvedchuk and Yanukovych, and launched sententious attacks at the Yushchenko administration that were embarrassing rather than devastating. He considered starting his own political party to run in the 2006 parliamentary elections. To qualify to join, he said prospective members would have to demonstrate 'criminal and moral cleanliness'. It is a pity he did not use such high standards when picking his associates during his term as president. That might have prevented the 'founding father' being remembered as the man who started

Ukraine off on the road to mass-scale corruption as well as ushering Leonid Kuchma on to the political scene.

Kuchma was born in a North Ukrainian village in 1938, trained as a mechanical engineer and later gained a doctorate related to rocket engineering. Undoubtedly a talented scientist, he embarked on a career designing and manufacturing rocket and space technologies at the Yuzhmash Design Bureau near Dnipropetrovsk. It was the world's largest missile-producing complex, which made the rocket stages for some of the Soviet military's most powerful conventional and nuclear weapons, including intercontinental ballistic missiles. His important position meant that Kuchma was completely trusted by the Communist Party and the KGB, had access to some of the USSR's top secrets, and enjoyed close ties with many other powerful industrial leaders.

From 1982 Kuchma worked as the technical director of the Baikonur cosmodrome rocket-launch site in Kazakhstan. He returned to Yuzhmash, this time as its boss, between 1986 and 1992, and in 1990, with the Soviet Union in turmoil, entered politics and was elected to parliament. Kravchuk chose him as prime minister in 1992–93 and Kuchma made a promising start. He had been in favour of gradual reform but was impressed by the way Poland had bitten the bullet and introduced extensive economic reforms that were painful in the short term but beneficial in the long run. Kuchma concluded Ukraine should follow the same shock therapy course but resigned in 1993 because his economic reforms were being blocked.

His reformist zeal seemed to wane and it was Kuchma's fellow Soviet-era industrial bosses who nominated him for president because they believed there would be no sudden changes under his rule. They were anxious to hang on to the feudal power their positions gave them and maintain close relations with Russia which they saw as the main market for their anachronistic industries, and in 1994 Kuchma beat Kravchuk with support from the industrial, Russified southern and eastern areas of the country.

There is no reason to believe that Kuchma became president specifically to loot his country. At home he liked strumming a guitar, playing with his grandchild, and drinking with his friends. Whatever his intellectual prowess, though – he is after all a rocket scientist – Kuchma's emotions appeared more than merely under control: they seemed unnaturally attenuated, his manner cold. He never betrayed, by word or manner, a strong affection for his country or people and the longer he stayed in power, the more contemptuous he seemed to grow towards the millions whose destinies he was shaping. One of the few times he displayed any sentimentality was during a television appearance when he reminisced fondly about his days in missile construction and seemed dangerously close to tears. For the most part he appeared to care for Ukraine as a proprietor cares for a lucrative business.

Roman Zvarych, who became justice minister for a period after the Orange Revolution, met Kuchma in his grand office soon after he became president. He said: 'Kuchma looked a bit lost and said he would welcome help and advice in his job. If the right people had come in then things might have turned out completely differently. But the wrong people got hold of him.'

In his election campaign Kuchma had promised economic reform, tough measures against corruption, closer ties with Russia and the introduction of Russian as a state language alongside Ukrainian. He was elected but he did not keep his promises. He reneged on his pledge to promote Russian to a state language and began a game of playing Russia off against the West and trying to extract favours from both as they courted Ukraine. But Kuchma never did anything which would allow Russian politicians, who had reverted effortlessly themselves to the vocabulary of Russian nationalism, to accuse him of 'nationalism'. His speeches in Ukrainian were often stilted and in everyday conversation with his colleagues or family, Kuchma used Russian.

When Kuchma became president he inherited a parliament where the single biggest group, but without an overall majority, was the Communist Party, which was hostile to capitalist reforms and to the adoption of a post-Soviet constitution for Ukraine and disliked the very idea of an independent Ukraine. He complained the chaos in parliament was preventing essential market reforms, but the confusion also worked to Kuchma's advantage because he could blame the quarrelsome parliament for all the country's ills. The comedy at the parliament also provided a diversion from the massive plundering of state resources that, under Kuchma's auspices, was franchised out to three main oligarch clans. These were based in Kyiv and in Ukraine's two largest industrial centres in the east of the country, Donetsk and Dnipropetrovsk. The three clans competed against one another, sometimes murderously, and Kuchma played the role of arbiter. The clans either had links with organised crime or they *were* organised crime. They were and are involved in, among other things, protection rackets, prostitution, the smuggling of heroin from Central Asia to the West and contraband cigarettes and alcohol from the West for the domestic market, and armaments plundered from Ukraine's vast arsenals. In some areas they controlled the customs officials at Ukraine's borders where goods flowed in from the European Union and where the potential for illegal profits was vast, depriving the country of legitimate tax revenue.

The people who benefited most and became super-rich were Kuchma's inner circle, who acquired enterprises, property and licences for lucrative projects at knock-down prices in auctions only the chosen few could take part in. They were expected to show their gratitude to their patron and in turn could expect to receive bribes for access to the president or for exercising their influence on behalf of others. In Ukraine they say a fish rots from the head downwards. As the acquisition of wealth became an obsession in the top ranks of government, corruption percolated down into the interstices of society at every level, and almost all bureaucrats charged a price for applying their rubber stamp. Setting up a business or buying an enterprise often required dozens of permits, and every official issuing them demanded a bribe. Sometimes they were apologetic, like the firemen who came to check fire safety at a newspaper office in Kyiv where I was working. They explained that as the government was neither paying for the upkeep or purchase of their equipment, nor paying them wages, they had to make money by demanding payments for fire safety certificates: no certificate and the premises would be shut down. Police cooperated with criminals or operated their own protection rackets. Plagues of traffic police stopped drivers in towns or on highways for spurious reasons and demanded bribes. On long journeys drivers would expect to be stopped more than once. Some just slowed down, rolled down their window, handed over cash and drove on without even stopping.

Parents of students at schools and colleges had to pay teachers and lecturers. Then students had to pay to be able to sit their exams. By 2004 students could pay to get a pass in their exams. Doctors and hospital staff were also not being paid and made their money by demanding payments. The government's social network for pensioners, the unemployed and the handicapped also did not pay out for months or even years at a time, and the sums were anyhow paltry. Most people were resilient and resourceful enough to cope somehow. Families pooled their resources, grew vegetables in country plots and looked after their elderly. But for thousands of childless pensioners it was a bitter struggle to keep hunger at bay and meant serious illness could be a death sentence.

As a thin raft of well-connected people hurtled along Kyiv's streets in Mercedes and BMWs, the underpasses below filled with beggars who looked like grotesque figures from a Fellini film: withered old men and women bundled up in grubby clothes, amputees – some in uniforms to show they were Afghan War veterans – sitting in wheelchairs or propped up against cold concrete steps, gypsy children with sad faces and old people's eyes. Those who had hands stretched them out pleading for money, others knelt in abject surrender, crossing themselves and mumbling prayers. Some of the women, with tins before them, sang songs.

Poverty and lawlessness combined to make Kuchma deeply unpopular as the presidential elections approached in 1999. But the opposition was badly organised and Kuchma received campaign cash from his grateful associates, and pressured government bureaucrats to use every possible means, however questionable, to boost his vote. He won after the only democratic candidate with widespread support, Vyacheslav Chornovil, died in a suspicious car accident.

It is not suggested that Kuchma ever ordered anyone to be killed. One doubts he ever had the stomach for cold-blooded murder. But he presided over a succession of governments which allowed a climate of lawlessness, murder and brute force to become so prevalent that the death of a prominent opposition politician, although bound to arouse suspicion, was met with impunity. Kuchma was, though, blamed for the deaths of many thousands of the impoverished, elderly or sick who died prematurely because they could not survive the policies of an administration which feverishly accumulated wealth for itself while neglecting the majority.

Kuchma described his first term in power as a period of learning and said that in his second and, under the constitution, final, term in office, he felt much better equipped to lead his country into the next millennium. He unveiled what appeared to be a genuine, far-reaching reform agenda for more ambitious privatisation of property and land and for the disbanding of collective farms. The political divisions in parliament were fiercer than ever, the Communists and Socialists boycotted Kuchma's inauguration and there were moves to impeach him.

Then, a year after his re-election, a political bombshell exploded – the decapitated body of a journalist who had campaigned against government corruption was discovered, and secret recordings seemed to implicate Kuchma in ordering the murder. One of Kuchma's bodyguards had slipped out of Ukraine and announced that he had covertly recorded hundreds of hours of the president's conversations. Ukrainians heard excerpts from the recordings that seemed to be the voice of their president ordering that the journalist, Georgiy Gongadze, should be dealt with. Kuchma denied, unconvincingly, that it was his voice on the recordings and the belief that he was involved grew as the investigating authorities dissembled and deceived.

The murder scandal overshadowed the remainder of Kuchma's term in office and crushed hopes for significant changes. Further damaging excerpts from the recordings were released throughout Kuchma's presidency which implicated him in corruption and illegal arms deals. The international consequences were that Kuchma became a pariah in the West, shunned by its leaders and increasingly pushed into the arms of Putin, the only major world leader prepared to meet him. Ukraine had declared its desire to join the European Union and later NATO, but Western leaders made it clear those ambitions were hopeless as long as Kuchma was president. In October 2003 Kuchma insisted on attending a NATO conference in Prague where other candidate countries were represented despite the fact NATO made it painfully obvious that he was unwelcome. He went anyway. The seating arrangements at previous NATO conferences had been in alphabetical order using the English names for countries, which placed the Ukrainian delegation between the UK and the US. Photographs and TV clips of Kuchma flanked by Tony Blair and George Bush would have provided a prestigious domestic PR nugget for the beleaguered Ukrainian president. But that was not to be, for on this occasion, in a humiliating snub to Kuchma, the French country names were used and the Ukrainians ended up next to Turkey whilst Grande Bretagne and Les Etats Unis were out of reach.

That was good news for the Kremlin and Putin soothed Kuchma's wounded pride by arranging in January 2003 for him to become chairman of the CIS. The organisation was as hollow as ever but provided Kuchma with an illusory sense of importance as he presided over the CIS's 'international' assemblies where the evenings featured lavish banquets and pleasing drinking binges with fellow leaders whose suits were Armani, whose democratic rhetoric was feigned, but whose souls were vintage Soviet.

It was not just Kuchma who was feeling isolated but Ukrainians generally were becoming concerned as the imminent enlargement of the European Union seemed to herald a new division of the continent with Ukraine again on the wrong side of the fence. The fact that eight former Communist countries (three of them – Poland, Slovakia and Hungary – Ukraine's neighbours), were to join the EU in the summer of 2004 only emphasised how hopelessly far behind Ukraine was trailing. The Kremlin sensed again that the situation was ripe to bind a dispirited Kuchma closer into its schemes and in September 2003, without much in the way of serious negotiations, Putin persuaded Kuchma to put his signature to an accord for the creation of a Single Economic Zone, the SEZ, consisting of Russia, Ukraine, Belarus and Kazakhstan. The accord committed its signatories to synchronising their legislation on tariffs, customs and transport to enable the free movement of commodities, labour and capital. Kuchma made it plain that his rejection by the West played a part in the decision to sign up for the SEZ. He said: 'Under the present conditions, when the European markets are closed for us . . . it's better to have a real bird in the hand than two in the bush.' Some usually obedient senior figures in the Kuchma administration spoke out against the accord warning that Ukraine's sovereignty and future acceptability to the EU would be jeopardised. Western diplomats in Kyiv considered the proposed union a crude attempt by Russia to keep Ukraine under its thumb and that its aim was to make Moscow the headquarters for a powerful post-Soviet grouping. US ambassador to Ukraine, John Herbst, warned: 'I think there needs to be a careful look at the way this agreement fits in with the aspiration of the Ukrainian government to join Euro-Atlantic organisations.' The proposed new SEZ union was to become one of the most controversial and passionately argued issues in the 2004 presidential election because it was seen as a battle over Ukraine's continued existence as an independent country, just as Putin, during his own successful re-election campaign earlier in 2004, flaunted the accord as proof that his ambitious plans to reassume Russian power and rebuild her prestige were meeting with success.

Kuchma's standing at home declined during 2003 as precipitously as his international reputation: the Gongadze murder scandal caused outrage and triggered mass protests calling for the president's resignation and prosecution. The results were that the oligarch cronies who had benefited so handsomely in his first term now saw in Kuchma's weakness a way to increase their influence and that his name became increasingly synonymous with spiralling corruption and a chilling increase in authoritarianism. Intimidation by the police or tax authorities grew and court judgments either went to the highest bidder or were made according to government instructions. Government intolerance to opposition increased and there was an assault on freedom of speech with intimidation and violence used against troublesome media and journalists. For most Ukrainians the repeatedly broken promises of economic improvement and a crackdown on corruption had become a bad joke. In a nationwide survey in 2003, nearly eighty per cent of Ukrainians said they believed members of the Ukrainian government were involved in coruption, and forty-four per cent said they had personally paid at least one bribe that year. Even according to Ukrainian official statistics, twenty-seven per cent of the country's people lived below the poverty line. The labour ministry said that three million people were out of work.

Up to seven million Ukrainians were estimated to be working abroad, many illegally or semi-officially, sending back money to keep their families afloat. Accurate information was sparse but there were large numbers in

Poland, Italy, the Czech Republic, Portugal, Britain, Spain, Turkey, the US and Russia. Ukraine's ombudswoman Nina Karpachova said that Ukrainians abroad belonged to 'the most discriminated against and least protected category' of citizens. Most worked ten to eighteen hours per day and were poorly paid or often cheated of their meagre wages. For example an estimated three hundred thousand worked semi-legally or legally in the Czech Republic. They were treated with disdain by many Czechs who viewed them as inferiors and there was usually no provision for compensation or medical care if they were involved in accidents or became ill. In a graphic illustration of this, the corpse of a Ukrainian worker killed in an industrial accident was dumped outside the Ukrainian embassy in Prague because the employer apparently did not feel it was his responsibility to arrange for something more dignified, and the dead man's friends could not afford to repatriate the body.

Many Ukrainian villages had virtually emptied of young people who went abroad to seek work. The elderly looked after the children left behind by their parents. In some villages a disproportionate number of women had left because they were in high demand as nannies, waitresses, cooks, cleaners, and domestic servants. Men joked that at village dances they had to partner one another as there were so few women.

An estimated two million of the people working abroad were young women aged under thirty, many of whom ended up in the sex industry. Some had made the decision to work as prostitutes themselves, but many were tricked into becoming sex slaves. The UN and Interpol said that by the early 2000s the trade in women had become one of organised crime's most lucrative rackets, netting between seven and nineteen billion dollars annually. Many of the women are lured abroad with promises of well-paid jobs as au pairs, models, or in the entertainment industry as dancers or singers. When they arrive at their destination, their passports are confiscated, they are raped and beaten, and forced into prostitution to pay their tormentors' 'expenses' for transporting them and arranging the bribes for their visas out of Ukraine. The women are too terrified to approach local police and in any case do not usually understand the local language. Many are only thrown out by their pimps after they contract HIV, at which point they are obviously no longer profitable.

Spread by prostitution and drug use, Ukraine has one of the highest HIV infection rates in Europe. The Kuchma-era government consistently shied away from admitting the extent of the problem. In 2005 the government said there were nearly 77,000 registered HIV carriers in the country, although international organisations say that HIV/AIDS is on the cusp of assuming catastrophic proportions. Some experts believe there were as many as half a million HIV-positive people in Ukraine in 2005 while the Ukrainian Institute of Social Studies said the number could reach 1.5 million by 2012.

While Ukrainian governments did little to counter the HIV/AIDS epidemic, some top officials in the health ministry were quick to try to loot tens of millions of dollars of aid provided by Western charities and international institutions like the UN-backed Global Fund. The experiences of a Ukrainian woman called Nadia, who works with a Western non-governmental organisation (NGO) charity setting up hospices for terminal AIDS victims, is instructive. She recalled that in 2003 her group applied for a relatively modest grant of one hundred thousand dollars to operate a hospice in Kyiv in a building which did not need any extensive work done on it. She said: 'I was surprised when we received an answer saying we could expect $1,360,000 for three hospices operating for two years in Kyiv, Odessa and Donetsk, to include money for major repairs on buildings.' Her group was told to prepare proposals for the project swiftly and turn up for a meeting with 'advisors' several days later. They were also told they would be given a contract worth almost one million dollars to operate a telephone hotline for people seeking advice about HIV/AIDS.

Nadia met with the 'advisors', who said they represented the minister and deputy minister, at an office at the health ministry. By their manner and expensive clothes, Nadia said it was obvious they were not ordinary ministry employees and indeed they gave her business cards showing they were owners of private companies in medical-related businesses. The NGO was informed it would get the grant but only if it paid a fifty per cent kickback to the 'advisors'. Though having no intention of proceeding, Nadia thought it was inadvisable to refuse straight away and, pretending to be unfazed, asked how the transaction would work without arousing the suspicion of the international fund donor. The 'advisors' said their lawyers were very experienced at handling such matters and would draw up paperwork showing the fifty per cent as payments for consultation and technical services. Nadia said: 'When, after a few days, I told them we had decided not to take up the grant, I received some very aggressive telephone calls.' She said she was frightened because a friend from another NGO dealing with the same 'advisors' had been threatened with death when she wanted to expose the crooked arrangement. Nadia said that her NGO had informed the international donor agency about what had happened and they had withdrawn millions of dollars from the health ministry. But the 'advisors' were unaware that their scam had been revealed because the donors did not tell the Ukrainian officials the real reason why they were cutting the money. The donors were concerned that exposure of the corruption would anger senior health ministry officials and hinder the work of foreign agencies and NGOs trying to help HIV victims. In January 2004, against this backdrop of suspicion and criminality, the Global Fund suspended funding HIV/AIDS programmes in Ukraine, voicing concerns over their 'slow progress'.

Kuchma's golden caste was growing drunk and arrogant with power. They not only felt themselves impervious to the law, but they owned the police and judges and could buy themselves out of any trouble. Senior police officers, working in collaboration with the oligarchs as well as operating their own rackets, became so wealthy that the Kuchma administration made money by selling jobs in law enforcement. A police colonel in the Kharkiv region told me a general's rank cost upwards of $250,000 but that even junior officers had to pay for promotion. He said: 'Everyone buying their rank sees it as an investment, an opportunity to make money by demanding bribes. The calculation works despite the fact they have to pass some of the money they make upwards to their superiors. That way the corruption is self-reinforcing. The only chance of getting rid of it is to fire everyone in the top jobs and hope that with better pay and the right atmosphere the junior officers will change their habits.' None of the murder cases and illicit deals that should have been investigated by the upper echelons of the police force led to arrests or convictions. The president and the elite could and did use the law with impunity to intimidate or crush their political and business opponents.

The oligarchs delighted in flaunting their wealth: they had expensive homes abroad, vulgar mansions in exclusive compounds in Ukraine and sped through cities surrounded by bodyguards in convoys of expensive four-wheel drives or armoured limousines. The police did not dare to stop them. They radiated danger and intimidation but denied using criminal methods or ordering beatings and murders.

The intertwining of government and criminality stretched even into the parliamentary chamber. Under the Kuchma administration, laws were crafted explicitly with loopholes to facilitate plundering. It was as if thieves had passed a law making theft, by themselves, legal. Legislation by parliament was often superfluous as Kuchma sometimes chose to govern by decree. The former prosecutor-general, Viktor Shyshkyn, said: 'The decree approached, in status, the authority of a law. You could change the law by decree. Decrees were used to regulate matters that were not hitherto regulated by law and by such means laws were installed. The ruin of Ukraine's economy began by these decrees and thanks to such decrees the opportunity opened up to create mafia gangs on legal foundations.'

Many of the new 'businessmen' bought votes to secure a seat in parliament so that they could both claim parliamentary immunity in the unlikely case anyone sought to prosecute them, and also influence legislation. Some MPs had their seats bought for them by oligarch patrons who then expected them to follow their instructions, while others would sell their votes in the right circumstances. Before the end of Kuchma's first term in office, Hryhoriy Omelchenko, a member of the parliamentary committee on fighting organised crime and corruption, had complained that more than a score of MPs would face criminal charges if they were stripped of their parliamentary immunity.

The most lucrative sector, and the most corrupt, was the energy business. Ukraine produces little gas and oil itself but transports huge amounts from Russia and Turkmenistan.

Russia buys much of the output of Turkmen gas at source and sells it on at profit; some of this gas is destined for the Ukrainian market but most of which is sold to Western Europe. The gas is owned by the Russian gas giant, Gazprom, while a Ukrainian state monopoly called Naftohaz buys gas for Ukraine's needs and controls the pipelines. The managements of both monopolies under Kravchuk, Kuchma, Yeltsin and Putin, have run the enterprises to enrich themselves and their political masters. The Ukrainian and Russian gas tycoons have cooperated in a variety of complex and opaque deals where cash or barter goods are moved around like cards in a three-card trick. Gazprom and Naftohaz officials have collaborated to depress by hundreds of millions of dollars Gazprom's tax obligations to the Russian state and recycle the money through foreign bank accounts among the corrupt benefactors. The two companies have collaborated on insurance scams when gas may or may not have actually gone missing. Because Russia was selling gas for Ukraine's needs at one hundred dollars less than the world price, vast profits could be made in any scheme which delivers that gas to the world market. Ukraine's gas monopoly has for years been accused of illegally siphoning off huge amounts of gas and selling it. Undoubtedly it has, and the missing gas has saddled the Ukrainian exchequer with a debt to Russia of some $1.4 billion. But the evidence points to the theft being carried out in collusion with Gazprom officials.

In 1996 and 1997 the man who masterminded the Ukrainian end of the system was Prime Minister Pavlo Lazarenko. Lazarenko's position had seemed impregnable until a dramatic falling-out with Kuchma, who became suspicious his protégé wanted the top job for himself. Kuchma set the law enforcement authorities on to Lazarenko who fled to the US in February 1999. There he asked for political asylum saying his former colleagues in the regime had ordered his assassination. Instead of giving him asylum, the US charged Lazarenko with fifty-three counts of money laundering and mail fraud involving $114 million he had allegedly acquired corruptly in Ukraine. The number of charges was later reduced to twenty-nine. Washington had been troubled by financial scandals involving the use of American financial institutions to launder huge sums of dirty money from the former Soviet states. The US was able to prosecute someone for a crime carried out in another country because some of the alleged dirty money had been transferred through American banks and other US financial mechanisms. It was also the first time someone who had occupied such an elevated political position was being tried in America since Panama's General Manuel Noriega, who was accused of drug trafficking and brought to the US after an American invasion of his country in 1989.

The 2004 trial in San Francisco provided a rare insight into the usually opaque criminal-political nexus in Ukraine.

Pavlo Lazarenko was born in 1953 in Dnipropetrovsk. After the fall of Communism he quickly adapted from his job as boss of a collective farm to rise swiftly in the new and murky world of politics and wild capitalism, displaying a ruthless talent for both. He became governor of the Dnipropetrovsk region during Kravchuk's presidency. One of his closest business allies, Petro Kiritchenko, who had been arrested separately in the US, said in evidence against him that as governor, Lazarenko extorted payments to allow businesses to operate in what he regarded as his personal fiefdom. Kiritchenko sought out Lazarenko in 1992 because he knew that without the governor's agreement he would not be able to expand his business. After lavishly entertaining him, Kiritchenko said: 'I agreed to give him fifty per cent of the profit and fifty per cent of the company. I didn't see any other way to develop the company.' He was made aware there could be grim consequences if he rejected the proposal.

Kuchma talent-spotted Lazarenko in 1994 and propelled him on to the national political stage, first in the cabinet and then in 1996 and 1997 as prime minister. The seemingly limitless opportunities for making money must have flabbergasted the newcomer to Kyiv.

One of the biggest schemes involved what until then had been an obscure Dnipropetrovsk company called Unified Energy Systems of Ukraine (UESU) run by another Dnipropetrovsk tycoon, Yulia Tymoshenko, who nearly a decade later was to become one of the heroes of the Orange Revolution. Lazarenko used his ties with Russia's giant Gazprom gas company to secure a lucrative monopoly for UESU to sell natural gas in Ukraine which gave it annual revenues of eleven billion dollars. UESU was credited with accounting for a quarter of Ukraine's entire economy.

An American former economic advisor to Ukraine during the Kuchma period, Anders Aslund, senior associate director of the Russian and Eurasian Programme at the Carnegie Endowment for International Peace in Washington, estimated that during his term in office Lazarenko used his position to steal up to a billion dollars. He said: 'He was the leader of a culture of pervasive corruption. I never encountered anyone who was as crudely corrupt as Lazarenko.'

The rich pickings being made by the Dnipropetrovsk clan aroused the jealousy of the other two clans, notably the one based in Donetsk, and gang warfare erupted. Lazarenko was fortunate to escape injury when a roadside bomb was detonated as his car drove by in the Ukrainian capital. In what many perceived as a related event, a leader of the Donetsk Clan, member of parliament Yuriy Scherban, was killed along with his wife and bodyguard. A man dressed in police uniform calmly walked up to them as they descended from a plane at Donetsk airport and riddled them with machine-gun fire before escaping.

But Lazarenko's mistake was to become too ambitious and he resigned after Kuchma discovered he harboured ambitions to run in the 1999 presidential election. Lazarenko used some of his wealth to get himself elected to parliament – thus securing immunity from prosecution – and to set up his own political party as a power base in preparation for the presidential campaign.

Although Lazarenko had now positioned himself as Kuchma's enemy, the president had to be circumspect in the way he dealt with the former prime minister because of Lazarenko's familiarity with the shady dealings of his inner circle. Investigations were launched into Lazarenko's business dealings and he correctly sensed it was the beginning of the sort of process he had himself often used to destroy his enemies. Things went from bad to worse in December 1998 when he was arrested entering Switzerland on a counterfeit Panamanian passport and charged with money-laundering offences. By now the Kuchma regime was accusing him of embezzlement. He jumped a three-million-dollar bail in Switzerland and returned to Ukraine where his parliamentary immunity protected him from arrest. Lazarenko now tried improbably to transform himself into a political crusader and announced he was going to run for president. As the Ukrainian parliament was preparing to lift his immunity, Lazarenko fled to the US, where he had surreptitiously moved his family when he was prime minister. His properties there included a $6.7 million forty-one-room mansion previously owned by comedian Eddie Murphy.

Kuchma and his circle were anxious about what Lazarenko

would reveal at his trial and tried to extradite him to Ukraine after issuing warrants for his arrest on charges of arranging at least two contract killings – those of his Donetsk rival, Scherban, and the head of the national bank Vadym Hetman who was shot dead by a professional assassin in 1997. According to prosecutors, Lazarenko had paid a criminal gang around one million dollars for the murders, and the killers themselves had subsequently met violent ends. Lazarenko was also charged with ordering two failed assassination attempts on high-ranking officials, of having profited by buying and selling gas contracts when he was Ukraine's energy minister, and of having siphoned off millions of dollars from state programmes as prime minister in 1996–97. Although there was no extradition procedure between Ukraine and the US, the Kuchma regime was, in any case, only one in a queue of those lining up to prosecute Lazarenko that included Switzerland and the tax haven Antigua.

The hearings before Lazarenko's trial were deeply embarrassing to Kuchma, as the prosecution and defence evidence depicted the stunning scope of Ukrainian corruption and turned the spotlight on many of the president's closest associates. Lazarenko pleaded not guilty and said that all the schemes he was involved in were regarded as legal in Ukraine and that Kuchma had sanctioned everything. Lazarenko's attorney, Daniel Horowitz, compared Kuchma to a brutal Mafia don saying, 'You have a country controlled by Mafia-like thugs who either buy off their opponents, jail them or murder them.' Amongst those they felt certain would prove their point and who they wanted to call as witnesses were the national security advisor Yevhen Marchuk, the former head of the Ukrainian gas monopoly Naftohaz, Ihor Bakaj, the former prime minister Valeriy Pustovojtenko, the deputy prime minister Mykola Azarov, Kuchma's advisor and presidential campaign manager Oleksandr Volkov and the president's son-in-law Viktor Pinchuk.

Lazarenko, who it emerged presented Kuchma and his wife on 'numerous occasions' with expensive gifts including a $42,000 watch, alleged the Ukrainian president was involved in a plan to divert IMF loans into a scheme that netted some two hundred million dollars, part of which went into Kuchma's 1999 re-election war chest. Most of it was allegedly deposited in the Belgian and Swiss accounts of people close to Kuchma.

Lazarenko was found guilty on all twenty-nine counts in June 2005 and appealed against the conviction – and a possible twenty years in jail – in a process predicted to last well into 2006.

Until the last moments of the Kuchma regime there was a feverish bout of privatisations with plum state assets going cheaply to members of the president's inner circle. The deal that caused the greatest public outrage was the rigged auction of Ukraine's biggest and most valuable steel-production complex, Kryvorizhstal, to Kuchma's son-in-law Viktor Pinchuk, in partnership with the country's most powerful oligarch, Rinat Akhmetov, head of the Donetsk Clan.

Those fixing the privatisation auction hardly bothered to disguise what was happening and the conditions were blatantly drafted to eliminate foreign rivals. One of the conditions demanded that any bidder must have produced at least one million tons of coke and two million tons of rolled steel in Ukraine for the previous three years, two of them profitably. One of the competitors thus barred from the auction had offered $1.5 billion for Kryvorizhstal, compared to the eight hundred million dollars Pinchuk and Akhmetov paid.

The hypocrisy and arrogance of this enchanted circle were staggering. The members were consumed with greed and ambition for power, oblivious to the grotesque incongruity of their lavish lifestyles compared with the miserable existence of so many of their compatriots. The poor and unconnected were treated as lackeys and peasants who could be bullied or trampled upon with impunity.

Kuchma presided over Ukraine's descent into a corrupt, sinister, semi-criminal state where the police and the justice system served those who paid most, the press was censored, and human rights were increasingly abused. His term in office saw the consolidation of a ruling structure whose main goals were the accumulation of power and wealth for a small number of cronies and allies, and the tools to maintain that power were fear, corruption and violence.

Ukraine's first president also bears much responsibility. Leonid Kravchuk not only failed to speak out against the defilement of his country but he became a leading member of the political party most closely associated in the public mind with corruption and thuggery.

An expert on crime and corruption in the region, Roman Kupchinsky of Radio Free Europe/Radio Liberty knows Kravchuk and senior figures, including intelligence chiefs, who served in both the Kravchuk and Kuchma governments. He said: 'Crime and corruption during the Kuchma era became a function of the state – like garbage collection or retirement payments. It was directed from the top by Kuchma and filtered down.'

However, what Kuchma did not suspect was that a microphone hidden in his private office at the presidential administration building had for months been secretly recording his conversations and meetings. The president's cynical complacency was about to be shattered by the shocking and damning recordings, which implicated him not only in corruption but also in murder.

Chapter Six

BEHEADED

Late on the evening of 16 September 2000, Georgiy Gongadze, a thirty-one-year-old journalist, left the central Kyiv apartment of Olena Prytula, his mistress and co-editor of an Internet newspaper, *Ukrayinska Pravda* (Ukrainian Truth). The government controlled much of the conventional press but the Internet had proved difficult to bring to heel. *Ukrayinska Pravda* had become particularly troublesome because of Gongadze's investigations into high-level corruption, which pointed to the involvement of the president himself. Gongadze had indeed come to the president's attention the previous election year when Gongadze had hosted a daily radio programme urging listeners to vote against Kuchma. Another time he asked Kuchma some embarrassing questions on a popular television discussion programme.

It was a cool evening for the time of year and Gongadze hurried to get to the family apartment before his wife Myroslava and their twin daughters returned home from a day out of town. Myroslava, who knew about her husband's affair, had forgotten her keys so he had to be there to open up. As he walked out of Prytula's building and headed for the Metro station, Gongadze looked around for anything suspicious. It was a habit he had developed several months before after noticing a Zhiguli car, full of young men in black leather jackets, that had trailed him to his meetings around the capital for days. On one occasion Gongadze had started to approach the vehicle but the driver sped off. Gongadze was certain that the men were undercover police, not least because of the way they were dressed. The secret police wear black leather jackets as an unchanging uniform, as anyone watching them leave the interior ministry HQ in droves to infiltrate protest rallies can observe. Gongadze had jotted down the car's number and handed it in with an official complaint to the interior ministry and the prosecutor-general's office. After that it seemed as if the surveillance had been called off.

When Gongadze told his friends about being followed they were concerned for his safety. But Gongadze was not easily daunted. He had been raised in Georgia, a country known for its tough people, by his Georgian father and Ukrainian mother. His father had been involved in the country's independence struggle which frequently deteriorated into armed clashes. The resilient and athletically built Gongadze, a former conscript in the Soviet army, worked bravely under fire as a medic in Georgia and knew how to handle a gun. He had visited Ukraine in 1989 to represent Georgia at a pro-independence conference and spoke Ukrainian impeccably, having been taught it by his mother. His exotic background, good looks and passion for the Ukrainian cause always won him a lot of female admirers and he married a Ukrainian woman in 1990, but the relationship did not last long. He travelled between Ukraine and Georgia where he not only fought, receiving serious wounds in 1993, but made documentary films about the conflict. In 1995 he returned to Ukraine where he began to carve out a niche as a fearless journalist and married his second wife, Myroslava, in 1997.

While other journalists in Ukraine had been beaten or killed, and Gongadze did not dismiss these dangers, everything seemed calm on the deserted streets that evening. But there were eyes watching him and they belonged to people better at concealing themselves than their predecessors in the car Gongadze had reported. When they emerged, it was too late for Gongadze to escape. Nobody – except those involved in the abduction – saw what happened but days later someone said they had heard a man's desperate cry for help at around the time the journalist left Prytula's apartment block. Perhaps when Gongadze saw the men coming for him some instinct warned him these were more than the usual government goons who might rough him up. As they forced him into a waiting vehicle, he may have recognised they were an execution party.

The next day Gongadze's wife and friends raised the alarm about his disappearance. In his various statements over the next six weeks, Kuchma vacillated over admitting if he had ever heard of Gongadze, although photographs existed of the two of them together. That set the pattern for years of official deception and obfuscation. Within days the authorities were claiming that Gongadze had been sighted the night after his disappearance at a popular Kyiv bar, then that he had been seen strolling along a street in Lviv, and later that he had bought a train ticket in Moscow. All of these sightings turned out to be false but each helped to sow confusion and wasted weeks of time as all the law-enforcement agencies – the police, prosecutor-general, and intelligence services – insisted on checking out even those leads that seemed obviously fabricated.

Late on 2 November two farmers discovered a hand sticking out of the earth in a wood near the town of Tarascha, fifty miles south of the capital. The next day police uncovered a headless corpse and took it to the town's mortuary where the conscientious coroner began an examination and contacted his superiors in Kyiv. When it was found, the corpse was in surprisingly good condition but the coroner, Ihor Vorotyntsev, did not have refrigeration facilities and wanted it taken to Kyiv where it could be preserved before decomposition set in. A ring, braclet and necklace with a half-moon pendant were found on or near the body.

On 6 November the police contacted Myroslava Gongadze and Olena Prytula, took details of the jewellery that Gongadze wore but did not tell them a body had been discovered. On 8 November Ukraine's chief coroner and the Kyiv prosecutor turned up in Tarascha and told the coroner to get rid of the body, by now badly decomposed. They then left. But the coroner knew the body was evidence of a murder and bravely delayed acting on the orders of these powerful officials.

Rumours that a corpse had been found began to surface in Kyiv and on 15 November, Prytula and other journalist friends of Gongadze's drove to Tarascha. The body was now in a state of extreme decomposition but Prytula had little doubt of its identity as she wore a pendant, a gift from her lover, fashioned from the other half of the metal moon found with the corpse. The coroner was also able to perform a test that, for Prytula, confirmed the identity of the remains. During a battle in Georgia's civil war Gongadze had received shrapnel wounds in his hand. X-rays showed that there was shrapnel in the hand of the corpse.

Prytula telephoned the interior ministry in Kyiv to tell them she believed Gongadze's corpse had been found. As she and the others set about looking for a coffin and a vehicle to transport the body back to Kyiv, police swooped on the makeshift mortuary and removed the corpse. The journalists feared that the body would now be disposed of. When opposition members of parliament asked questions the next day about the location of the corpse, the interior ministry said a murder inquiry had been launched and attempts were being made to identify the body. The deputy minister cast doubt on the rumoured identity of the headless corpse claiming it had been in the ground two years and was shorter than Gongadze. The Tarascha coroner's report which indicated the victim had been dead for a far shorter time was annulled, his computer files were destroyed, and he was warned to keep his mouth shut.

Kuchma and his officials must have felt a twinge of anxiety but believed they could prevaricate and muddy the waters until the matter was forgotten like other deaths and unexplained disappearances. On 28 November, however, an extraordinary announcement rocked the administration to its core and startled the nation. It emerged that one of the president's bodyguards, Major Mykola Melnychenko, had secretly been recording the president's conversations with a digital minidisc recorder concealed, he said, under the sofa in Kuchma's inner office. He had left Ukraine with his wife and daughter and was now at a secret location in Europe, having released excerpts from the recordings which showed that Kuchma had raged about Gongadze for months before his disappearance and ordered his security chiefs to punish him.

The leader of the Socialist Party, Oleksandr Moroz, a politician with a rare reputation for honesty and one of Kuchma's rivals in the previous year's election, had helped Melnychenko leave Ukraine and now played an audio cassette to his astounded colleagues in parliament in which they recognised a voice that seemed to be the president's discussing Gongadze with interior minister General Yuriy Kravchenko, and ordering him to deal with the journalist by a method he outlined thus: 'The Chechens should kidnap him and take him to Chechnya by his dick and demand a ransom

. . . Take him there, undress him, the fucker, leave him without his trousers, and let him sit there . . . He's simply a fucker.' Kravchenko assures Kuchma that he has just the crew to deal with Gongadze, a group he calls his 'eagles' and who he says are completely amoral and 'will do whatever you want'.

Other recordings featured the president talking about Gongadze to people identified as the chief of the intelligence service, Leonid Derkach, the head of his presidential administration, Volodymyr Lytvyn, and his campaign manager and fund administrator, Oleksandr Volkov. The men's speech was often like the inarticulate ramblings of drunkards with Kuchma setting a tone of high crudeness; his interlocutors would pitch in with 'the bastard', 'scum' or 'the fucker' by way of agreement with and encouragement for his profanities. Kuchma and his men insisted that the recordings were all faked and the contents, therefore, calumnies. Later the denials were modified and Kuchma allowed the possibility that it was indeed his voice but maintained that the recordings had been edited to generate conversations that had never taken place.

If Kuchma claimed not know who Gongadze was, he certainly knew the man responsible for the political storm raging around him. Mykola Melnychenko, a young former KGB officer, had been part of Kuchma's retinue as a bodyguard since 1994 and it was his familiarity and ability to blend in that allowed him to record the unsuspecting president's most private exchanges.

Melnychenko had gone to ground somewhere. Like most journalists interested in Ukrainian issues, I was eager to meet him and find out more about the man that had made such sensational allegations. Although he was contacting some journalists by telephone to pass on information and fresh excerpts from the recordings, he was understandably reluctant to meet face to face, but he trusted the Ukrainian service of the American-funded Radio Liberty. Radio Liberty, the BBC, and Germany's Deutsche Welle radio stations broadcast to Ukraine in Ukrainian and had reputations for honest and independent reporting, unlike much of the country's own media. My wife, Iryna Chalupa, was deputy head of the Ukrainian service and a well-known and respected voice in Ukraine, and it was thanks to her that I made contact with Melnychenko's intermediary, a man called Volodymyr Tsvil.

I had met Tsvil before, during the 1999 presidential elections, when he was an aide to Socialist Party leader Moroz. Now he was Moroz's link to Melnychenko in his hiding place. We met at a hotel in Prague, and Tsvil agreed that Iryna, *New York Times* Moscow correspondent Patrick Tyler and I could meet Melnychenko the following day. We were to set off early the next morning but were not told where we would be going.

We left Prague with me following Tsvil's car in my own. Tsvil took great pains to ensure that we were not being trailed, and our three-hundred-mile drive involved doubling back on ourselves and executing a number of unorthodox manoeuvres, including stopping on the side of a busy highway and reversing to the previous exit. Anybody who might have been following us and tried to imitate our dangerous and illegal move would have made themselves very obvious. We finally arrived at a country inn near the town of Ostrava, close to the Czech border with Poland, and were shown to a private room in a restaurant on the second floor. In a short while Melnychenko himself turned up in disguise; he wore a raincoat, dark glasses hiding greyish-green eyes, and a long woman's wig, which covered his own short brown hair. Accompanying him were two men of military bearing who said they were Ukrainians living in the Czech Republic and were guarding Melnychenko because they supported his actions.

Melnychenko was very impressive at that first meeting. Born in 1966 in a village south of Kyiv, he had intended to make a career in the Soviet army but during his conscript service, his ability and enthusiasm meant that he was offered the chance to join the KGB – an opportunity he seized. His rigorous training included weapons, martial arts, some spy craft and the techniques required of a bodyguard. He was also trained to detect hidden recording devices and de-bug rooms – very useful knowledge to anyone planting a bug. He performed well, received good marks from his tutors and was assigned to the KGB's Ninth Directorate, which provided bodyguards for top Communist officials. He served in the detachment guarding Gorbachev, and after the Soviet Union fell apart, returned to his native Ukraine and became part of Kuchma's security retinue in 1994.

We sat down to a typical Czech meal of pork cutlets and potato dumplings. Melnychenko drank a little red wine but stuck mostly to mineral water. Our conversation lasted some seven hours and the room darkened as the short winter day turned into evening.

He said that he initially admired Kuchma and was part of his protection detail on foreign visits to Greece, Vietnam, the Emirates and Indonesia. He even went on a training course organised in part by the American Secret Service in VIP protection. But gradually he became disenchanted as, standing in the background in Kuchma's private office, he overheard those around him concocting corrupt schemes, accepting bribes and dealing ruthlessly with political and business rivals. 'It became clear that there was no greater criminal than Kuchma in the country,' he said. 'For him Ukraine was a huge business and he turned the country into one giant protection racket.'

He decided to make secret recordings of Kuchma's conversations to expose the corruption and used his knowledge of surveillance techniques to install a microphone connected to a digital recording device in a sofa, he said, in Kuchma's private office. Over the following months he made around one thousand hours of recordings.

Melnychenko said he was not sure what exactly he was going to do with the material until he heard about the disappearance of Georgiy Gongadze, when he remembered Kuchma fulminating against the journalist to senior security officials. He took some leave and spent around two weeks sifting through the recordings. By the middle of October his evidence, pieced together with other information, convinced him that Kuchma was linked to the disappearance. Melnychenko then started planning his departure from Ukraine even before Gongadze's body was discovered. He left his job, explaining that he had been offered a lucrative post as a security consultant. He chose Moroz as his confidant and collaborator because, from what he had seen, the Socialist Party leader seemed to be a man of integrity. He discussed whether to pursue the plan with his wife, Lilya, who agreed it had to be done because she could imagine the torment Gongadze's wife was going through.

Melnychenko got passports for himself, his wife and four-year-old daughter. His cover story to his colleagues was that he needed to go abroad to get medical treatment for his daughter and also to receive training for his new job. As an added precaution, Moroz provided him with a special passport issued to state officials which would prevent his luggage, containing the recordings, being searched.

Melnychenko left copies of excerpts with Moroz and also a video-taped statement which was later broadcast in parliament. The family flew to Poland on 26 November 2001, and then took a bus from Warsaw to the Czech Republic, staying in a series of apartments in remote locations. The Ukrainian authorities issued a warrant for Melnychenko's arrest, and he was worried that he and his family had become targets for assassination by Ukrainian secret services or by hitmen sent by some of the corrupt businessmen linked to Kuchma who might suspect, correctly, that they figured in the recordings.

Gongadze, the recordings showed, was probably being followed by both undercover police and agents of the Ukrainian SBU secret service. In one excerpt the then head of the SBU, Leonid Derkach, told Kuchma: 'We're all over him [Gongadze], monitoring all his communications, checking out all his Kyiv contacts. He's already crept over to Moroz.' Another recording has interior minister General Kravchenko indicating his people had also placed him under surveillance. Melnychenko believes the journalist unwittingly bought himself a few extra weeks of life by lodging his complaints about being followed. The deputy chief of Kyiv police, General Petro Opanasenko, looked into the matter and discovered the number plate belonged to the security services. Kravchenko told Kuchma he intended to fire Opanasenko because the general seemed intent on investigating the complaint.

On the weekend Gongadze disappeared, Kuchma, Kravchenko and Volodymyr Lytvyn, the head of the president's administration, were hunting outside Kyiv. A few days later – according to Melnychenko – the recordings have Kuchma asking someone whose voice is difficult to identify whether Gongadze was dead or alive and saying he should be found because it looked bad for the president. None of the recordings have Kuchma explicity ordering Gongadze's death, but Melnychenko construed from them that four days after the journalist's disappearance Kuchma already knew Gongadze had been killed and was putting on a show for his interlocutor. 'Kuchma can be a very good actor and he is a very cunning man,' he said.

Melnychenko's final assessment is that Kuchma did not actually want to have Gongadze killed, but he had undoubtedly put in motion the events that led to his death and subsequently given instructions for the elaborate cover-up.

He portrays Kuchma as a wily and talented chameleon sometimes assuming a gangsterish manner of crude language and threats, while at other times taking a passable shot at charm. Melnychenko never claimed any close relationship with him but had plenty of time to study Kuchma who, he said, consciously promoted to important positions people with criminal records or other murky back-grounds he could use to pressure or blackmail them. The president had, however, fallen into the thrall of some oligarchs and there were occasions when the tables were turned on him. He said Kuchma had treated him courteously, sometimes asking him to fetch a bottle of Ukrainian Hetman vodka for guests and would affectionately ask his 'guardian pigeon' to leave when he wanted private conversations with visitors.

In contrast to his insatiable appetite for money, the president's tastes in food were almost spartan and he preferred the traditional Ukrainian delicacy of smoked garlicky pig fat, *salo*, to caviar or smoked salmon. He did have a fondness for vodka, something the Ukrainian press knew about but could not publicise. On one occasion the president turned up the worse for drink at a press conference following an event when alcohol had been served generously. He swayed about and found it difficult to string together his sentences. Afterwards the security agencies confiscated photographs and TV film of the event. Melnychenko recalled that Kuchma's aide and controller of funds, Oleksandr Volkov, supplied him with tablets that Melnychenko never identified.

Melnychenko depicts an almost obsessively greedy man who enjoyed presents from people seeking favours. He saw Kuchma receiving suitcases stuffed with dollars and even historical Scythian gold artefacts. 'One grateful businessman gave Kuchma a yacht for his sixtieth birthday. It was kept in Ukraine and required a crew of four, but Kuchma did not like it very much. He prefers having people give him country houses.'

When gifts were not forthcoming Kuchma had a vengeful streak and would order the crushing of businesses whose owners supported his political opponents. Melnychenko said: 'The thing that disgusted me most was that Kuchma has ruined lots of businesses that could have provided work for ordinary people and could have brought economic benefit to Ukraine. He wanted everyone to pay protection and if they didn't he wanted to put them out of business.' The oligarchs were obliged to pay financial tributes and during the 1999 election campaign Kuchma forced them to make large contributions to his campaign funds. 'He would say that he needed twenty or forty million dollars and he would receive it in cash the next day,' said Melnychenko.

The recordings show another vindictive streak to Kuchma when they link him to attacks by thugs on political opponents including a member of parliament, Oleksandr Yelyashkevych, whom Kuchma is heard calling 'a fucking

Yiddish sprout'. The SBU chief, Derkach, agreed to Kuchma's bidding 'to fuck him up'. I met Yelyashkevych in London in 2005 and he told me he was attacked by a man who struck him with a karate-type blow which, if it had landed differently, might have been fatal. When Yelyashkevych was in the forefront of attempts to impeach Kuchma, the president is heard on a recording saying he would be hit again so hard that he would never be able to get up. In 2002 Yelyashkevych fled to the US where he received political asylum.

Melnychenko believed members of the 'amoral' unit that Kravchenko called his 'eagles' were responsible for killing Gongadze. He said they had also been used during the 1999 election campaign in a carefully choreographed terrorist attack designed to discredit Socialist Party leader Moroz, then one of Kuchma's main rivals. Grenades were thrown at a buffoonish candidate, Natalya Vitrenko, leader of the Progressive Socialist Party. Vitrenko and her party were regarded as politically irrelevant and some suspected she was funded by Kuchma to split the Left's vote. Vitrenko was slightly wounded and, extraordinarily, the usually incompetent police speedily arrested suspects linked to the local Socialist Party election agent. The government-controlled press produced an avalanche of pieces suggesting that Moroz was resorting to terrorist tactics in his bid for the presidency, a slur that undoubtedly damaged his showing in the election.

Melnychenko knew about the regime's involvement in these dirty tricks, and the operation against Moroz particularly offended him because he regarded Moroz as one of Ukraine's few hopes for a decent future. Melnychenko said that he could have ignored what was going on and built a comfortable life for himself and his family by starting a business or by selling his information to some of the oligarchs. 'Even though I worked for the president I wasn't detached from the misery of the life of ordinary people, most of whom have to survive on a pittance. I believe every person has to make a choice at some stage. I had to decide whether to make money and keep quiet. I decided to try to stop this type of corruption.' He said he felt honour-bound as an officer and patriot to do what he did. 'I am a soldier of my country and I am not concerned about my own life. I am ready to sacrifice my life for my country. Each day that I was making these recordings I didn't know whether I would live to see the end of that day. I had no financial or any other support from anyone whilst I was doing this with the exception of the moral support of my wife.'

At that first meeting Melnychenko said that although he was concerned about his family's safety he did not intend to apply for political asylum because he hoped the revelations about Kuchma would force his impeachment or otherwise topple him. He was expecting to return to Ukraine within weeks to testify in court against him. But in case the need arose to apply for asylum, he asked me to put him in touch with British officials, and for Patrick Tyler to organise contacts with the American government.

The recordings linking Kuchma to the journalist's murder prompted a wave of revulsion and the largest demonstrations in Ukraine since the country's independence. Kuchma's regime had been accused of plenty of other crimes and there had been other murders, including those of journalists, but never before had there been such seemingly irrefutable evidence. The revelations sparked a protest campaign called 'Ukraine Without Kuchma' which kept up pressure on the president throughout the remainder of his term in office and, in uniting diverse political groups, provided something of a dress rehearsal for the Orange Revolution. But Kuchma was not ejected from office as Melnychenko hoped or expected. Meanwhile, Moroz, having exploited Melnychenko's political capital, decided he had served his purpose and left him stranded in the Czech Republic, his small life savings long since exhausted, living on the charity of Tsvil and some of his friends. Melnychenko chose political asylum in the US and was flown there in April 2003.

After recovering from the initial shock of what Melnychenko had done, Kuchma decided to brazen it out, maintaining that either the recordings were completely fabricated or the sequence of words and phrases had been altered by sophisticated digital editing to impute crimes against innocent people. Using its extensive control over the media, the regime was able to minimise the impact of the recordings among ordinary Ukrainians. But Kuchma was embarrassed by reports in the foreign press. In an extraordinary move for an incumbent president, Kuchma protested his innocence in a letter to the *Financial Times*, writing 'The death of a journalist, although tragic, is not grounds for my political adversaries to accuse me of murder.' He made no mention of Melnychenko or the recordings. At the same time the regime and people close to Kuchma, especially his son-in-law, oligarch businessman Viktor Pinchuk, put much effort into a PR campaign to suggest the murder and recordings were part of a conspiracy to discredit the president and to hamstring Ukraine's economic and political development. They hired Kroll, a well-known US company of risk consultants and investigators, to look into the matter. Kroll's report claimed the recording had been tampered with. Independent tests in the West, including by the FBI, concluded that the recordings were authentic, while DNA samples from the headless corpse indicated the body was that of Gongadze. Later most Ukrainians who had followed the story were appalled when a Western newspaper correspondent, Charles Clover, presented a documentary, shown on Ukrainian TV and which was most likely funded by people close to Kuchma, which vindicated the president.

Melnychenko only ever made public a fraction of the recordings he said he possessed. He said that some of the material concerned Ukrainian national security and named people working abroad for the Ukrainian intelligence agencies. He also strenuously denied that anybody else but him had decided to make the recordings or that he received financial and technical help to carry out the bugging.

However, as time went on, nagging doubts about his story grew. Various theories circulated about Melnychenko's motives. The Kuchma regime maintained that mysterious forces were out to discredit Ukraine and destroy its chances of building a stronger relationship with the West. Many Ukrainians thought that Russian intelligence forces were behind both the Gongadze murder and the recordings in order to strengthen Russian influence over Kuchma. Others believed that Ukrainian security services, working in league with the oligarchs, had collected the damaging recordings to black-mail Kuchma, especially as he had hinted that he might tackle corruption and thus their ability to increase their wealth. Some thought the recordings were originally intended to help the presidential ambitions of one of the 1999 candidates closely linked to the intelligence service. Few believed Melnychenko when he said that he had acted on his own.

In my first meeting with Melnychenko he hinted that at least one other person in Kuchma's entourage had helped in ensuring the hidden microphone remained undiscovered. The Kroll report cast doubt on Melnychenko's version of how the recordings were made. It seemed unlikely that a digital recording device or even a microphone could remain undetected all that time in one place, but it also seemed natural that Melnychenko might want to send some disinformation to those investigating his actions, especially to protect any assistant who was still in place.

But there were other puzzling aspects to Melnychenko's subsequent behaviour and statements. After he received political asylum in the US, he claimed the FBI had warned him of three separate assassination plans. He could nevertheless be seen strolling around the Ukrainian district of downtown New York seemingly unperturbed. On one occasion he was approached by two visitors from Ukraine, friends of mine, who recognised him walking in Manhattan. He had never met them before but he took up their invitation to go for drinks in a nearby bar – hardly the actions of a man worried about his safety. In the US he was known to keep company with a Ukrainian businessman who himself had links to two of the top, and most odious, oligarch figures in Kuchma's coterie, MP Hryhoriy Surkis and his long-time business partner Viktor Medvedchuk, the head of the presidential administration and the man many believed effectively ran the country. There were credible rumours that Medvedchuk and Surkis had tried to buy the recordings from Melnychenko. What is suspicious is that the only publicised excerpt of the recordings that features Medvedchuk makes him look as innocent as an altar boy. The former head of the Ukrainian parliamentary commission on the Gongadze case, Oleksandr Zhyr, distrusts Melnychenko and believes that Medvedchuk and Surkis either helped set up or were aware of the plot to bug Kuchma. He said it was possible that 'before becoming public knowledge, the major's recordings had been listened to at a football stadium near Kyiv'. The reference was to Surkis, who counted Dynamo Kyiv Football Club among his many properties.

Melnychenko didn't only attract the interest of Ukrainian oligarchs. He began to receive money from Russian business-man Boris Berezovsky, who was living in Britain after fleeing Russia because of his bitter clashes with President Putin. Berezovsky, one of Russia's richest men, made his money following the wild privatisation of Russian industry, and the funds for Melnychenko were ostensibly to allow him to transcribe the remaining recordings. In the summer of 2005, former Ukrainian president Leonid Kravchuk accused Berezovsky of secretly helping to fund Yushchenko's campaign the previous year. Yushchenko's aides dismissed the suggestion and said the money had gone to a democracy-building fund, which was perfectly legitimate under the law. A parliamentary committee was formed to investigate the matter.

I met Melnychenko briefly for the second time in London in 2003, and he was evasive and agitated. He would not give a clear answer as to why he was drip-feeding information from the recordings instead of handing over complete copies for independent verification and release to the public. He was no longer denying that he had been given serious help to obtain the recordings. It was becoming difficult to decide whether he had lied to people like me and put on an elaborate show with himself as hero, or whether, despite the mounting evidence that he had collaborated with or worked on the orders of others, he had been driven by honourable motives. He was under immense psychological strain and may have discovered that he had unwittingly been somebody's puppet. Certainly people like Moroz, whom he once trusted, had proved themselves unreliable.

Whenever the effect of Melnychenko's damaging revelations seemed to be receding, he would provide more ammunition for Kuchma's enemies by releasing further information. In the autumn of 2002, as America drew closer to conflict with Iraq, Melnychenko released excerpts of recordings in which Kuchma seemingly approves the sale to Saddam Hussein of a sophisticated 'passive radar' detection system that could help Iraqi forces destroy British and US planes. It was called Kolchuha, from the Ukrainian word for the chain mail worn by medieval warriors.

The recordings purported to be a conversation between Kuchma and the head of Ukraine's state arms export company, Valery Malev, in July 2000. According to a transcript of the recording, Malev told Kuchma: 'We were approached by Iraq through our Jordanian intermediary. They want to buy four Kolchuha stations and offer one hundred million dollars up front.' Malev suggested that after the system was smuggled into Iraq, Ukrainians with forged passports should be sent to oversee its installation. 'Just watch that the Jordanian keeps his mouth shut,' Kuchma replied. 'Who is going to detect it?' asked Malev. Kuchma, once convinced the operation will go undetected, answered: 'OK. Go ahead'.

As usual, the Ukrainian government questioned the authenticity of the newly released recordings and denied the system had ever been sold to Iraq. However, the US State Department said it was convinced the recording was authentic although it was not certain the sale in fact happened, a view confirmed by a Ukrainian official, speaking in confidence, who told me: 'The recording of Kuchma approving the Kolchuha sale to Iraq is genuine, but Ukraine did not actually go ahead with the sale.' The Ukrainian administration's dilemma, he said, had been how to convince the world it did not sell the system, while admitting that Kuchma, in a severe error of judgment, had been personally willing to do so.

Suspicion only increased when Ukraine admitted that it

sold three Kolchuha systems to Ethiopia. Military analysts were quick to point out that Ethiopia, one of the world's poorest countries, did not need such a sophisticated and expensive system, and suggested Ethiopia was a staging post for eventual delivery to Iraq. It also emerged that Malev, the arms salesman talking to Kuchma in the recording, died in an accident not long after the conversation.

The net result of this scandal was that America withheld fifty-four million dollars in aid grants to Ukraine. The American ambassador to Ukraine, Carlos Pascual, explained that it was punishment for Kuchma authorising the deal, and more severe penalties were threatened if evidence came to light that Ukraine had actually transferred the system. 'If there had been a transfer, that would automatically trigger sanctions in American law and it would be a violation of UN sanctions. We are not at that point,' he said.

Kuchma, already facing international condemnation over the Gongadze murder, felt himself sinking deeper into isolation, and after the fighting seemed to be over in Iraq, Ukraine responded to Washington's plea for other countries to send troops, and sent out 1,800 peacekeepers. The move was interpreted as penance.

Volodymyr Tsvil, the person who led me to the first meeting with Melnychenko, said in 2004 that Melnychenko's bugging activity was known to people who had headed the Ukrainian intelligence services during the Kuchma regime. The men in question included Yevhen Marchuk, Ukraine's Soviet-era KGB chief who went on to be the first leader of the SBU, Volodymyr Radchenko, another vintage Soviet figure from military intelligence, and the man in charge during the Orange Revolution, Ihor Smeshko. 'Don't look for other traces in this affair, neither American, nor Russian nor European. It's all a homegrown product,' Tsvil said in his memoirs.

Tsvil said that Melnychenko had told him the idea for bugging Kuchma's office was first mooted in 1997 by the president's security detachment, supposedly to test their own safeguards against secret listening devices. The equipment was put in place, recordings were made for a while and then the experiment was stopped, although the equipment remained. Melnychenko and some of his like-minded colleagues decided to start secretly recording Kuchma in earnest. According to Tsvil, Melnychenko first offered access to the recordings to Marchuk in 1999 when the latter was a fierce political opponent and rival presidential candidate of Kuchma's in that autumn's election. Marchuk, according to Tsvil's version of events, was interested and had some meetings with Melnychenko. But Marchuk did not get enough votes in the first round of the election and, without batting an eyelid, switched support to Kuchma in return for the promise of a plum job as chief of the council for national security in the new administration.

Marchuk then apparently broke off contact with Melnychenko, but did not betray him, and in early 2000 Melnychenko approached Moroz who agreed to collaborate with him.

But four years later both Tsvil and Melnychenko, by their own accounts and those of witnesses, were meeting with Ukrainian intelligence and members of Kuchma's entourage. Tsvil, somewhat ingenuously, claimed that the meetings had been prompted by patriotic motives to find a way to avoid Ukraine's legitimate state interests being harmed by the recordings. But his and Melnychenko's behaviour made it obvious neither was being completely forthright. Or perhaps they no longer knew what the full truth was.

Both the Gongadze case and Melnychenko's own tale took more twists after the Orange Revolution, and the former bodyguard's behaviour disappointed Ukrainians who hoped that he would finally help put the journalist's killers behind bars. Instead of returning to Ukraine with his recordings to testify, Melnychenko kept stalling. I met him for a third time in the spring of 2005 in London. He arrived in a bullet-proof, chauffeur-driven Mercedes belonging to oligarch Boris Berezovsky, accompanied by two bodyguards.

Melnychenko seemed more distracted than ever, had put on weight, and had a decidedly unhealthy pallor. The company he was keeping had definitely chipped away at his credibility. He said two of the new Ukrainian government's senior figures were mentioned in the recordings and might try to destroy the evidence or him. Melnychenko persisted with his refusal to return to Ukraine even after receiving a personal guarantee of safety from President Yushchenko. Prosecutor-General Svyatoslav Piskun visited the US in July 2005, but a planned meeting with Melnychenko to take an affidavit and transport the original recordings to Ukraine fell through with both men blaming the other for the failure.

By early 2005 rumours abounded that Berezovsky, who wanted to live in Ukraine but was being refused permission by the new authorities, had possession of a complete set of recordings and was trying to use them as a bargaining chip. One Ukrainian newspaper, *Zerkalo Tyzhnia*, warned that what was happening was transforming Melnychenko's actions 'from a heroic deed into something absolutely different. And a national tragedy has been transformed into a farce.'

Melnychenko finally and dramatically returned to Ukraine at the end of 2005 saying he wanted to see Kuchma and 'his criminal band' brought to justice. But, as always with Melnychenko, he seemed to generate more riddles than answers.

But the Gongadze scandal remained Kuchma's most enduring political nightmare. When Melnychenko's recordings first hit the headlines, the Kuchma regime's strategy was to fend off awkward questions about the Gongadze murder by saying everyone had to wait for the outcome of an investigation by law-enforcement agencies. He rode out the mass demonstrations calling for his resignation and prosecution and the international pressure for the case – a symbol of the regime's criminality – to be solved. The Parliamentary Assembly of the Council of Europe (PACE) condemned 'the lack of results in bringing to justice those responsible for the murder of the journalist, Mr Gongadze' as did the European Union. In January 2001, Reporters Without Borders concluded that 'Gongadze was murdered because he was a journalist. Everything seems to have been done to prevent that truth from being revealed.'

The pressure for answers came from many directions, including the US, Britain and human rights organisations, but the Ukrainian authorities continued to buy time with ridiculous stories. First they disputed that Gongadze was dead at all, and even cast doubt on a DNA test, saying it had only determined with 99.6 per cent probability that the decomposing corpse was his. On several occasions officials declared the case solved and announced that they had apprehended Gongadze's killers who, they claimed, were common criminals with no political motives. Details about the accused were always scanty: one set were said to be two gangsters known as 'Cyclops' and 'Sailor', while another couple of culprits were supposedly drug addicts. After enough time had been wasted, the authorities would mention that their information had proved wrong and they were pursuing a fresh lead. None of the suspects was proved even to have existed, but apart from a few exceptions, notably

Gongadze's own Internet newspaper, the Ukrainian press was too intimidated or lacking in resources to pursue its own inquiries.

Soon after Gongadze's disappearance in 2000, parliament set up its own committee to investigate the matter, headed by Oleksandr Lavrynovych. Under Lavrynovych's diligent guidance, the committee got nowhere and Kuchma duly appointed him, perhaps with intentional irony, as the country's justice minister. In late 2003, however, it seemed as if there might be some genuine progress. The recordings had implicated Interior Minister Yuriy Kravchenko and suspicion had fallen on an interior ministry police general. General Oleksiy Pukach was arrested on 23 October, by the then prosecutor-general, Svyatoslav Piskun. But Piskun was rapidly removed from his post by Kuchma, and Pukach released from custody. Kuchma then appointed a new prosecutor-general, Hennadiy Vasilyev.

Vasilyev, a lawyer and businessman from Donetsk, was closely associated with the country's most powerful oligarchic clan, based in Donetsk and led by Rinat Akhmetov. Vasilyev would distinguish himself in the cynical way he perverted the law. He declared immediately that previous investigations into Gongadze's murder had failed to turn up anything useful and the process would have to be 'started from a clean slate'. That increased suspicion that Vasilyev had been appointed to put a brake on the investigation, which indeed proceeded to disappear from view. Vasilyev fired or retired some two thousand employees around the country who seemed inclined to pursue criminals, including many who had been working on the Gongadze case.

Like many other journalists I was trying to make sense of this smoke-and-mirrors world of politics, law enforcement and intelligence, when suddenly it seemed as if ghostly arms had reached out of one of the mirrors and pulled me through to the other side. A member of the Ukrainian parliamentary opposition telephoned me in Prague and said that if I came to Kyiv, I would get a very good story for the newspaper I worked for, the *Independent*. There was no more he could tell me on the telephone. The caller was a friend I had trusted for many years and I bought a plane ticket to Ukraine the next day.

I met my friend in a small park not far from Independence Square. We had a brief talk and he told me that it concerned the Gongadze case. My heart sank a little because I could not imagine what fresh interesting information he could offer me. We then went to meet the man my friend said would hand over the information. The meeting was in an Irish bar and restaurant called O'Brien's, and when the contact came in, there was no question about his identity. I recognised him immediately. All three of us switched off our mobile telephones and handed them to a fourth person who left before we started talking. I was told that the security agencies had equipment that could use an unsuspecting person's mobile phone as a listening device even when it seemed turned off. The lively music being played also helped obscure our words.

I was told that some of the senior investigators from the prosecutor-general's office had been dismayed by the appointment of Vasilyev because they were certain he would destroy the extensive evidence already gathered in the case. It pointed to specific individuals alleged to have been involved in the murder, and some of the investigators had surreptitiously photocopied the evidence. I would be given a set if I was interested. I was. The next day we met again at O'Brien's and I received a large bulging manila envelope inside a plastic bag.

I went to the apartment where I was staying and impatiently laid out the envelope's contents. What I saw were more than two hundred pages of official documents dealing with the Gongadze investigation. Most of the pages were copies of interviews with witnesses, most of them police and other employees from the interior ministry. The first and last pages of the statements contained official preambles and the signatures of everyone taking part in the interview. The actual statements were on plain, numbered pages with each initialled at the bottom by the interviewee and interrogator. However, some of the pages were written by hand and a few of the documents were on the official paper of the SBU intelligence agency surmounted by a trident crest.

Even a cursory assessment of the pages was sufficient to know that this was a treasure trove of sensational material proving senior police involvement in Gongadze's disappearance and obstruction of the case at the highest levels. There followed three days of careful reading to ensure I understood everything properly. Most of the statements were in Ukrainian and were easy to follow, but I needed a dictionary to cope with Russian text, and help to decipher Russian handwriting. Some of the documents were statements by different witnesses dealing with the same incident, and some of the same names were mentioned in different documents. I prepared a chart which cross-referenced the information, including dates, and gradually produced a diagram mapping Gongadze's final days.

The central revelations of the documents were as follows:

- Ministry of Internal Affairs (MVS) undercover police teams carried out surveillance on Gongadze for weeks until the time of his abduction. Evidence from some of those involved in the daily surveillance includes detailed descriptions of their routines,.their coded call signs and the number plates of vehicles used.

- Official records including the names of the team watching when Gongadze was actually abducted were destroyed, contrary to correct procedure, on the orders of the arrested (and quickly released) General Oleksiy Pukach.

- Pukach took orders directly from the then interior minister, Yuriy Kravchenko, the man a furious Kuchma is heard on the recordings ordering to deal with Gongadze. Witness statements by MVS staff and information from the Ukrainian SBU intelligence service confirm Pukach ordered surveillance of Gongadze.

- MVS staff testifed Pukach ordered a halt to the operation against Gongadze hours after the journalist disappeared, even though the fact of the abduction did not emerge for days and his corpse was not discovered for weeks.

- Investigators for the prosecutor-general's office were convinced that the initial investigation into the murder by the then prosecutor for the Kyiv Province, Volodymyr Babenko, was conducted in a way intended to sow confusion, keep the location of Gongadze's corpse secret, and prevent the killers' apprehension. The investigators were certain Babenko lied in his statements to them.

- A former senior MVS officer, Ihor Honcharov, who was in custody for working with racketeers, said he had proof the killing was done by gangsters linked to a Kyiv crime lord who carried out the murder at the bidding of the MVS. He said that MVS surveillance personnel watched the abduction, knew those involved, and did not attempt to prevent the kidnapping.

- In his statements, Honcharov repeatedly expressed fear he would be murdered, and the documents contain strong evidence that, after extensive interrogations, he was.

- MVS staff say it was not uncommon for them to be ordered to commit illegal activities, but in those cases instructions were issued verbally and a written record was seldom kept. They frequently worked for private clients, oligarch businessmen and politicians, who paid large sums in cash for people to be followed, their communications tapped using sophisticated MVS resources, and sometimes to be intimidated.

The revelations in the documents were fascinating because many of them were from the people taking part in the surveillance, and I could almost hear their voices as they described events using the jargon of street-hardened police. Some spoke defiantly about their roles, while others sounded as if they felt sullied by what they had been drawn into. Witnesses who had been part of the undercover teams following Gongadze said they were working on instructions from General Pukach, who was so involved in the case that he sometimes went on stake-outs. It was clear Pukach and the other MVS personnel were acting on the orders of Minister Kravchenko.

The documents provided a mass of information about the manner in which Gongadze was observed and finally abducted. One of the undercover agents, Volodymyr Yaroshenko, said that about twenty-five people were involved in the surveillance teams, which used cars equipped with five sets of number plates each that would be regularly changed. When Gongadze noticed he was being followed by men in a Zhiguli car he noted down the vehicle's number, but in one of the bodyguard's recordings, Kravchenko tells Kuchma not to worry because the number seen by Gongadze was out of date – that is, it had already been replaced by one of the spare sets of plates.

Another agent, Hryhoriy Serhienko, confirms the surveillance was ordered by General Pukach and continued until Gongadze's disappearance on 16 September 2000. Serhienko says on that day, General Pukach told him to forget that there had been any surveillance operation against Gongadze and to forget he had ever heard of the journalist. Serhienko asked what he meant, and Pukach told him he would find out and he should bear his words in mind. Serhienko said that an MVS agent, Oleksandr Muzyka, from the police department fighting organised crime, worked with a powerful Kyiv crime family. He believes that the final surveillance team watched Gongadze being abducted or themselves handed over the journalist to the gang members who murdered Gongadze.

Yet another MVS officer, Serhiy Chemenko, attested to investigators that the surveillance operation stopped on 17 September 2000, without any explanation. After news emerged about Gongadze's abduction and death, he and other MVS officers suspected their own organisation was involved in the journalist's murder.

An MVS captain, Vitaly Hordienko, said the surveillance, known in MVS jargon as an *uliana*, included gathering information about the layout of Gongadze's apartment and the routes of approach and departure he used. Hordienko said records concerning the surveillance began disappearing within hours of Gongadze's abduction, and other MVS staff, including a senior official, Anatoly Osypenko, and General Pukach's office manager, Lyudmyla Levchenko, said the general ordered the destruction, contrary to regulations, of records logging the names and work shifts of teams watching Gongadze.

Some of the documents dealt with the interrogations of the former senior MVS colonel, Ihor Honcharov, who was in custody in 2003. Honcharov, who denied he had collaborated with mobsters, claimed inside knowledge of a government plot to abduct and murder Gongadze. He said the murder was carried out on the orders of Kravchenko who was doing Kuchma's bidding.

In a letter smuggled out of prison, Honcharov claimed that his superior, Serhiy Khomula, had threatened to kill him while he was in custody if he gave the names of colleagues linked to the Gongadze killing. Honcharov said that a special police unit formed by Kravchenko had taken part in the illegal operations. This was likely the 'eagles' group Kravchenko boasted about in some of the secretly recorded conversations and which was reportedly made up of serving and retired police and military officers, and members of organised crime groups.

Honcharov's testimony painted a horrifying picture of what Ukraine's law-enforcement agencies had become during the Kuchma years. He said that Kravchenko, Pukach and other senior police officials regularly worked with criminals and that much of the interior ministry's forces, including the department set up to deal with organised crime and corruption, far from combating gangsters, had organised themselves into the country's premier criminal ring.

Honcharov repeatedly expressed his fear that he would be murdered and that the killing would be portrayed as suicide or illness. Only a few weeks later, on 1 August 2003, he died. The official version was that he died of a heart ailment. He was quickly cremated. However, among the documents handed to me were copies of the autopsy and tests performed for the government by six experts showing Honcharov had received head injuries and had been injected with a drug called Thiopental. The drug is an anaesthetic for women in labour, and is also used in psychotherapy to induce a relaxed state. Experts said there would have been no legitimate medical reason to use the drug.

I used the material to write a series of articles for the *Independent* in June 2004. But there were some documents from the prosecutor-general's office and the intelligence services that I did not publish at the time because I thought doing so might endanger people. The deputy chief of the SBU intelligence agency, General Yuriy Vandin, wrote in a June 2003 letter that the agency's investigations showed that General Pukach was personally and directly involved in supervising the operation against Gongadze. The letter named three men in the surveillance squad taking orders from Pukach. In October 2003 the SBU sent information to the investigators detailing Pukach's contacts with a Kyiv-based gangster.

Another letter is from Deputy Prosecutor-General Shokin to his chief, Piskun, on 10 July 2003. In it he complains that the MVS chief and other senior MVS personnel were actively obstructing the work of a special task force created the previous year on Kuchma's own orders, and comprised of representatives from the prosecutor-general's office, the SBU and the MVS. Members of this group were being followed, their phones had been tapped and they feared for the safety of their families. The letter says that documents related to Gongadze's surveillance had already been destroyed illegally and the rest would follow. Kravchenko, the interior minister when Gongadze was killed, had been replaced, and his successor Yuriy Smyrnov refused to cooperate in the investigation despite personal, written requests from Prosecutor-General Piskun.

The first reactions from the Ukrainian government upon seeing my articles in the *Independent* were the familiar bluster of knee-jerk denials. A representative of the prosecutor-general's office, Serhiy Rudenko, said, 'We are very dubious about publications with quotations from anonymous sources, or from mythical employees of law-enforcement bodies.' He insisted that the Gongadze affair was being 'thoroughly investigated' and when asked about General Pukach and the accusation he had ordered the destruction of documents about the Gongadze case, Rudenko said: 'If there had been any proof of the guilt of this individual, then the appropriate investigative procedures would have been taken against him.'

The following day the Ukrainian authorities were forced to admit the documents in my possession were authentic, and the prosecutor-general launched a criminal inquiry into who had leaked them to me. Rudenko, meanwhile, blithely announced that the dead witness Honcharov had suffered spinal injuries and that, without publicly announcing it, the prosecutor-general's office had in fact opened a criminal case the month before 'into officers at Remand Centre Number 13 exceeding their authority and inflicting deliberate bodily harm that led to the death of Honcharov'. Rudenko went on to say the prosecutor-general's office had reviewed the Honcharov letters and statements and found them immaterial to the Gongadze case, despite Prosecutor-General Piskun, before he was removed, telling a Kyiv television station that Honcharov's information had been 'very useful to us'.

A few days later, the prosecutor-general's office again attracted mockery when it declared yet another person had confessed to killing Gongadze – 'During questioning the man said he had committed the murder of Gongadze. His statement fits the circumstances of the murder at the time and other key moments, which are already in the public domain. He said he had decapitated him.' The man, known only as 'K', had supposedly been previously prosecuted for murders. Like 'Cyclops' and 'Sailor' before him, 'K' also quietly faded away without his full name or other details being made known.

The precise events surrounding Gongadze's murder might never be clear, but by piecing together information from the documents it is clear that a surveillance team was watching Gongadze at the moment that he was abducted, probably by being bundled into a vehicle by men soon after he left his girlfriend and co-editor's flat. He may have been grabbed in the courtyard of the building before he even reached the street.

Although the log of the last team to follow Gongadze has been destroyed, the names of the twenty-five people in the surveillance group over the period are known. The composition of the final team should not be difficult to discover, especially as some of the witnesses seemed genuinely shocked at what had happened. That last surveillance team either saw who snatched Gongadze or took part in the abduction.

The team working under Prosecutor-General Piskun, who was fired by Kuchma, believe that Gongadze was tortured before being killed. One theory is that he was being tortured by a Kuchma aide to make him reveal who had leaked documents for his story about money transfers out of the country.

The investigators and others who have studied the evidence believe Gongadze died within hours of being abducted, and not far from where he was last seen, possibly in a Kyiv warehouse or in the car. Gongadze was physically fit and no stranger to action, and some people think he may have been shot dead as he struggled to escape from his captors. Decapitation is not a method commonly employed by Ukrainian murderers. It is possible he was decapitated after death, because a bullet was lodged in his head and would have identified the officially issued service pistol that fired it.

The Tarascha coroner recorded that the body looked fresh and had not been in the ground very long, suggesting that the corpse may have been kept refrigerated somewhere else, perhaps in Kyiv, in the weeks between Gongadze's disappearance and the discovery of the remains in Tarascha. The town is in the constituency of Socialist Party leader Oleksandr Moroz. Some theorise the site was chosen with the intention of somehow discrediting Moroz, though there is no evidence for this.

The revelations in the *Independent* caused an immense stir in Ukraine and were immediately translated and reprinted in the Ukrainian media not under government control, especially the Internet. People were not surprised there had been a cover-up but that, for once, the cover-up had been exposed. The documents showed that Kuchma's regime was riddled to the core with lies, and that senior figures in the administration, including Kuchma, had conspired to hamper and derail the murder investigation. It was clear that Interior Minister Kravchenko had directly ordered the police operation against Gongadze and knew everything about the killing. As layers of secrecy and lies were peeled away they revealed many of the usual suspects lurking around other shifty schemes that had earned Ukraine such a bad reputation.

The disclosures came just a few weeks before the 2004 presidential election race officially began, and the opposition used the information to put acute pressure on the Kuchma administration. During the Orange Revolution, Yushchenko forced Vasilyev's sacking and Piskun, who returned to his old job, resumed the investigation into Gongadze's killing.

Of course, proof of the ruthless methods the government was willing to use to stay in power were daunting. But it was apparent that the government had not succeeded in cowing everybody into submission; even amidst the corruption and intimidation that infected every area of officialdom, there were still people of integrity who wanted to uphold the law and to behave honourably. The Gongadze case symbolised for Ukrainians everything they hated most about Kuchma's regime. Kuchma's ruffians wanted to show that they could bury Gongadze's ideals, and it was a shattering blow to them when Gongadze's spirit seemed to return with an even greater force on the eve of elections that would change everyone's life. Gongadze's killing and the pledge to bring his murderers to justice became one of the Orange Revolution's most powerful rallying points.

I moved the leaked documents out of Ukraine and wrote the stories in Prague. I then scanned all the documents and transferred them on to compact discs, which I distributed to people campaigning for press freedom and justice for Gongadze. They were posted on the Internet so that anybody could inspect them. Despite the Ukrainian authorities' anger at the disclosures, I wanted to return to Ukraine to report the forthcoming presidential election campaign. The prosecutor-general said repeatedly in public that he wanted to question me but he had made no attempt to get in touch with me. So I decided to go to Ukraine and test the waters.

I flew to Kyiv and then took a plane to Crimea to do a story about the ethnic tension there, and to watch Yushchenko campaign on the peninsula. At first the authorities did not react at all, and I thought that they perhaps preferred to pretend I was not in the country. However, one evening I returned to my hotel in Simferopol, the Crimean capital, and waiting on the landing was a youngish man, dressed entirely in black, who introduced himself as an investigator from the prosecutor's office in Kyiv. He handed me an invitation for questioning from the prosecutor-general in Kyiv and politely told me that I could be compelled to attend if I did not go voluntarily.

I arrived for my appointment at the prosecutor-general's office on the morning of 12 August and was led into a cramped office. The investigators were courteous but not overly friendly; the older of the two asked most of the questions while the younger noted down the answers straight into a computer. As each page filled up he printed out my statement, we checked that the answers had been correctly recorded and I signed the bottom of the page. It was peculiar to be generating a witness statement whose format was identical to the dozens of documents I had pored over a couple of months before. My statement, though, was a good deal less interesting as it mostly consisted of refusing to answer the questions and explaining my refusal by saying I would not give away the source of the leaked materials.

My two investigators made no attempt at any really spirited or aggressive questioning. I had told them at the start that if the British embassy and my wife did not hear from me every two hours on my mobile phone, they would sound the alarm. I was conscious that no Ukrainian interviewee would be allowed to phone anyone from the interrogation room and that, in relative terms, I was being treated with kid gloves. The only disagreeable thing was that I was not offered anything to drink for more than seven hours. The investigators sternly informed me that publicising confidential state documents was against the law and asked what I thought about breaking the law. I replied that I did not feel guilty about committing a minor offence in a country where state officials from the president down were constantly breaking the law and somebody like General Pukach, who was implicated in murder, was free. I have a sneaking suspicion that they agreed with me. After more than nine hours we called it quits; I was allowed to leave but had to return the next day. I turned up, this time with two large bottles of mineral water, to the amusement of my interrogators.

On the occasions one of them left the office, it was obvious they were discussing my replies with their superiors: the older one would return with new questions jotted down in his notebook that were different in tone and very probably suggested by Vasilyev himself. To several of those I replied innocently that they seemed more stupid than his own questions and I was sure somebody else had formulated them. I hoped that Vasilyev was listening in and seething. The investigators concluded the second day's questioning by telling me they were releasing me but it was possible I could be called in again. I never heard from them after that.

The Orange Revolution leaders promised that if they came to power they would vigorously investigate the Gongadze killing. Whilst progress has been made, many unanswered questions and loose ends remain. In the spring of 2005 three of the four policemen the authorities alleged killed Gongadze were arrested. But General Pukach managed to flee abroad. The interior minister, Yuriy Kravchenko, who is on the secret recordings discussing with Kuchma what to do about Gongadze, was found dead with two bullets in his head on a March morning in 2005, hours before he was supposed to appear for interrogation at the prosecutor-general's office in the same building where I was questioned. The official verdict was suicide.

But the key suspects implicated in the recordings and still alive – Kuchma, Parliamentary Speaker Volodymyr Lytvyn, and former spy chief Leonid Derkach – were not charged. Lytvyn was set to be a possible ally of Yushchenko in the 2006 parliamentary election while there was strong suspicion that Kuchma had negotiated some sort of immunity. Hryhoriy Omelchenko, meanwhile, chairman of the parliamentary committee investigating the murder, said there was enough evidence to indict senior officials, including Kuchma, who he called 'the main organiser' for conspiracy to kidnap at the very least.

The irony is that many people who have studied the case, inevitably dubbed Kuchmagate, do not believe the president intended the journalist should die. In the secret recordings he never actually gives orders to kill Gongadze, only to scare him. Some have speculated Gongadze was killed by overzealous figures in Kuchma's administration who misinterpreted his desires, like the knights who slew Thomas Becket and turned him into a martyr after believing Henry II's anguished cry 'Who will rid me of this turbulent priest' to be an exhortation to murder.

Others say a group, possibly the crooked oligarch businessmen benefiting from corrupt rule or pro-Moscow personnel that permeated all Ukraine's security structures, decided to find a way to discredit and blackmail Kuchma because he had indicated he would steer away from corruption and lawlessness and towards the West in his second term.

Whatever the genesis of the drama that ended in Gongadze's murder, if there is not a demonstrably just conclusion to the affair the credibility of those who led the Orange Revolution will be damaged, since its very occurrence owed much to the scandal, something those leaders themselves realise. The man who for a time was SBU chief in the new government, Oleksandr Turchynov said: 'The death of Gongadze really shook up and changed the country. Without Kuchmagate, there likely would have never been an Orange Revolution four years later.'

Chapter Seven

CANDIDATES OF RECORD

When he began his second term in office, Kuchma promised
he would turn over a new leaf. In his inauguration speech on
30 November 1999, he outlined a wide range of reforms to
reshape the country and announced, 'In the context of
strengthening national security I lend particular significance
to the fight against corruption and criminality.' Ukrainians
hoped that meant he would curb the avaricious plundering
of their country's economy and stem the corruption and
lawlessness that had metastasised throughout society.

Kuchma also needed to buff up his reputation with dismayed Western governments and institutions. The president
seemed to be sticking to his word when in December 1999
he startled Ukraine by appointing to prime minister Viktor
Yushchenko, the head of Ukraine's national bank. The
youthful Yushchenko had hitherto shied away from politics
and was not allied to any of the clans which competed for
supremacy and influenced government policy. Although
still relatively unknown, Yushchenko was already respected
among opposition politicians and foreign financiers
because of his professional competence and a reputation for
honesty.

Yushchenko had been head of the national bank since
1993, introduced Ukraine's new currency, the *hryvnia*, in
1996 and tamed inflation with a tight monetary policy.
Ukrainians, used to the pilfering ways of their officials,
looked with admiration and some awe upon the man who

controlled such huge sums of money without stealing any of it.

Kuchma thought he could kill two birds with one stone by appointing Yushchenko. He knew Yushchenko's appointment would be welcomed by Ukrainians, Western governments and financial bodies like the IMF, World Bank and the European Bank for Reconstruction and Development. He felt he could also check Yushchenko as a potential political rival because the prime minister's powers were very limited compared to those of the president, who could appoint ministers, as well as regional governors and even local county heads.

Yushchenko could, however, choose his own deputy and his astute choice was Yulia Tymoshenko, who had previously come to prominence as Ukraine's richest woman oligarch. He also gave her the all-important energy portfolio. The iron-willed and charismatic Tymoshenko was strikingly pretty and had an appetite for figure-hugging designer clothes. Tymoshenko was not only alluring but also intensely loyal, although she came from a background, which, at first sight, did not make her an obvious choice as deputy for the new corruption-fighting prime minister.

Tymoshenko is undoubtedly tough psychologically, as well as physically – she goes for long runs most mornings before starting work. She is also charming and her disarmingly self-deprecating comments, often accompanied by a schoolgirl giggle, seem very ingenuous. She likes to compare her story to a fairytale, complete with impoverished origins. She was born Yulia Hryhyan in 1960 in Dnipropetrovsk, an only child who was brought up by her mother who she says was the biggest influence in her life. Tymoshenko rarely talks about her father except to say that he was not around to bring her up. Even by the prevailing

Soviet standards, Tymoshenko said they were considered poor and were able to afford few comforts in their tiny flat in a dilapidated high-rise. Her mother did seamstressing work to make extra money and Tymoshenko, as a schoolgirl unable to afford new clothes, used to sew her own. 'I was delighted when other girls admired my dresses and asked where they could get the same things,' she said. 'They never suspected I made them myself.'

She did well at school and went on to study economics at Dnipropetrovsk University. Tymoshenko said that she was not a politicised person when she was young and thought little about whether her country should be independent. 'I don't want to disappoint anyone but I suppose I was just an ordinary Soviet teenager and just accepted the way things were. I wasn't a big Ukrainian patriot. My biggest concern was to try to help my mother make ends met.'

When she was eighteen she met another student, Oleksandr Tymoshenko, and by the following year they were married and she had their only child, a daughter, Evgenia. The couple continued their studies and took onerous jobs for paltry wages in their spare time; one of Yulia Tymoshenko's jobs was shifting and stacking tyres twice the size of a man.

In the late eighties as the Soviet Union began to open up to private enterprise, the Tymoshenkos seized the opportunity to work for themselves. They bought some video recorders and made pirate copies of Hollywood blockbusters like the *Rambo* movies, which they sold or showed in makeshift screening venues. With the profits from that and a bank loan secured for them by her father-in-law, who was well-connected with the local Communist Party, they started trading in petrol and were then set on the road to becoming the largest electricity provider in Ukraine.

In this part of the Tymoshenko fairytale story her version

diverges from the one provided not only by her detractors but also by some of her friends. Tymoshenko insists that as head of a company called Unified Energy Systems of Ukraine (UESU), which in 1996 was credited with an annual turnover of eleven billion dollars, she never made more than five thousand dollars per month and always worked with Ukraine's interests at heart. Ukraine's exchequer also apparently did not make much from UESU. In fact UESU did not pay a penny in taxes according to a parliamentary investigation in 1996.

She may have been on a tight personal budget but Tymoshenko moved between her palatial home and businesses in convoys of Mercedes limousines, guarded by a phalanx of bodyguards. She also managed to send her daughter to Britain to be educated privately at an expensive school followed by a prestigious university. In 1997 Tymoshenko sent one of her company's four private planes to pick up a friend of mine, author and journalist Matthew Brzezinski, to take him from Moscow to Dnipropetrovsk for lunch and back the same day so he could interview her for his book *Casino Moscow*. In pride of place above the desk from which she ran a web of some two thousand interrelated companies, Matthew noticed a photograph, in a gilded frame, of the Ukrainian prime minister, Pavlo Lazarenko.

Although she later downplayed his role, Lazarenko was the catalyst for the success that made Tymoshenko probably the wealthiest woman in the former USSR and earned her the nickname 'The Gas Princess'. Tymoshenko unquestionably possesses considerable business acumen, but she admitted that she also sometimes exploited her head-turning looks. It is possible the same method helped arouse Lazarenko's interest in a close financial partnership.

When he was chosen for government by Kuchma,

Lazarenko gave Tymoshenko a monopoly for buying and supplying Russian gas to Ukraine. Ukraine's giant Soviet-era industries were in disarray and suffocating, and the managers had no idea where to procure raw materials or how to find buyers for the goods they manufactured. Most of all they could not pay for the electricity to allow their factories to work. Tymoshenko solved all their problems by providing energy and finding customers for their goods. She took many of the payments in barter and paid for much of the gas through similar deals, which are notoriously opaque, especially from a tax perspective. In 1996 and 1997 it is estimated that UESU's earnings represented twenty-five per cent of Ukraine's total economy.

For her part Tymoshenko insists that she did nothing criminal and that estimates of her wealth were greatly exaggerated. She claims that by 1997 she and her company had come under pressure from Kuchma and his associates because she was refusing to pay bribes.

In 1996 she decided to run for parliament. She said that she originally chose to go into politics, like many other business people, to be able to better protect her commerial interests. Members of parliament also receive immunity from criminal prosecution. Touring her constituency exposed her to the poverty to which most Ukrainians had been condemned, while a small number of people became fabulously wealthy. She said she entered a house in a village that had broken windows and seemed deserted. Inside she found a barefoot elderly woman. 'She actually apologised to me for being alive and being a burden to other people. She said she was praying she would die soon. That woman's pain has haunted me ever since.'

Those who question Tymoshenko's version of events say that initially she had no problems about Kuchma's political morality, and difficulties only arose because of business clashes. Speaking in 2005, Tymoshenko told me it was the type of rule that Kuchma had instilled in Ukraine that dismayed her. She maintains that soon after winning her seat, her view of Kuchma became more critical. 'I realised an honest politician could simply not be on the same side of the barricades as Kuchma. He was destroying Ukraine's national interests, there was complete deception, complete corruption, and an absolute absence of any justice,' she said.

Tymoshenko's deteriorating relations with Kuchma coincided with the president's worsening relations with her mentor, Lazarenko. In 1998 Lazarenko's party, with Tymoshenko as one of its leading lights, went into parliamentary elections as opponents of the Kuchma government.

As Lazarenko began his bizarre travels, which ended awaiting trial in San Francisco, Tymoshenko formed her own *Batkivschyna* – Fatherland – Party and launched a vigorous political war against Kuchma that involved mass demonstrations and calls for his impeachment. She accused him of using the courts and intimidating her family and colleagues to persuade her to fall in line. 'When they started ruining the business I had two choices: to come to an agreement with Kuchma or to oppose him in the knowledge that everything I had would be destroyed in a ruthless manner. I chose opposition. They utterly destroyed everything, they left nothing, but I was determined not to do anything that would bring me dishonour.'

Many were sceptical about Tymoshenko's apparent conversion to selfless servant of the people, but Yushchenko chose to believe that, whether for simple or complex reasons, she did not want to go down in Ukraine's history as another shady oligarch and recognised that her poacher-turned-gamekeeper skills would be invaluable for the success of his anti-corruption campaign. The partnership was the beginning of an extraordinary political relationship that was destined to propel them, a few years later, on to the world stage with the Orange Revolution as the dramatic backdrop.

When Yushchenko took office, Ukraine's gross domestic product had plummeted by more than fifty per cent and there had not been a single year of growth. The standard of living had spiralled inexorably downwards during the years of independence, and by 2000 the average wage in Ukraine was less than sixty dollars per month; unemployment stood at around a quarter of the working-age population.

Tymoshenko used the knowledge that came from her experience of the energy business to hamstring some of the oligarchs' most lucrative illicit schemes, and largely thanks to her endeavours Ukraine, in 2000, for the first time since independence, had a budget surplus – a huge one, to boot – of about $1.5 billion.

Yushchenko used this to repay the massive wage arrears for public employees that had accumulated, in many cases for years, and did the same with unpaid pensions. He also introduced sweeping economic reforms that finally set Ukraine upon the path that Kuchma and Kravchuk had been promising for years. Yushchenko had cemented his reputation for honesty and the opinion polls showed he had the highest popularity ratings of any Ukrainian politician.

Kuchma was always suspicious of anyone who looked to be developing an independent power base, especially his own appointees, and his relations with Yushchenko and Tymoshenko deteriorated. Tymoshenko had become a very costly thorn in the side of many of the energy oligarchs, including two who were now very close to Kuchma, Hryhoriy Surkis, one of the biggest players on the energy markets, and his partner Viktor Medvedchuk, the deputy parliamentary speaker, and leader of their pro-presidential SDPU(U) party.

Kuchma removed Tymoshenko from her post by presidential decree on 19 January 2001, and shortly afterwards had her thrown in jail on corruption charges where she joined her husband and other close colleagues already jailed on the president's instructions.

'They put me in a filthy little cell that hadn't been cleaned for years,' she said. 'I demanded a rag and a bucket of water and I cleaned my cell thoroughly and then hung the rag over the spyhole. I told the wardens that if they took away that rag, I'd go on hunger strike.' The rag stayed and so did Tymoshenko, who remained imprisoned for six weeks until a Kyiv court ordered her release because it decided there was no case to answer.

Tymoshenko said she was certain she would not stay long in prison because of an almost mystical faith in her destiny. 'I had a task to perform in life, and I believed that my goal was pure and, therefore, attainable – to topple Kuchma's regime and to begin building for Ukraine the sort of life my country deserved.'

Kuchma's vindictive behaviour firmly fixed the animosity between the two on a very personal plane, and from that point Tymoshenko was to become his most implacable enemy.

Yushchenko's dismissal was a tougher nut to crack because the prime minister had made the first demonstrable improvements to Ukraine's economy since independence and his 'clean hands' image made it difficult for Kuchma to remove the prime minister from his post blithely. But the oligarchs wanted a return to crooked business as usual. Their hold over Kuchma increased after the Gongadze murder scandal erupted and the president did not object when the deputy parliamentary speaker, Medvedchuk, publicly announced that he would push through a no-confidence vote in Yushchenko's government that would force the prime minister's resignation. Medvedchuk had assembled a sordid coalition of the two groups most stridently opposed to democracy in Ukraine – the oligarchs and the Communists. The oligarchs hated Yushchenko because the anti-corruption campaign was hitting their pockets, while Ukraine's dinosaur Communists loathed Yushchenko because he wanted closer relations with the West and a functioning market economy.

In April 2001 this unholy alliance forced Yushchenko's resignation. Thousands of opposition supporters outside parliament listened on loudspeakers to the proceedings within. The crowd booed and whistled when the vote went against the prime minister and they waited expectantly to see if Yushchenko would come out to meet them.

A few minutes later Yushchenko walked out past lines of police and metal railings to talk to his hushed supporters through a public address system set up in a van. His oratorical skills had never been his strong point, and his manner was generally more like a lecturer who wanted to ensure his students understood the subject, rather than a fiery rabble-rouser. On this occasion too Yushchenko's speech was almost matter-of-fact, as if he had just walked out of a disappointing conference about interest rates rather than out of government. But his short address was nevertheless stirring because he was so obviously speaking from the heart.

Yushchenko did allow himself one uncharacteristic flourish at the end of his speech when he assured his audience that this was not the end of something but rather the beginning of a new phase, and that he was only 'leaving in order to return'. It was perhaps the moment when

Yushchenko stopped being someone who wanted to bring about change from within, to a person who was now firmly in the opposition camp. The streets reverberated to affectionate cries of 'Yushchenko!', echoes of which would come to haunt Kuchma and his accomplices. Less than half a mile away in the presidential administration building, Kuchma had watched the parliamentary proceedings on television. By throwing Yushchenko to the wolves, a spineless Kuchma had demonstrated that his second term would only deepen the delinquency of the first. But he may have been disturbed to notice that far from snuffing out the former prime minister's political existence, his dismissal from office strengthened Yushchenko's political stature because ties to the government no longer tainted him. Kuchma himself had also forged the alliance between Yushchenko and Tymoshenko that was to prove so powerful a few years later.

Things were sliding from bad to worse for the president. There was a steady flow of revelations from the bodyguard Mykola Melnychenko, and if the excerpts from the secretly recorded conversations were not damaging enough, Kuchma's implausible denials made even his opponents cringe. In one interview for American television news, Kuchma affected a persecuted look and ostentatiously crossed himself as he pleaded innocence, claiming that unknown forces plotting 'a provocation' against Ukraine were setting him up. Melnychenko had said Kuchma was a proficient actor, but the Ukrainian president's performance on prime-time news was both unconvincing and embarrassing.

Meanwhile, journalists continued to die in mysterious circumstances or suffered beatings and intimidation. Less than a year after the murder of Gongadze thousands of people attended the funeral in July 2001 of television journalist and manager Ihor Aleksandrov who died after being savagely clubbed by assailants with baseball bats as he entered the TOR television company in the East Ukrainian city of Slovyansk. Aleksandrov, director of TOR, was known for exposing corruption and investigating organised crime in the Donetsk region.

In the run-up to the 1999 presidential elections, Aleksandrov's television station was one of the few in the country that gave ample opportunity for opponents of President Kuchma to voice their views. At the time of his death he was resisting pressure to sell a controlling share of his television station to a company he believed would limit TOR's editorial independence.

Aleksandrov's murder was the eleventh of a journalist during Kuchma's rule, and brought to around forty the number of reporters who had died violently or in suspicious circumstances since Ukraine's independence.

Nobody accused Kuchma of direct involvement in the murder of Aleksandrov in the way that he was being linked to Gongadze's death, but he was blamed for helping to create a dangerous climate for determined journalists. Ivan Bokyj, a former journalist who had become a member of parliament, said Aleksandrov's murder was made possible because criminal organisations had increased their power since Kuchma's re-election. He said: 'In Ukraine there is no democracy. The characteristics of today's government are oligarchic and criminal. The things that happen to our brother journalists are just the way the regime deals with such people and will continue to do so as long as it remains in power.'

International groups defending journalists' rights condemned the Kuchma government. Reporters Without Borders ranked Ukraine 112th out of 139 countries in terms of journalistic freedom and government efforts to guarantee freedom of expression. The Committee to Protect Journalists placed Kuchma on its list of the world's ten worst enemies of the press in 1999 and again in 2001.

There had been an unsuccessful attempt to impeach Kuchma in 1998. At the end of 2000, the Kuchmagate scandal, combined with concerns about corruption, authoritarianism, and impoverishment, triggered a protest campaign called 'Ukraine Without Kuchma' which dogged the president for the remainder of his term in office.

Yushchenko had never displayed avid political ambition, and perhaps this reticence endeared him to his countrymen. Meanwhile the fractured opposition needed a figure to coalesce around, and Yushchenko's consistent popularity in opinion polls made him the natural choice. In 2002 he led an opposition coalition called Nasha Ukrayina – 'Our Ukraine' – into that spring's parliamentary elections. The coalition of Western-oriented centre and centre-right parties advocated democratic, market and human rights reforms, pledged to fight corruption, and sought eventual membership of the EU. Yet despite Kuchma's huge unpopularity he was able to manipulate the election to secure a majority for his supporters in the 450-seat parliament.

As in his own 1999 re-election, the main weapon Kuchma used against the opposition was what was known in Ukraine as admin-resource, short for administrative resources. Admin-resource entailed leaning on every level of official and threatening them with the loss of their positions unless they coaxed or intimidated enough people into voting the required way. As a starting point, that meant every official threatened to fire their underlings unless they also pulled out all the stops to get the correct result – a lot of votes in a country where a large proportion of the workforce are still state employees. The system was also applied to colleges and universities where students were threatened with expulsion unless they voted as ordered by the head of their institution. Hundreds of thousands of conscripts in Europe's second largest army were routinely coerced into voting for the regime's candidates, as were patients in hospitals and prison inmates. Admin-resource even penetrated into the private sector by threatening to launch crippling tax inspections or strangle businesses with red tape.

In addition to admin-resource, the parliamentary election system in 2002 was especially prone to manipulation. In those elections half the seats were distributed on the basis of national proportional repesentation, while the other half were filled by the candidates who gained most votes in the electoral constituencies. Where the winner was the person with the simple majority of votes in a constituency, fixing the outcome was relatively easy. The recordings secretly made by Kuchma's errant bodyguard, Melnychenko, have Yanukovych gleefully confiding to the president that using the first-past-the-post type of election, rather than the proportional representation form, you could 'get an orangutan into parliament'.

Many of the candidates poured huge amounts of money into quite openly buying votes or bribing election officials to fake the count or ignore ballot stuffing. Many of these candidates campaigned as independents and only showed their true colours after the election when they joined the pro-Kuchma camp in parliament. Some who fought the election on the opposition ticket later defected, reportedly for large bribes.

In March 2002 these abuses produced a victory for Kuchma. Nasha Ukrayina, led by Yushchenko, won the biggest share of the popular vote in the proportional ballot –

23.57 per cent – with second place going to the Communist Party, which secured twenty per cent. However, Kuchma's party held the greatest total number of seats -182 – because it was so successful in the majority-vote elections where bribery and underhand means were prevalent.

The conduct of the elections was criticised by independent monitors and international bodies. But the dramatic testimony to the strength of the opposition was that despite the fraud, Yushchenko's Nasha Ukrayina won 117 seats, knocking the Communist Party into third place for the first time since independence.

Opposition confidence had been boosted and the pace of events was increasing. On the second anniversary of Gongadze's murder, Nasha Ukrayina, the Yulia Tymoshenko bloc, the Communists, and the Socialists called anti-Kuchma rallies in Kyiv and around the country which the government tried to frustrate by banning demonstrations in central Kyiv and disrupting train, bus and private car travel into the capital. To discourage demonstrators, television reports implied there would be violence as they showed hospitals stocking up on medical supplies. Very few channels reported anything about the eventual demonstrations. Those that did said the protests were small – in fact tens of thousands took part and the next day police violently broke up a tent camp of protestors and arrested scores of people.

In this atmosphere of growing hostility, Kuchma's eye was already on the 2004 presidential election and how he could either stay in the top job himself or otherwise arrange things to retain power. Under the Ukrainian constitution, any president is allowed only two terms in office. So Kuchma decided to change the constitution. In 2000 he held a referendum to give him the authority to strengthen presidential powers, decrease the number of MPs from 450 to three hundred, remove their immunity from prosecution and create a second parliamentary chamber that he would control. He secured popular approval for the amendments because voters were fed up with a squabbling parliament, the majority of whose members were despised as crooks. But the parliament refused to ratify the amendments.

On Independence Day 2002, 24 August, Kuchma unveiled a new strategy, believed to have been masterminded by his new head of administration, Viktor Medvedchuk. It took an opposite tack to the previous scheme and consisted of constitutional amendments that would give parliament more power. Under the prevailing system, the president appointed cabinet ministers, regional governors, judges, prosecutors, tax inspectors and police officials, without approval from parliament, which could only veto the appointment of the prime minister. The proposals would shift the lion's share of political power after Kuchma's term expired from the presidency to a prime minister elected by the majority in parliament. It was obvious Kuchma intended to be that first sinewy prime minister.

The backroom dealing, horsetrading, and sometimes brawling, continued for months, with opinion polls showing that voters believed the proposals were a trick so that Kuchma could retain power.

Kuchma's public stance was that he would not seek a third term, but it looked as if he was hedging his bets and wanted to have the option to run if necessary. The obliging constitutional court ruled that Kuchma's first term, which started in 1994, did not count because it began before the new constitution's approval in 1996 and that he could therefore run for a further five-year term.

By this time the parliamentary shenanigans were attracting the attention of many governments. On 24 December the

EU expressed 'deep concern' over the events in parliament and said, 'In the current political circumstances, proposals to amend the constitution could adversely affect the trust and confidence of voters in Ukraine's representative democracy, especially in the year of election . . . the EU is convinced that it is important to hold a really free, fair and transparent presidential election.' The EU said it would be keeping an eye on Ukraine and the future of relations between Kyiv and Brussels depended on how the election was conducted.

Another European body, relatively unknown, was beginning to play an increasingly important role in the battle for Ukraine's future. The organisation was the Council of Europe and in particular the Parliamentary Assembly of the Council of Europe (PACE). The Council of Europe, based in the French city of Strasbourg, is a separate institution from the EU and was founded in 1949 to set and monitor human rights and democracy standards in countries that applied for membership. No country has been accepted into the EU without first proving its eligibility for the Council of Europe. Ukraine and the other newly Communist-free countries saw membership of the Council of Europe as a way of establishing their democratic credentials and intention to join the EU. The Council of Europe was pleased at the prospect of a renewed lease of life, having sunk into obscurity in the eighties, and offered bargain-basement membership, which seemed to compromise some of the previously high criteria for entry. Conspicuously, Russia was granted membership in February 1996 despite its army regularly slaughtering and raping Chechen civilians. The Council justified relaxing the rules by advancing the questionable argument that the roguish new entrants would pick up good habits from the example set by virtuous older members.

For countries like Ukraine, excluded from the clubs which wield real power like the EU, World Trade Organisation, or the G7, membership of the Council of Europe became intricately bound up with prestige and internal propaganda. It provided an important interface with Western Europe through a body of which Ukraine was a full member, and not merely a guest or associate. Ukraine could point to membership of the Council as proof to its own people that the country was moving upwards in international society. The corollary to this was that Kyiv had to take censure from Strasbourg seriously.

The Council of Europe had already expressed concern at the apparently slapdash way the investigation into the murder of Gongadze was being handled. In early January 2004 the PACE member monitoring events in Ukraine, Danish parliamentarian Hanne Severinsen, said she could not understand how Ukraine's constitutional court had ruled Kuchma could seek a third presidential term when 'both the current and the former constitution talk about only two terms'.

A week later Severinsen came to Kyiv and talked to the players in the mounting dispute. Yushchenko told her that the opposition still did not know the names of the 276 deputies who purportedly supported the amendments to the constitution and implied the count was incorrect. He said the government's behaviour was tantamount to an attempted state coup and that if it were successful, an 'emperor' would run the country. 'The main political problem,' he said, 'is the concentration of authority with a total lack of accountability . . . When we're talking about fundamental human values, then we believe they're worth fighting for.'

The Council of Europe then took a determined stand denouncing the attempts to alter the constitution ahead of the election and threatened to suspend Ukraine's membership of the Council if it did not create conditions for a free and fair presidential poll. Kuchma responded by saying Ukraine would not give in to any 'ultimatum'. 'We realise that Ukraine needs the Council of Europe no less than the Council of Europe needs us. This makes any ultimatum inappropriate,' he said. In February 2004 the Communists and Socialists backed the government proposals on constitutional change. But in April another boisterous session of parliament, which again degenerated into fist fights, failed to pass a vital stage of the controversial bill. Yushchenko accused pro-presidential members of parliament of breaking the law. He said: 'They voted with one objective, to hand vast presidential powers to the prime minister. This decision is a way to preserve the current regime.' He claimed coercion had been used in the vote and he had seen a list of parliament members who were blackmailed into supporting the changes by threats to use the tax administration to ruinously investigate their businesses. Tymoshenko also chipped in, saying the regime wanted to make the new president a monkey taking commands from the oligarchs.

But time had run out for the government to ram through the constitutional changes before the upcoming election, and the Kuchma regime felt it as a huge confidence-sapping defeat. As the opposition opened its campaign in July 2004, with one of the biggest political rallies ever seen in Ukraine, disquiet seeped into the corridors of the presidential administration building.

Losing the presidential election in Ukraine, and in other former Soviet republics, implies much more than a loss of political power. Ukraine and others in the region are still in the infant stages of democracy. In the West where democracy has developed over centuries, the opposition is referred to as 'loyal' and is treated courteously, in theory anyway, by a governing party holding temporary stewardship of a mature institution. However, most of the former republics of the Soviet Union had no experience of democracy, and government – whether by Communists or tsars – had meant a tyrannical exercise of power that treated opposition as treachery. Many Ukrainian politicians still view politics in that way, and although they mouth democratic slogans, their spirit is autocratic. Some members of parliament, like the Communists, are full of contempt for the notion of Western parliamentary democracy. Interruptions by fist fights, physically blocking access for opposing speakers in a debate, and even ripping out microphones from sockets are all tactics regularly used in the Ukrainian parliament.

Losing the election would also imply the end of the cosy corrupt arrangements that had enriched the elite. For some in the regime the emergence of democracy and the rule of law meant they would face the risk of confiscation of ill-gotten assets and prosecution and imprisonment for corruption, thug tactics, illegal arms sales and murder. For these people the election involved extremely high stakes: it was a fight for survival.

But if they succeeded in retaining power, the consequences for Ukraine would be tragic. It would mean the entrenchment in power of criminals hiding under a patina of democratic procedure, as if Al Capone had managed to have himself elected president of the US in the thirties. And if they won this time, everyone feared that the regime's top priority would be to emasculate all real political opposition and independent media and tighten their grip on society so that nobody could ever challenge them again.

Kuchma had got the constitutional court to grant him the right to run for a third term as president but he saw that in opinion polls about the popularity of the country's politicians he never made it into double figures; he was realistic enough to realise that even a terrific amount of cheating could not guarantee him an election victory. Ukraine did have a functioning and stalwart political opposition; the press was not completely suppressed and Internet publications especially were able to resist censorship. There were murders and intimidation was rife, but Kuchma had not unleashed the sort of repressive forces at play in Belarus and Russia because he knew that would have led to complete isolation of his regime by Western governments. He knew that many of his oligarch supporters would ditch him if their businesses suffered international economic sanctions imposed in punishment for government excesses.

Kuchma had hinted for a long time that he would back Prime Minister Yanukovych for president, but he delayed making this official in order to keep his own options open for as long as possible. A conference of Kuchma's political allies picked Yanukovych as their candidate in April 2004 at a session in which the president took part. Stepan Havrysh, one of Kuchma's leading loyalists in parliament, said that Yanukovych's electoral programme would be to 'complete political reforms in Ukraine and implement constitutional changes'. Even then Ukrainians suspected it was part of a murky game plan that would somehow see Kuchma remain at the helm.

It had been almost certain since the parliamentary elections in 2002 that Yushchenko would be the presidential candidate from the largest opposition group, Nasha Ukrayina. The only question was whether the main opposition parties could find enough common ground to field a single candidate for the 2004 election, thereby consolidating their votes. Yulia Tymoshenko, who had once declared she was ready to do Yushchenko's laundry if bidden, made it clear that she wanted a unified opposition to field one candidate. She did not abandon all hope of becoming that single candidate, but promised to abide by the decision of the opposition coalition and when it chose Yushchenko, Tymoshenko kept her word but secured a secret promise she would become prime minister if Yushchenko won.

Improbably the Communist and Socialist parties also spoke about joining forces with the other opposition parties and even signed a pact to that effect. However, when it became clear that neither Communist leader Petro Symonenko or Socialist Oleksandr Moroz stood any chance of becoming the unified opposition's candidate, they decided to go it alone.

In all, twenty-six candidates registered for the elections. Some were genuine contestants but many others were funded by the regime and called 'technical candidates' who were used to diminish Yushchenko's chances, either by dividing his potential voters or by packing every level of the election-monitoring mechanism with their representatives who would collaborate with the regime to pervert the results. But many months before the first round of the elections in October 2004, there was little doubt that the contest would end in a showdown between Yushchenko and Yanukovych. There was no difficulty in recognising who was who: Yushchenko used to keep banking records while Yanukovych had a criminal record.

Viktor Yanukovych was born in 1950 in Yenakyive, a rough neighbourhood near Donetsk, to a family of Belarusian immigrants. His mother died when he was two years old and he was brought up by his grandmother. People who lived in the area, notorious for crime and hooliganism, said Yanukovych fell in with a bad crowd who were involved in petty crime, including the theft of valuable fur hats. He was imprisoned in a jail for minors and soon after his release jailed again after being convicted for involvement in an assault.

By 1980, though, he was in charge of local bus transportation and had been admitted to the Communist Party. Clearly Yanukovych was already getting some very high-level backing because in 1972, just two years after his release from prison, he represented the USSR as a racing driver in Monaco. In those days – the height of the Cold War – only the most trusted Soviet citizens were allowed to go abroad. A former criminal who served a prison sentence at the same time as Yanukovych claimed the future prime minister had been an informant on other inmates, thus securing privileges for himself whilst behind bars, and possibly favours once he was out.

But being an informant does not entirely explain his good fortune on being admitted into the Communist Party, which rarely accepted those with a criminal past. One of his sponsors into the party was very high level indeed, a former cosmonaut, Georgi Beregovoi, who was a member of the Soviet parliament from Yanukovych's area and had apparently met Yanukovych and decided the young man needed a break. To anyone who lived through those years, this heartwarming tale of one of the Soviet elite reaching down to help a lowly ex-criminal sounds very implausible, but Beregovoi died years before Yanukovych came to political prominence and so was not able to explain why he helped him.

Even in Soviet times, Donetsk had been known for the nexus between its politicians and organised crime, and Yanukovych's opponents said he became acquainted with the region's criminal elite early on. After the fall of

Communism, the criminals grew bolder and by 1996 their domination became an undisputed fact of life in the region. Donetsk has always boasted that it was different from the rest of the country and even many of its law-abiding citizens take a peculiar pride in what they would describe as their region's roguish, rather than downright criminal, reputation.

Donetsk and the minerals-rich Donetsk Basin, Donbas, is home to Ukraine's strongest oligarchic clan led by Rinat Akhmetov, reputedly Ukraine's richest tycoon. Akhmetov, who took over the family business after his employer was shot dead in a gangland killing, controls most of the region's metals and coal industries as well as the Shakhtar football club. Before the presidential election his fortune was estimated at between $1.7 billion and $2.4 billion. Akhmetov and Yanukovych have a long relationship and Yanukovych owes him his wealth and propulsion on to the political stage. Akhmetov is known as the regional political kingmaker and Yanukovych became the region's governor in 1997 with his blessing.

During his rise to political prominence Yanukovych kept quiet about his criminal record, which only came to light in curious circumstances. Volodymyr Bojko, one of the fearless journalists who continued to risk his neck despite threats and the knowledge of what had happened to others, was arrested and jailed for ten days in the summer of 2002 for writing about corruption in Donetsk Province's tax service, police force and prosecutor's offices. In prison he met a veteran inmate who told the astonished Bojko that he had once been behind bars with the region's current governor, Yanukovych.

Bojko was released after protests from journalist, opposition and human rights groups, who were worried he would become another statistic in the tally of the country's dead journalists. Once out of prison Bojko published the previously unknown snippet from Yanukovych's CV which was immediately reproduced by other independent media. There was a convulsive reaction, said Bojko, from the governor's administration. 'An intermediary came to see me and demanded that I publish a retraction saying that the information was not true. He made it very clear there would be dire consequences if I didn't cooperate.' About a week later Bojko was called in to see one of Yanukovych's associates who told him the information about a criminal past had been concocted to discredit the governor. The man explained there was a photograph of Yanukovych reading a newspaper in Monaco during the period he was supposed to be in jail, and that allegations about his second imprisonment were also lies. 'Why are you telling me about some newspaper?' said Bojko, 'I never said which years Yanukovych was imprisoned. As to his second jail term, this is the first time I've ever heard about it.' The crestfallen official became speechless as he realised he had not only failed in the cover-up but had handed Bojko more fascinating information about Yanukovych's past. Bojko was never bothered about the matter again, something he attributes to Kuchma's public intervention on his behalf. The Ukrainian president had suffered from the outcry after Gongadze's murder and the more recent killing of TV station director Aleksandrov, and let Yanukovych know the country did not need another high-profile journalist meeting a similar end.

Yanukovych is around six feet four inches tall, weighs about eighteen stone, and lists sport, particularly boxing, as his hobby. He has a reputation for a fiery temper and is thought to have used his boxing skills on hapless colleagues or underlings. In Donetsk a muscular management style is expected and even admired. As nerves frayed during the election campaign, tales emerged, which he made little effort to deny, that Yanukovych had beaten up some of his top colleagues. One story had him knocking down a senior administration figure in a lift, while the transport minister was hospitalised after a similar explosion of fury.

Before diving into the whirlpool of political life in Kyiv, however, the busy governor apparently found time for academic pursuits and in 2001 graduated from the Ukrainian Academy of Foreign Trade as a master of international law and later as a doctor of science, then a professor. Like most people from Donetsk, Yanukovych primarily speaks Russian and his Ukrainian is notoriously poor. He made numerous spelling mistakes in Ukrainian when he wrote his CV for parliament. He was unable to spell 'prime minister' (his job at the time), his wife's name, and his title of professor, which he spelled with a double 'f'. During the subsequent presidential campaign and the mass demonstrations, his detractors referred to Yanukovych as the 'Proffessor' on mocking placards.

When Yanukovych was nominated by Kuchma for prime minister he made a handwritten CV available to parliament in which he addressed his offences. He said that he was in fact innocent of any wrongdoing in 1968, having agreed altruistically to take the rap for an older friend who would, as an adult, have drawn a far more severe penalty. The second incident involved violence against the victim of a robbery.

When he subsequently stood for president, however, Yanukovych neglected to mention his criminal record in the publicly available CV he was obliged to furnish. When challenged he said that was because the offences had been quashed in 1978 after a court review found him innocent of all wrongdoing. The judicial authorities in Donetsk from those years, speaking in 2004, did not recall quashing the offences although the records of the cases had disappeared. In 2005 the Donetsk prosecutor's office opened a criminal case into forgery of documents cancelling Yanukovych's criminal record. Investigators found that some time between 2002 and 2004, unidentified court personnel had forged two resolutions of the Donetsk regional court dated 27 December 1978 purportedly quashing the sentences.

Not all reports of Yanukovych are unflattering though. A person who got to know him quite well said: 'Of course everyone who deals with him is aware that he could destroy you if he wanted to. He has a fearful reputation, you don't want to cross him, but he is not a sadist. He plays by the rules the clans have established and he thinks of himself as a fair person.' The man, a journalist who was opposed to the rule of the clans, met Yanukovych at his offices when he was governor. The journalist had readied himself for an unpleasant encounter and was surprised that Yanukovych conducted himself politely. During the course of their conversation, the journalist mentioned his mother was in financial difficulties and when he walked out he found a thousand dollars tucked into a pocket of the coat he had left in the antechamber. He said: 'There was a note saying it was for my mother.' The journalist said he considered returning the money – a year and a half's wages for an average Ukrainian – but kept it. 'I did not alter my reports about what was happening in Donetsk,' he said. 'I worried there would be demands for me to earn the money but that did not happen. I know the system he and his fellow clan members built in Donetsk can be ferocious and I think it's wrong, but I do respect him as a man.'

Viktor Yushchenko was born in 1954, far from the political power centres of Ukraine or the Soviet Union, in the northern village of Khoruzhivka in the country's Russian-speaking Sumy region. During World War Two, Yushchenko's father was called up into the Red Army and after being captured by the German forces was incarcerated in several places as a prisoner of war, including the notorious concentration camp at Auschwitz. Yushchenko said that for the rest of his life his father had a loathing of large dogs, reminders of the vicious guard dogs patrolling the barbed wire perimeters of the camps.

Yushchenko was born a year after the death of Stalin, and the period that followed saw a relaxation of the terrifying secret-police grip on the USSR under its new leader Nikita Khrushchev. The crude and pugnacious Khrushchev was no liberal and had been the Communist gauleiter in Ukraine where he worked ruthlessly to destroy any traces of Ukrainian nationalism, but in comparison to the savagery of Stalin's rule, the Khrushchev era brought hope. Khrushchev exposed some of the horrors of the Stalin years but was careful to lay the blame for them on the dictator, not on Communism. Even the modest changes introduced by Khrushchev were too much for many of the old guard to stomach, however, and he was replaced by more orthodox Communists, one of whom, the drab, granite-faced Leonid Brezhnev dragged the Soviet Union into an ultimately economically ruinous arms race and a new period of intense repression.

Yushchenko studied at the Ternopil Finance and Economics Institute in West Ukraine, most of which, prior to the war, had never been under Russian or Communist rule and where Ukrainian guerrillas had still been fighting Communist forces when he was born; it had remained a place whose inhabitants were always consciously and patriotically Ukrainian – a haven for dangerous anti-Soviet nationalists.

Here Yushchenko came into contact with Ukrainian culture and traditions that were vibrant and part of ordinary life, and his fondness for Ukrainian history and culture grew. In West Ukraine he met people who had lived under the more benign rule of the Austro-Hungarian Empire and, between the wars, Poland. Notions of freedom, political diversity, and a relationship between endeavour and reward had not been eradicated to the extent they had been in East Ukraine, which had also experienced the horrors of mass purges and the artificial famine in the thirties. Yushchenko admits that his time in West Ukraine influenced him deeply. He once said, 'If burning myself to ashes could help Ukraine . . . I would be happy to do it.'

After a job as an accountant at a collective farm in the village of Yarove, Yushchenko was called up to do his national service and he served as a border guard. One of his publicity leaflets later showed a picture of the young Yushchenko in Soviet army uniform with a Kalashnikov rifle slung over his shoulder; the caption pointed out that Yanukovych had no similar photograph in his family album because people with criminal records were not allowed to serve in the armed forces or carry guns.

In 1976 Yushchenko returned to the Sumy region and worked in a local branch of the state savings bank of the USSR until he transferred to Kyiv to lead a department in the state agricultural bank. In 1987 he was spotted by the head of the bank, Vadym Hetman, who became his patron and in 1993 nominated Yushchenko as chairman of the national bank. His success in curbing inflation and introducing a strong new currency, the *hryvnia*, in 1996, brought him into the spotlight for the first time and the national bank became his launching pad into politics when Kuchma chose him as prime minister.

The handsome Yushchenko was never short of women admirers and he has been married twice. He has two adult children from his first marriage and three younger ones from his second marriage to an American woman of Ukrainian descent, about whom his enemies used to attack him, suggesting the attractive blonde was a CIA agent sent to snare one of Ukraine's up and coming figures and turn him into a puppet of Washington. Katya Yushchenko denies that she ever worked for the CIA but in the spring of 2001, as the combination of oligarch businessmen and Communist Party members of parliament were pushing to dismiss Yushchenko, a Russian government TV station, ORT, which is beamed into Ukraine, claimed that she was an American spy.

The show was broadcast the next day by a Ukrainian TV channel taking orders from leader of the Social Democratic Party, Viktor Medvedchuk, the man who became Kuchma's closest confederate. Katya said: 'They alleged I had been sent to Ukraine to meet Viktor Yushchenko and bring him to power, that he was nothing until I came along and made him what he was today – basically an American lackey. They implied that the secret recordings of Kuchma were all a part of this vast American conspiracy.' She took the case to a Ukrainian libel court which found in her favour.

Katya Yushchenko was born in Chicago in 1961 to Ukrainian refugees who wanted their daughter to know about her Ukrainian cultural heritage. She told me: 'I had to blend two lives – American schools and American education and many American friends, and at the same time we spoke Ukrainian at home and held to many Ukrainian traditions. I attended a Ukrainian Saturday school and attended Ukrainian churches. I went to Ukrainian dance classes and other cultural activities.'

At university in Washington she trained for the United

States diplomatic corps and then earned an MBA from the University of Chicago in 1986. During Ronald Reagan's second term in office she worked as an advisor on Eastern European ethnic affairs in the White House and in the State Department's human-rights office. In 1991 she joined an American aid group based in Kyiv and later worked with a financial group helping Ukrainian financiers brought up on defunct Communist-era economics get to grips with capitalism. As part of that job she organised a trip for ten Ukrainian bankers to travel to the US, and aboard the plane found herself in the same row of seats as the head of the delegation, national bank governor Viktor Yushchenko.

Yushchenko asked a colleague sitting between them to swap seats 'so this young lady can tell us where we are going and what we are going to do'. She said: 'He remembers that conversation because he says I was prickly as a porcupine. I did not know much about him at the time and I assumed that as he was a banker from the Soviet system he could not know much about the free market, and I said I was going to teach him about it.'

She recalled with the infectious laugh that often punctuates her speech that he knew much more than she expected. Yushchenko was still married at that time and Katya said that their romance did not start until some time after that meeting, 'although I couldn't help noticing what a good-looking man he was'. But they did keep in touch when they returned from America and she said she was very impressed when, by chance, she discovered that he was discreetly providing financial support for orphanages, a women's psychiatric home and various cultural projects without seeking public plaudits for his philanthropy.

Even after the start of the election fray, many opposition supporters were worried that Yushchenko lacked the killer instinct needed for victory. He is a naturally polite man with a ready smile, but initially his public oratory was often insipid. It did not seem a question of weakness but rather an unpolitician-like reticence to view things in black and white. To his advantage, though, this mild approach served to reassure supporters that he was not an extremist Ukrainian nationalist who hated Russians or Russian-speakers, as his enemies tried to portray him.

Luckily for Yushchenko, none of his serious rivals could mesmerise an audience either. Communist Petro Symonenko and Socialist Oleksandr Moroz, himself nurtured in the stifling bosom of the Communist Party, both boasted a droning, pompous delivery matched by hackneyed content. Yanukovych, despite his roster of academic qualifications, came across as unrefined and slow-witted. By comparison Yushchenko appeared charismatic and intelligent.

Yushchenko may be able to master complex figures but he frequently displays remarkable disorder and indecision. He is notoriously late for appointments and thinks nothing of keeping scores of people waiting hours before appearing at a meeting or press conference. Sometimes he just fails to turn up altogether. Part of his popular attraction was undoubtedly that he did not behave like other politicians. He never courted publicity and his interests and hobbies reveal a surprising range of skills. Yushchenko, who in 1997 received the Global Finance Award as one of the world's top five central bankers, enjoys books, music, films and theatre, and is a good painter. His wife and friends say that even in the midst of tense political crises he would retreat to his workshop to indulge his love of carpentry; he built much of his family's country cottage outside Kyiv himself. Other hobbies include bee-keeping and archaeology – particularly of the Trypillian Civilisation. One of his heroes is Winston

Churchill, another statesman who painted and enjoyed working with his hands. Yushchenko told friends his favourite television viewing was the Discovery Channel.

Yushchenko avoided, for as long as possible, any direct attacks on Kuchma. While prime minister he claimed that his relationship with Kuchma was akin to that between a father and a son, and even after being ejected from office he frequently visited Kuchma.

In 2003 he was still reluctant to pin all the blame for Ukraine's ills on Kuchma. In an interview, he told me: 'To personalise politics or identify Ukraine's problems with one or other name is not completely honest, because although some individuals do bear an immense personal responsibility for what's happened to democracy here, we must remember that a political system has been created that is based on clan interests, and if there isn't change such a clan system can lead to horrific consequences.' Opinion polls, though, told a different story: Ukrainians did blame Kuchma precisely for creating the corrupt, clan-based political system that was destroying their country.

Chapter Eight

DIRTY FIGHTING

Almost exactly a year before the first round of the 2004 presidential election, a plane carrying Viktor Yushchenko and some seventy colleagues from the Nasha Ukrayina opposition coalition landed at the airport in Donetsk, the capital of Ukraine's industrial powerhouse, the Donbas region. The politicians had arrived for a long-planned convention to lay out the opposition's political plans to the people of East Ukraine whose support was vital. The meeting, at one of the city's largest concert venues, was to be followed by a rock concert.

There were no musical bands or dignitaries waiting at the airport's single, dilapidated terminal building to greet the visitors, most of them members of parliament, who had flown in from Kyiv. Donetsk was the home of President Kuchma's ally and heir-apparent, Prime Minister Yanukovych. The powerful Donetsk oligarch clan, of which he was a leading member, had ensured that for months almost all the regional media coverage was hostile to Yushchenko; most of the inhabitants did not even know the opposition wanted to hold a rally in their city.

The airport staff were also ostensibly unaware about the arrival of the flight because it was more than an hour before mobile stairs for the descent of passengers could be found, a delay smugly attributed to technical reasons. When Yushchenko and his group finally entered the terminal building, armed police and an abusive crowd faced them. The previous day's preparations for the rally and concert were dramatically halted by police who said they had to spend the entire day searching for a bomb that an anonymous caller said was hidden somewhere in the building. There was, of course, no bomb but on the day of the conference itself a hostile crowd occupied the hall, many of whom were very obviously drunk. The police, far from trying to clear the crowd, were helping to organise it.

Many of the demonstrators were students or traders at Donetsk markets who told local reporters that the city government had promised to waive business licence fees for three days, or give them small payments of four or five dollars and free drinks for turning up. They were not there for political reasons. In impoverished Ukraine, rent-a-crowds come cheap. The market vendors were threatened with the loss of their pitches if they failed to appear at the anti-Yushchenko rally. Observers reported that each group of ten to fifteen demonstrators was shepherded by a young man who led them in chanting slogans. A hard core, though, seemed very committed, waving Russian flags and yelling insulting remarks about the Ukrainian language.

Yushchenko and some of the parliamentary deputies decided to drive into the city to complain to the mayor of Donetsk, Aleksandr Lukianchenko, and on the way were treated to the sight of advertising billboards showing giant caricatures of Yushchenko in Nazi uniform extending his hand in a Fascist salute. The poster caption had him calling for the 'purity of the nation'. Mayor Lukianchenko smirked that he had banned the opposition rally on safety grounds, and it became clear the meeting would have to be cancelled. He was doubtless pleased to have done the bidding of the Donetsk Clan, as was Yanukovych, who revelled in the opposition's setback.

The pattern of trying to prohibit or otherwise wreck opposition events was thus set early on. But even within the regime's inner sanctum Yushchenko had his supporters, and he was receiving even more disturbing reports about plans to use violence against the opposition generally and against himself personally. On 24 October 2003, Yushchenko made a statement in Kyiv that he had learned his political opponents were plotting to kill both him and other leaders and activists of the Nasha Ukrayina group. 'There are projects under which killers have already arrived and taken appropriate measures that cannot be described as jokes,' he said. He also described how pressure had been building up on parliamentary deputies suspected of wanting to join Nasha Ukrayina. He said he had 'seen men crying' who told him they had received death threats if they did not join the pro-Kuchma bloc in parliament.

Yushchenko was in no doubt that the government was responsible for the attempts to wreck his party's meetings. He distributed copies of a confidential document, apparently originating from the presidential administration, bearing the unwieldy title 'For the minimisation of the political and social impact of the forums being held by the Nasha Ukrayina bloc'. It set out instructions for local authorities to obstruct rallies, to prevent appearances by Yushchenko and his supporters, to prevent well-known local figures taking part in the rallies, to make available only small, remote venues, and to infiltrate anti-Yushchenko stooges into those venues. The man masterminding the plans to sabotage the opposition was the head of Kuchma's presidential administration, Victor Medvedchuk.

Medvedchuk, who like Yushchenko was born in 1954, had in his teens taken part in a voluntary organisation for people who wanted to aid the police and KGB – a sort of perverse

Boy Scouts for prospective secret policemen and snitches. He continued in this auxiliary role after he entered the law faculty at Kyiv's Shevchenko University and in 1973 he and one of his colleagues were arrested after they hospitalised a teenager in Kyiv they had overheard making drunken disparaging remarks about the ruling Communist Party. Were it not for the intervention of the Communist-connected father of Medvedchuk's comrade, they might have faced jail.

After completing his studies he rose swiftly in the world of Soviet lawyers. In 1979 he was appointed as the defence lawyer for the prominent Ukrainian independence activist, poet Vasyl Stus, a defence he opened by saying his client was guilty and that 'all of Stus's crimes deserve punishment'. His lame plea for leniency consisted of asking for the poet's fine work at a shoe factory and his ill health to be taken into consideration when sentencing him. Stus received ten years in prison to be followed by five years' 'internal exile' and died in a forced labour camp. It is true that it would have been difficult for Medvedchuk to make any kind of spirited defence of his client without himself risking punishment. Stus, however, had said he did not want Medvedchuk to represent him and the lawyer could have used that as a pretext to withdraw. Instead, he insisted on representing Stus and defending him in the peculiar way which earned his client what turned out to be a death sentence.

After the fall of Communism, Medvedchuk used his legal skills to take advantage of the rich business opportunities the financial and political chaos afforded. He built his wealth in partnership with a number of other businessmen – collectively called 'The Magnificent Seven' – whose activities encompassed a huge variety of ventures including energy, raw materials and agricultural produce, property, timber, alcohol, tobacco and various imports. Medvedchuk's role was to deal with the legal aspects of The Magnificent Seven's business.

Medvedchuk and his partner in The Magnificent Seven, Hryhoriy Surkis, swiftly established close relations with the first Ukrainian president, Leonid Kravchuk, and in 1993 Medvedchuk became an advisor on legal matters to the cabinet of ministers. The next president, Leonid Kuchma, who won the 1994 elections, had initially been hostile to Medvedchuk's circle because of its powerful influence and his own loyalties to the Dnipropetrovsk Clan. But Medvedchuk managed to win him over and not only preserve The Magnificent Seven's business interests intact but increase their potential by being appointed to senior advisory posts by the new president. Medvedchuk became advisor on employment and production in 1995, advisor on tax policy in 1996 and a member of the president's high council on the economy in 1997.

Medvedchuk and Surkis made the Social Democratic Party of Ukraine (United), the SDPU(U), their parliamentary power base. Medvedchuk's talents were eventually to prove so appealing to Kuchma that he appointed him head of his presidential administration.

In his office at the sprawling presidential administration complex on Bankova Street, Medvedchuk now had his hands on the most important levers of power. He became responsible for the president's schedule and thus for access to Kuchma. He controlled the administration's bureaucracy, its liaison with parliament, and the appointment of advisors to the president, the press section and the president's representatives in the regions. He showed himself adept at balancing the interests of the rival Dnipropetrovsk and Donetsk business groups and his own Kyiv Clan. Despite their small number in parliament, members of the SDPU(U) were given chairmanship of many influential committees and party members gained powerful positions in local government.

Medvedchuk swiftly came to be perceived as a ruthless, cynical operator and was sometimes called Ukraine's Cardinal Richelieu. One Western diplomat said in 2003: 'It's possible that Kuchma actually follows plans drawn up by Medvedchuk and that Medvedchuk is the real power in the land.' More colourfully, the leader of a party that was part of the Nasha Ukrayina coalition, Yuriy Kostenko, said of Medvedchuk: 'That man is the nearest thing to Satan that most people will meet on this earth. He will do anything to maintain his power.'

Medvedchuk himself had never concealed his ambitions to succeed Kuchma as president. His then party colleague and business partner, Oleksandr Zinchenko, told a newspaper in August 2001: 'Our party doesn't disguise the fact that we are heading to the 2004 presidential elections with our own candidate and that's the leader of our party, Viktor Medvedchuk.' But by 2003 his outrageous behaviour was reflected in opinion polls which showed he was deeply unpopular and too distrusted to stand a chance of being elected, even with the considerable advantages of admin-resource. That year Zinchenko himself became so repelled by Medvedchuk's behaviour that he left the party and later became Yushchenko's election campaign chief of staff.

Despite concern from his colleagues that Medvedchuk would become ungovernable, Kuchma continued to shower him with honours, awarding him Ukraine's top medals and even senior military ranks. Medvedchuk also cultivated excellent relations with the Kremlin and was seen as one of its most important lobbyists in Ukraine. When in the summer of 2003 Medvedchuk got married for a third time, to a young and pretty television presenter, the lavish ceremony was presided over by an Orthodox bishop and televised on Ukraine's three largest television channels like a royal wedding. The guests included President Kuchma, Prime Minister Yanukovych, others from The Magnificent Seven and the Russian prime minister.

By late 2003 Medvedchuk was shunning press interviews and preferred to work behind the scenes. He did not deign to answer Yushchenko's accusations that the presidential administration had drawn up careful plans to undermine the opposition by foul means. The presidential administration's head of the press and information policy department, Serhiy Vasyliyev, suggested the document in Yushchenko's possession was a fake and should be forensically examined. He said: 'From the moment the opposition started to attack the presidential administration there have been many declarations about various documents, but they are unsubstantiated accusations made by political enemies.'

With a few exceptions, most of the press did not cover opposition events and ignored the opposition's complaints about the government's ham-fisted methods to suppress Nasha Ukrayina's message. The previous year, evidence had emerged how the government was using every means available to censor information about the opposition, but now a leaked document shocked even the cynical. Sporting another convoluted and innocuous-sounding title, 'Additional commentaries for the events of Week 36 for official use', the document was handed to opposition member of parliament Mykola Tomenko by a senior television executive in August 2002. It turned out to be one instalment of a circular for media editors called *temnyk* – derived from the Ukrainian for 'theme' – which spelled out in detail how sensitive subjects should be handled and which issues should not be covered at all. The copy Tomenko had been given was the thirty-sixth issued that year and set out how the media should cover more than thirty forthcoming issues and demonstrated how anxious the government was to discredit Yushchenko:

Item 6. **The opposition is preparing to organise street demonstrations on 16 September.** This issue to be covered only by newspapers and Internet publications. Television is asked not to cover it. It is suggested to revive the scandal surrounding the war cemetery in Lviv to divert the city's inhabitants' attention away from the demonstrations . . .'

Item 18. **A press conference is being called (by opposition groups about the demonstrations).** Ignore it . . .

Item 19. **An (unofficial) commission on journalistic ethics is conducting its work around Ukraine.** Ignore it . . .'

Item 27. **A round-table meeting is to be conducted about political reform.** Exclude any theses put forward that contradict the president's initiative (about parliamentary reform) . . .'

Serhiy Vasyliyev once again denied there was censorship and said the accusations were intended to discredit Ukraine. He suggested Tomenko could have faked the document.

One of Ukraine's most respected television news personalities, Danylo Yanevsky, told me when the documents were made public that the government instructions were regularly sent to the largest newspapers and all the television channels. He said: 'In Soviet times if you didn't stick to the government line you were sent to prison or the Gulag. Now it's more subtle and there is the appearance of press freedom, but all the major media is tightly controlled by Kuchma's people. You can make a lot of money if you obey the instructions, or face intimidation, get a beating or lose your job if you don't.' Yanevsky said that during presidential and parliamentary elections, Kuchma's administration sent its people to supervise output directly at newspapers and television channels and predicted, correctly, that the same thing would happen for the 2004 presidential elections.

Later that year, in October, more than a hundred Ukrainian journalists, dismayed by what they said was increasing government interference, formed an independent union led by Andriy Shevchenko, another well-known television broadcaster who had resigned his well-paid, high-profile job in disgust at the censorship being imposed upon him. Shevchenko said the first time he saw one of the confidential *temnyk* instructions he thought it was a spoof. He was, however, dismayed and appalled when he saw that all the television channels in their evening news bulletins that day followed the instructions to the letter. He said: 'What I can say precisely is that I and a thousand of my colleagues have no doubt where the pressure comes from. It comes from the presidential administration and its regional bodies. It strikes me as a citizen of this country that such a situation is very frightening.' He added that in addition to censorship, the government bugged journalists' phones and often used intimidation against them.

Other journalists were quick to confirm that the eight-to-ten-page *temnyk* arrived weekly by fax or e-mail without an official letterhead or stamps or signatures that could identify its origin. Human Rights Watch, which investigated the issue, reported in 2003: '*Temnyk* instructions direct television editors and journalists to cover events in ways that portray President Kuchma and the SDPU(U) favourably and that minimise or eliminate negative or controversial information about pro-presidential figures. In addition, the guidelines instruct newsmakers to present negative or misleading information about opposition politicians and parties, or ignore them altogether.'

The human rights watchdog observed that political pressure on the media had increased soon after Medvedchuk became head of the presidential administration and created the department for information policy. 'In this period top station managers and editors also received more frequent phone calls from figures within the presidential administration insisting on compliance and threatening repercussions for stations and individuals who disobeyed the instructions. As a result, leading editors no longer simply established editorial limits but also exercised stricter oversight of the news content and pressured journalists to produce one-sided news, threatening them with negative consequences for non-compliance.'

By the late nineties most of Ukraine's media was privately owned and, according to the National Council for Television and Radio Broadcasting, consisted of approximately eight hundred television and radio stations, four thousand print media sources, five hundred Internet news sites and thirty-five news agencies. Only four percent of television and radio stations and nine per cent of print media outlets were state-owned in 2003. But despite this theoretical diversity, most of the important media outlets were in the hands of people who owed loyalty to Kuchma or were afraid of angering the president or his associates. Disobeying the *temnyk* directives invited intimidation and risked exposure to incessant tax inspections and a cascade of other government measures designed to bring a recalcitrant news organisation to its knees.

In March 2003 the government shut down Radio Kontinent, an independent Kyiv-based radio station that carried news programmes in Ukrainian from the BBC, Voice of America, Deutsche Welle and Polish Radio. All these stations could broadcast on short-wave frequencies but they made arrangements with local stations to retransmit their programmes on superior quality and easily-accessible FM, a system controlled with licences issued by the government. The journalists in Radio Free Europe/Radio Liberty (RFERL)'s Ukrainian service were doing an outstanding job providing voters with information about the opposition and had thus incurred the government's wrath. The authorities manufactured charges that Radio Kontinent had not complied with licensing regulations after the station agreed to rebroadcast RFERL programming. Radio Kontinent's chief, Serhiy Sholokh, told of a meeting when he was summoned by people connected to Kuchma's administration: 'The first thing they told me was that if I put RFERL on air that would be the end for me and the end of the radio station. They proposed that if I secretly worked with them all my legal problems would end, that is all the proceedings against Radio Kontinent, and that I'd be like a fish in butter – I'd have money and everything else I needed.'

He realised he had to play along with them. 'I agreed to all their demands so that I could have a chance to leave the country,' he said. After he left, security forces raided the radio station, arrested three of his staff and confiscated equipment. Sholokh said: 'That was an act of revenge because they understood they could not get at me physically. They simply wanted to destroy Radio Kontinent. This was simply an attack by bandits.'

Socialist member of parliament, Yuriy Lutsenko, who secured the release of the three staff, said: 'What we are witnessing is the final attempt to destroy freedom of speech. They are shutting not just opposition media but also any independent mass media. The Ukrainian government is preparing not for elections but for the appointment of their next president of Ukraine, the next Kuchma.' Yushchenko said: 'In the run-up to the presidential election, the authorities are seeking totalitarian influence on information sources – that is why they resort to such blatant actions.'

The closure came only months after another Ukrainian station, Radio Dovira, suddenly announced it was stopping broadcasts of RFERL programmes after a Kuchma loyalist took control of the station. Elsewhere, the director of a radio station in the city of Poltava, north-east of Kyiv, was killed in a car accident on his way to sign a broadcasting agreement with RFERL.

The government was once again criticised by Western governments, the EU and the Council of Europe after the *temnyk* instructions were exposed. But the regime signalled it was ready to suffer some international censure, and even penalties, to stay in power.

Russia, meanwhile, was making the most of Kuchma's isolation to secure business concessions and increase its influence. By 2004 Kuchma was increasingly dancing to the Kremlin's tune and drawing back from Ukraine's commitments to join the EU and NATO as fast as possible. Meetings between Kuchma and his Russian counterpart, Putin, were frequent, like long-lost lovers making up for time, and cartoons began appearing suggesting a family relationship between the two leaders, who both have curiously weasel-like features. Belarus dictator President Lukashenko, given a wider berth by polite international society than even

Kuchma, also approved of the Ukrainian president's budding tyranny but Kuchma thought Lukashenko was de trop, even by his standards.

Almost alone of European leaders, the Polish president Alexander Kwasniewski did not abandon relations with Kuchma. Poland emerged as Ukraine's most stalwart international friend and consistently advocated that Ukraine should not be left languishing on the wrong side of a new Iron Curtain in Europe, encouraging Kyiv while others scorned. Kwasniewski, a former Communist himself, understood well the factors at play in Ukraine, especially the influence of Russia. His perspicacious grasp of the situation and graceful behaviour not only did much to heal ancient wounds between the two countries, but when tensions threatened bloodshed in Ukraine, he was trusted by Kuchma to be a key broker for a peaceful resolution. The former Soviet Baltic republics, Latvia, Estonia and Lithuania, also remained on good terms with Kuchma, with the Lithuanian president Valdas Adamkus also playing an important role in the most critical hours of the Orange Revolution. Having left Lithuania in the forties after taking part in his nation's anti-Soviet resistance movement, Adamkus spent most of his life in America, returning when the independence movement reignited in his homeland. He was elected president in 1998 and I met him a few days before the start of his first term as he was preparing to surrender his US citizenship, a bitter-sweet moment. It was obvious that his country was gaining an extremely able and charismatic leader who bridged the world between modern Lithuania and the Lithuanian diaspora. Ukrainians in Ukraine and further afield envied the Poles and Lithuanians for having leaders of such calibre. These two men would, in 2004, also earn the gratitude of Ukrainians who struggled for democracy.

As the election approached, the dirty tricks and attacks against the opposition intensified, and a mayoral contest in a small town that would normally have attracted little attention turned into a bruising and bloody trial of strength between the regime and the Nasha Ukrayina opposition.

The ancient town of Mukachevo, with a population of around ninety thousand, is in the West Ukrainian province of Transcarpathia, an area of stunning beauty – mountains, meadows, forests, and rushing rivers – but also great poverty. The province also abuts two EU countries, Hungary and Slovakia, and whoever controls local customs officials can make a fortune. Medvedchuk's SDPU(U) party had managed to buy support in the region and one of its men was the governor, but Nasha Ukrayina enjoyed an intuitive, grass-roots backing. In past regional elections for various posts, opponents of the SDPU(U) candidate had frequently found their candidacy ruled out at the last moment, on a technicality, by electoral commissions or court officials following SDPU(U) instructions. It looked as if it was going to happen again when in early April all ten members of the electoral commission succumbed to a mysterious illness that for several days prevented them from including the opposition candidate's name on the ballot papers.

In his role as SDPU(U) chief, Medvedchuk was determined to retain his hold over the lucrative region and as head of the presidential administration he saw the April 2004 mayoral election in Mukachevo as a dry run for the tactics the regime was planning to use in the presidential battle later that year. It was a chance to cow the opposition by flaunting the government's admin-resource techniques, accompanied by a display of physical intimidation. The Kuchma administration also wanted to test the outside world's reaction. Nasha Ukrayina recognised that the Mukachevo contest was loaded with symbolism and picked up the gauntlet thrown down by Medvedchuk and the Kuchma regime. The two candidates on 18 April were a Nasha Ukrayina member of parliament, Viktor Baloha, and Ernest Nuser, who was supported by the SDPU(U).

In the run-up to the election, large numbers of leather-jacketed skinheads appeared in the town creating a tense atmosphere which frightened many people from venturing out on election day. These supporters, who like the anti-Yushchenko demonstrators in Donetsk were organised around group leaders, congregated outside the voting stations, imparting in various unsubtle ways to those entering the buildings that it would be unwise to vote for the Nasha Ukrayina candidate. In the evening, knots of these thugs invaded many of the thirty-six voting stations, attacking people and smashing furniture. Polling stations had Nasha Ukrayina members of parliament present as observers, and some of these, along with other observers and journalists, were assaulted, while international monitors were intimidated. The local police either colluded with the thugs or took no action; none of the vandals was arrested.

Even so, independent exit polls gave Baloha sixty-two per cent of the votes compared to thirty per cent for Nuser and many Nasha Ukrayina supporters were preparing to celebrate when the city election commission declared Nuser had won with a majority of about five thousand in a turnout of 29,700.

The standard method in Ukraine is for the votes to be counted at the individual stations by the local election committee members who represent all the interested political parties. The committee's head has to certify the tally of votes in a document called the protocol. Some of the local officials, however, were too scared to sign the protocols because they showed the Nasha Ukrayina candidate had scored the most votes. The protocols from the thirty-six voting stations were then to be added up for the final result at the city's election commission, which was also supposedly composed of people representing both political forces taking part.

It was to the election commission's headquarters that a group of Nasha Ukrayina members of parliament went to investigate the result. There they got short shrift and were attacked by riot police and the omnipresent thugs. Six MPs were among the scores of people injured during the violence that day. Nasha Ukrayina MP Yuriy Pavlenko, one of those attacked, said, 'The most horrible thing about the raids was that police did nothing to stop criminal gangs. When police begin to attack members of parliament, it's time to admit that Ukraine has long ago passed the stage of being a "manipulated democracy" and has moved closer to totalitarianism akin to that of Nazi Germany.'

The next morning when Nasha Ukrayina representatives turned up again, they were told that all the protocols from the polling stations had been stolen from the election commission office during the night by unknown burglars. Hence, claimed the commission, the declared results could not be recounted, ignoring the fact that there were still supposed to be copies of the protocols with each of the heads of the thirty-six local polling station committees.

The state television channel and the private stations, except for Channel Five, showed none of the violence or the roving gangs in Mukachevo and blandly announced that regime candidate Nuser had won. Iryna Bekeshkina, a sociologist from a group called Democratic Initiatives which monitored the city's election, commented: 'After my trip to Mukachevo I was nagged with a vague feeling that I'd seen all of this somewhere before but I couldn't recall where. Then when I was watching the news it came to me, of course, it was Orwell's Oceania from his novel *Nineteen Eighty-Four*, except now the year was 2004.' Bekeshkina compared the Ministry of Truth broadcasts that *Nineteen Eighty-Four*'s hero, Winston, watched to the distorted reality conjured up by the *temnyk* directives. 'You know, after the election commission announced the results, I wondered a trifle malevolently how they were going to explain the ballots. I thought it was impossible to fake such a large number. What a naïve person I am. There weren't any ballots because they were stolen.'

Yushchenko met with President Kuchma to protest about what had happened and to demand a fresh election, the removal of the new interior minister who controlled the police, Mykola Bilokon, who owed his position to Yanukovych and Medvedchuk, of SDPU(U) Transcarpathian Province Governor Ivan Rizak, a Medvedchuk flunky, and Medvedchuk himself for what he called 'gross violations' of election laws. Kuchma, of course, took no action against any of the officials.

However, many more members of parliament than the regime had anticipated showed disquiet about the Mukachevo events and they formed a committee to investigate. The parliamentary commission found that voting results from twelve of the city's thirty-six polling stations were tampered with while being transported from district polling stations to the election commission headquarters and that the election ballots and protocols had disappeared.

One of the investigating MPs, Roman Zvarych, said: 'Crude and hasty falsifications were done by deducting votes from Baloha and either adding them to Nuser's count or invalidating them. For example, at Polling Station Number 3, there were 996 votes cast for Baloha, 496 for Nuser and ninety invalid ballots. These were transposed into ninety-six votes for Baloha, 996 for Nuser and 490 as invalid.' Piecing together the events on election day and the night that followed, the investigation concluded that the regime-backed thugs had swung into action when the exit polls, whose results were revealed before voting ended, indicated the government candidate was heading for defeat.

Parliament also received startling information about the events on polling night from a police sergeant who spoke out regardless of the risk to his safety and likelihood of losing his job. Mykhailo Dzhumelia had been on guard at the election commission offices when the deputy police chief, Vasyl Shvenda, ordered him and the other officers to leave their posts. Dzhumelia testified that Nuser's aide, Andriy Lohoyda, had previously taken the keys to the room where the ballots were kept and returned them two hours later indicating that copies of the keys had been cut. The sergeant said Lohoyda worked in concert with Shvenda.

Dzhumelia said he was suspicious at being ordered to leave the room with the ballots unguarded, especially after the violence that had erupted at the polling stations. When he discovered the theft he informed his superiors about the duplicate keys and his illogical orders, and testified to the prosecutor-general's office, investigating on Kuchma's orders. Prosecutor-General Hennadiy Vasilyev, the man who claimed there were no clues to who murdered the beheaded journalist Georgiy Gongadze, ignored Dzhumelia's testimony and reported before parliament that his investigation showed no fraud in Mukachevo. Viktor Yanukovych remained loyally silent and did not seem at all perturbed by the Mukachevo drama.

Many of the ingredients, therefore, that the administration would use during the presidential elections – intimidation, fraud, ballot stuffing or ballot disappearance, corruption, harrying the media – were tested out in Mukachevo. The experiment should nevertheless have showed its instigators that there were serious flaws in their strategy because the wider ramifications of the affair were beyond their control. The parliamentary investigation's discoveries appalled many MPs. Opposition leader Yushchenko, addressing parliament, said that the administration's blatant manipulations in Mukachevo were an insult to every member of parliament and an invitation to surrender. 'I ask you to get off your knees and make a conscious decision. Or are you willing to continue receiving these slaps in the face?' Some of them did make a decision and the faltering pro-regime majority in parliament splintered. Kuchma could no longer steamroll measures through the parliament and the opportunity for last-minute legislation to alter election rules in favour of the regime melted with the dissolving majority.

The events were also heartening for the opposition because they provided proof that, despite intimidation, people were willing to vote for the candidate they wanted and that there were officials like Sergeant Dzhumelia who were brave enough to expose the dirty tricks. Yushchenko called Dzhumelia 'a hero' and said: 'After Mukachevo, there is no doubt that the regime will fight by any means it can to retain political power in Ukraine. But we are ready for the worst-case scenarios, which are yet to come during the campaign.'

At the end of May, the administration's experiment in Mukachevo turned into a fiasco when Mayor Nuser, facing daily demonstrations and the contempt of his fellow citizens, resigned citing death threats. Eventually a Nasha Ukrayina candidate won another mayoral election in the city.

The government knew that it would face criticism from

abroad but calculated that fear of pushing Ukraine into Russia's arms would limit it to a mild rap over the knuckles. But the response was stiffer than expected. The Organisation for Security and Cooperation in Europe (OSCE) representative monitoring Mukachevo, Gerald Mitchell, had seen the violence and said: 'This blatant attempt to disrupt the election proceedings is an attack on the fundamentals of the democratic process.' The EU and Washington expressed concern. The Council of Europe abandoned the delicate 'diplomatic' responses usually associated with such bodies and denounced the Mukachevo events as an 'unfortunate dress rehearsal for the upcoming presidential election'.

Although at Mukachevo the regime acted as if it did not care about the presence of foreign election observers, who were ignored or even barred from entering election stations, Kuchma was anxious not to be assigned the same odious status as Belarus's detested president. The opposition's conclusion from the Mukachevo experiment was, therefore, that it was essential to have as many foreign observers as possible monitoring the run-up to the presidential election and the polls themselves. From then on pleas for election monitors became a recurring opposition theme. Yushchenko's ally, Yulia Tymoshenko, said international reaction was 'crucial to protect democracy in Ukraine'. Prime Minister Yanukovych duly promised that Ukraine would accept international election observers and that his government would ensure 'an immaculate vote'.

The election campaign began officially in July. Around fifty thousand people came to listen to Viktor Yushchenko on 4 July on a hillside near Kyiv's Pecherska Lavra, the ancient Monastery of the Caves. The golden church domes of the religious complex, sparkling in the sun, made a spectacular backdrop for one of the largest rallies in the country since independence. Thousands of orange pennants emblazoned with the word *tak*, which means 'yes', and Nasha Ukrayina's horseshoe symbol, denoting good luck, fluttered above the heads of an enthusiastic crowd. Yushchenko pledged to end corruption and lawlessness, raise living standards, and improve the social safety net. He promised to create five million jobs in his first term and cut the time conscripts serve in the army from eighteen months to a year, with students serving only nine months.

Yushchenko chose as the manager of his campaign the deputy parliamentary speaker, Oleksandr Zinchenko. From 1996 Zinchenko had been a leading member of Medvedchuk's SDPU(U) and one of the main instigators in easing Yushchenko out of his post as prime minister in April 2001. But Zinchenko underwent a profound change in his politics and attitude to life generally after a grave illness in 2002. He resigned from the SDPU(U) in mid-2003 and spoke out against the constitutional changes Kuchma wanted to bring about in order to extend his reign. In April 2004 he led the parliamentary investigation into the violent disruption of the Mukachevo mayoral election and condemned his former SDPU(U) colleagues who 'put into action the principles of Joseph Vissarionovich Stalin' and demanded the dismissals of regional officials. His appointment by Yushchenko to such an important position signalled that membership of Nasha Ukrayina was open to anyone regardless of their past and that the opposition was a broad coalition of views. Indeed Yushchenko said the contest was not an ideological one but that 'in reality there is only one conflict in Ukraine today, between those in power and the people', and he warned that 'the government is sowing the seeds of division in society'.

The Yushchenko rally was ignored by most television

channels or portrayed in a way that perverted the truth. The pictures showed only small knots of people and did not give a true idea of the size of the gathering. In addition some of shots homed in on people who were drunk and suggested that Nasha Ukrayina had attracted people to the rally by offering free vodka. Nasha Ukrayina organisers denied they were giving out alcohol and said the drunks had nothing to do with the political meeting.

The only television channel consistently running sympathetic pieces about Yushchenko and critical ones about Yanukovych and the regime generally was Channel Five, owned by an Nasha Ukrayina parliamentary deputy, Petro Poroshenko. He had defected in 2000 from Medvedchuk's SDPU(U) and was himself an oligarch of considerable wealth who, apart from Channel Five, counted among his holdings a car manufacturer, a shipyard and Ukraine's biggest chocolate company. Channel Five would be one of the most important factors in the election contest, broadcasting accurate information to a mass audience when the other television channels were either transmitting government lies or had been frightened into silence. An angry government put a lot of effort into shutting the station down, and Poroshenko and the Channel Five staff were to show considerable resilience in the coming months.

The prime minister, by contrast, had no difficulty getting himself on television and a few days later Yanukovych was broadcast on all channels announcing what he said would be a low-profile bid for the presidency. He said that he would carry on working as usual and allow his record and achievements to speak for themselves. Yanukovych also promised to quell corruption and although his pro-Russian sympathies were well known, he said he would court closer relations with the West. Few, however, believed that Yanukovych really intended to take such a relaxed approach to the election, a scepticism borne out not only by the thousands of posters of the prime minister that rapidly appeared on billboards across the country, but by the intensive way the admin-resource methods were employed.

Nasha Ukrayina and international bodies both monitored the election coverage in the Ukrainian media, which showed an overwhelming bias in favour of Yanukovych and a pattern of ignoring or denigrating Yushchenko. That pattern had been established even before the election campaigns officially began. Nasha Ukrayina monitored TV and radio for a number of weeks in May and said the results showed Yushchenko was being subjected to what it called 'media isolation'. In the third week of May a record of news coverage, excluding Channel Five, revealed that Kuchma was mentioned 517 times, Yanukovych 501, and Yushchenko twenty-seven times.

In August the human rights watchdog International Helsinki Federation for Human Rights reported that state-owned TV channels 'routinely convey negative portrayals' of Yushchenko and newspapers often published 'strongly propagandistic' materials in favour of Yanukovych. Yuri Murashov, the head of Ukraine's branch of the group, said it had logged numerous violations in the run-up to the election including pressure on state employees such as factory workers, regional officials and students to support Yanukovych.

The classic admin-resource tactic was to threaten people who depended on the state for their jobs, education, or welfare. Employees were warned they would lose their jobs and students were threatened with expulsion. The threats were used to force people to collaborate in voting scams on election days and to bring out crowds for rallies to provide a counterweight to the mass meetings being held by the opposition. A poll at the end of July conducted by the Razumkov Centre, an independent think tank in Kyiv, found that four per cent of people across the country claimed they had been forced to take part in forums, rallies or conferences in support of Yanukovych. More people had to take part in such events in East Ukraine where the overall average was eight per cent. Kharkiv – the second biggest city in Ukraine and a region with a very high proportion of undecided voters – had the most intensive turnout with twenty-seven per cent pushed into taking part.

The regime's policy on propaganda seemed to be of the 'throw enough dirt and some of it will stick' school. The government also tried to disrupt the opposition's campaign by stirring up fears of terrorism, planting explosives and weapons in cars and premises belonging to opposition workers, and by setting off bombs.

Within their own ranks, the regime also insisted on complete obedience to the cause: in September, the defence minister, Yevhen Marchuk, was fired for apparently refusing to guarantee that the armed forces would be ordered to vote for Yanukovych. He was replaced with a former defence minister, Oleksandr Kuzmuk, who was a close Kuchma acolyte.

But the electorate had become more savvy with each election, and the opposition had urged its supporters to record and expose the ways the government was preparing to steal the election. Video cameras were used openly or clandestinely to film electoral abuses and the resulting footage was frequently shown on Channel Five or as clips on Internet publications. In a Western country the effects of the films would have been devastating for the government candidate, but in Ukraine, where the authorities controlled most of the mass media, the impact of the revelations was limited; part of the problem was that the overwhelming majority of Ukrainians, as opinion polls showed, expected the regime to play dirty and to cheat and so were not surprised by proof that it was flagrantly breaking the law. But over time the footage showing the authorities had a cumulative effect that enraged many hitherto apathetic or apolitical Ukrainians who now recognised that the government regarded them with absolute contempt.

One secretly filmed clip shows a college rector haranguing students about the election and threatening them if they do not vote for Yanukovych. Another film shows students faking thousands of signatures for the Yanukovych camp on forms each of the twenty-six presidential candidates had to provide to the Central Election Commission (CEC) demonstrating that at least half a million people supported their candidacy. At a training college for government bureaucrats the head of the facility is filmed instructing his audience how they are to vote on multiple occasions for Yanukovych. The official warns his charges they need not return to work if they have not taken part in the scam.

The government also funded the candidacies of a clutch of people called 'technical candidates' who stood no chance of winning but, apart from splitting the opposition vote, had the right to have representatives on the electoral commissions which would supervise the vote at each level, beginning with the thirty-three thousand individual polling stations and going all the way up to the CEC in Kyiv. These representatives were an important ingredient in manipulating the election results. The technical candidates also qualified for slots on television and radio, which they used to attack Yushchenko. Two of the original twenty-six candidates dropped out before the first round of the election.

In the election itself the technical candidates did not muster anywhere near half a million votes, so it is clear that the signatures of their 'supporters' were faked. The regime provided the one-hundred-thousand-dollar deposit each candidate was obliged to pay and which was refunded only to those who received at least four per cent of the vote – beyond the reach of candidates whose supporters were fictitious.

The government made no attempt even to appoint as head of the CEC somebody who inspired confidence among all the parties. Instead it installed a person who was obviously the regime's creature. One of the senior opposition leaders, Mykola Tomenko, said millions of dollars had been set aside for bribing some of the commission members, including a twenty-one-million-dollar payment for one person. But the full, astonishing scale of the government's arrangements to control the CEC were only to emerge after the first round of the election.

Another subtle, insidious technique had technical candidates expound extreme right-wing, Fascist, anti-Russian and anti-Semitic views expressing support for Yushchenko and thus tainting him by a non-existent association as an extremist nationalist even though he repeatedly condemned all racism and anti-Semitism.

As the first round of the election approached, the government sought to create a climate of fear and warned that opposition forces were preparing to resort to violence and terrorism if their candidate lost. In Kyiv and other cities there was a spate of explosions where property was damaged but nobody was hurt.

In August two explosive devices went off at Kyiv's Troyeshchyna market injuring fourteen people and killing one woman. Police subsequently arrested four people and the Kyiv police chief, Oleksandr Milenin, announced that two of them were opposition supporters. Milenin said the motive for the blasts was to 'influence the political situation' and create 'social tension' among the electorate. Police exhibited leaflets in support of Yushchenko's presidential bid among the evidence confiscated from the suspects. After an appropriate delay the suspects were released because there was not a shred of evidence against them; it later transpired the bombing was linked to a gang war over control of the market.

While setting its attack dogs to intimidate and beat up opposition activists, the regime repeatedly warned that the opposition was determined to reproduce 'the Georgian scenario' of the previous year's 'Rose Revolution' which ousted Eduard Shevardnadze. Kuchma advisor Volodymyr Malynkovych said: 'Some of Yushchenko's people think in terms of victory or die . . . they're asking people to take to the streets in order to determine the election results. They want approximately the same thing as what happened in Georgia to occur.' The deputy interior minister, Mykhailo Korniyenko, joined the chorus warning 'there will be no Georgian scenario in Ukraine' and vowed 'if the need arises, the police will use force to prevent it'.

Attributing bomb blasts and terrorist activity to Yushchenko sympathisers became a recurring government theme. A week before the first round of the elections on 31 October, Yushchenko's campaign chief, Zinchenko, accused top government officials of stirring up dozens of violent incidents and planting weapons and explosives. The Yushchenko camp warned that 'bankrupt and criminal government officials' intended to use 'unconstitutional and un-democratic' means to keep the current ruling elite in power. Many in the opposition worried that the surge in violence and the fear being promoted about possible terrorism was intended as a pretext for the imposition of a state of emergency and to annul a Yushchenko victory.

At the Kyiv headquarters of opposition activists Pora, an umbrella organisation for groups mainly composed of young people and students, police claimed to have found grenades and dynamite. The group was later to become one of the most vibrant elements of the Orange Revolution protests. Its leaders made no bones about receiving grants over the years from Western organisations supporting civil development and democracy in Ukraine. The grants amounted to tens of thousands of dollars but the regime and its supporters, particularly in Russia, claimed Pora was controlled by the US and the CIA and that it had received far greater amounts in subsidies. Pora's leader, Vladyslav Kaskiv, said the group had set up a nationwide network of activists who wanted to see the end of the Kuchma regime. It had run training workshops to familiarise its members with their rights under the law and to discuss the most effective ways to work in the forthcoming elections. Pora organised innovative demonstrations and was responsible for imaginative protest literature, T-shirts, badges, and placards. Its striking black and yellow logo cropped up everywhere. The 'o' in Pora appeared as a clock with its hands set at fifteen minutes to midnight – a warning to the regime that its time was up.

Pora's premises were raided several times and weapons or explosives produced during the searches. Scores of its members were beaten or detained. Pora maintained that explosives and weapons were planted, and the authorities habitually released anyone detained after three days – the maximum allowed before charges had to be brought – without explaining why they were not prosecuting people who they claimed to have caught with guns and explosives.

The list of violent incidents grew larger by the month. In August the Lviv premises of a pro-opposition newspaper, *Postup*, were razed in what police confirmed was an arson attack. On 19 October, less than two weeks before the election, an explosion devastated the office of Prosvita, an organisation promoting education projects and known for supporting Yushchenko. Earlier that month a truck full of opposition election literature was stopped by ten police armed with automatic weapons and forced to a car park where men in civilian clothes unloaded the materials, doused them with petrol and set light to them.

Meanwhile, the regime's technique of inverting the truth was applied assiduously. The chief of staff of Yanukovych's election team, Stepan Havrysh, who bears a resemblance to Robert De Niro, displayed a remarkable talent for acting. With a straight face he told a sceptical press conference a few weeks before the election that the opposition had committed more than 1,600 breaches of electoral campaign laws, and that its sympathisers were planning violence. Gravely he warned that the government had information that terrorist acts were planned and said the opposition was opening a dangerous 'Pandora's box'. Curiously, none of the 1,600 breaches made it to court. It was a similar story with the trumped-up weapons charges. The government knew its cases were so ridiculous that even the normally pliant courts were likely to throw them out.

When not threatening them, Yanukovych tried to win over officials by offering sizeable pay rises a few weeks before the election. He paid particular attention to the interior ministry, which controls the police and its own crack troops, and it was known that many of their most senior officers were in his pocket. Yanukovych called hundreds of interior ministry officers to a conference in Kyiv at which he promised them lavish pay increases. The interior ministry, headed by the stridently anti-opposition Mykola Bilokon, said it would not baulk at using force against anyone who wanted to challenge the results of the election. In a sinister announcement the police said they had prepared new methods of crowd control, which had been 'approved by the ministry of health'. On the eve of the first round Bilokon bragged that he and his senior officers would soon toast Yanukovych's victory with three days of drinking.

To help obtain that victory the regime had invested large sums of money in what the opposition called 'black technologies'. Nasha Ukrayina sympathisers discovered two warehouses containing an estimated ninety tons of offensive propaganda material intended to discredit and smear Yushchenko. Opposition members of parliament entered the premises, one of which was controlled by the son of a prominent Kuchma ally, after tip-offs and found millions of items which portrayed Yushchenko as an American lackey or accused him of wanting to start a civil war. The material included posters of Yushchenko's face superimposed over the head of Uncle Sam in a parody of America's famous army recruiting poster. The caption read: 'Are You Ready for Civil War?' Other material featured a mosquito, clothed in the American flag, sucking on a map of Ukraine. Another image depicted Yushchenko as a rodeo cowboy riding Ukraine.

The opposition's scope for conveying an untrammelled version of their cause to the electorate was limited. Because they were denied access to most television, Yushchenko and his allies in the coalition embarked on a punishing schedule of public meetings that took them across the country. One of their main messages was that the country's destiny was at stake and that a Yanukovych victory would deepen Ukraine's corruption and hand it over to the control of criminals.

Yulia Tymoshenko became one of the biggest draws at election rallies. People were fascinated by the petite and beautiful woman politician's robust style, where her impassioned diatribes were often leavened with humour. She told election rallies that the oligarchic clans aimed to use Yanukovych to hang on to their power, money and domination of Ukraine. She warned: 'And if we don't realise this then Yanukovych will not just come for five years, because in five years they will eradicate from Ukrainian territory any different views, and they will come for ever and will rule Ukraine always.'

Yushchenko said that mass fraud was being planned for the election and he called for as many foreign observers as possible, saying: 'Remember that the thing that cockroaches and cheats fear most in the world is light.' He and other opposition members became worried by the increasing violence being used against them and by the attempts to portray Nasha Ukrayina activists as terrorists. Two weeks before the first election round, Yushchenko told of his fears that widespread violence would be used because Yanukovych's only strategy was mass falsification of the vote. 'However, whatever they do the falsification isn't going to work and I don't exclude that after unsuccessful falsi-fications, they are going to opt for force.'

A rally on 23 October aimed at focusing attention on just those plans for falsification brought the largest number of people out for a demonstration in Ukraine for a decade. Between 100,000 and 150,000 people marched two miles from the centre of Kyiv to the election commission building. People came from all over Ukraine to attend, despite govern-ment attempts to create obstacles: those trying to catch trains to Kyiv were told there were no tickets, yet trains arrived in the capital empty; police intercepted buses carrying Yushchenko supporters and tried to take them off the road for spurious reasons.

Yushchenko told supporters his opponent was trying to divide Ukrainians by language and religion. 'With the approach of election day, it becomes more obvious that all the government's efforts are to no effect. They can't buy us off, they can't fool us, and they can't divide us. Yanukovych has no chance of an honest victory. Now he wants to intimidate the citizens of Ukraine with the prospect of violence.'

Yushchenko regularly appealed to police and other branches of Ukraine's security forces not to assist in election falsification and to refuse to carry out illegal orders to intimidate or use violence against opposition supporters. He said he knew police officers and other officials might face difficulties by refusing to obey commands but implored them to show courage for a few weeks, after which he promised all who had issued illegal orders would be removed by the new regime. The police at public rallies usually faced the crowd and had their backs to the speaker. It was possible, often, to see the impact such words had on them, especially the younger police. Their faces became deliberative and frequently, very frequently when it was Yushchenko himself, they turned to look at the speaker on the platform and to listen attentively. That happened in the east and south of the country as much as anywhere else. The police in Ukraine knew the appalling reputation they had for corruption and dishonesty, and that they were disliked or held in contempt by their neighbours. There had been telling indications before that many were unhappy with the situation and wanted to discharge their duty honestly. Yushchenko was seemingly offering them a way of doing that.

The aftermath of the rally followed the by now familiar routine of government-sponsored unrest. After Yushchenko left the stage, five men wearing orange paraphernalia and handkerchiefs over their lower faces, ran amok smashing windows at the electoral commission building and hurling smoke grenades. Nasha Ukrayina security stewards caught them as they ran away and wrestled them to the ground before handing them over to police. Yushchenko staff were convinced the men were provocateurs intent on triggering violence.

A group of Nasha Ukrayina supporters remained outside the electoral commission building as Yushchenko led a delegation of some fifteen of his MP supporters in talks with electoral officials. After uniformed police guarding the building suddenly disappeared inside, a group of around forty men in the traditional garb of leather jackets and skinhead haircuts attacked the Nasha Ukrayina supporters. A fight ensued and Yushchenko's supporters tackled three of the thugs. Two were found to be carrying pistols and all of them had identification cards showing they were from a special police undercover unit.

The men were handed over to ordinary police at the CEC building. Later a heavily armed group from a police special forces unit called Berkut forced their way into the building in an attempt to free the three apprehended men. Yuschenko himself and other MPs barred their way and blows were exchanged. The confrontation was captured by TV cameras which showed a uniformed man shoving Yushchenko, who gave as good as he got. The following day police maintained that their men, undercover and disguised as hooligans, had been carrying out legitimate security operations.

Undercover police had already been discovered spying on Yushchenko while he was campaigning in Crimea in August. His police bodyguards from the interior ministry apprehended a group of men they had spotted following them. The men tried to escape and after they were searched it was discovered they were undercover police from the same ministry. Inside their car was a long-range directional microphone, video camera, and recordings of Yushchenko's private conversations over the preceding few days. Inside the trunk were five different sets of number plates for the car – as in the vehicles which had trailed Gongadze. The authorities grudgingly admitted the men were their agents but said they had been sent to keep an eye out for Yushchenko's safety.

A few weeks later there was a more ominous incident when a truck nearly drove Yushchenko's car off the road when he was trying to overtake it on a motorway. Yushchenko constantly worried his wife and entourage by insisting on driving his own car because he said it relieved the tension of his hectic schedule. A number of prominent opponents of the government had died in suspicious car accidents over the years and Yushchenko's colleagues were convinced the narrowly avoided tragedy was more than an accident. In September something even more serious was to happen that could not be dismissed as an accident.

Chapter Nine

POISON AND THE MARK OF THE BEAST

Yushchenko and his family had received warnings and death threats as the election campaign picked up. Anonymous notes and telephone calls warned that they would come to harm if he did not withdraw from the election race. Yushchenko was told his daughter would be kidnapped. They discussed the threats and decided to ignore them. Yushchenko and his wife also dismissed advice that the children should leave the country until the elections were over. His two adult children from his previous marriage took part in the rallies in support of Nasha Ukrayina while his and Katya's three young children also stayed in the country and even joined their father on the speaker's platform at some political gatherings.

Besides driving himself around on the campaign trail, Yushchenko also dismissed the extravagant security measures that many oligarchs and politicians threw around themselves. Katya said that both of them believed in God and they prayed nothing bad would happen.

Notwithstanding that, Katya told me she had long had a premonition that her husband's enemies would try to destroy him physically if they could not ruin him politically. But nothing had prepared her for the nightmarish discovery in September 2004 that her husband had been poisoned. The substance narrowly missed killing him but it had horrific consequences and Katya watched as her husband's previously handsome face underwent a painful transformation.

The poison that was used is called dioxin and was probably administered in food or drink, some time in September. Yushchenko himself thought it happened at a secret dinner on 5 September he had with the head and deputy head of the country's SBU intelligence service at the latter's luxurious countryside villa near the capital.

Yushchenko had asked for the meeting to sound out the intelligence chiefs, to enlist their help in preventing an escalation of the violence that was already being used against his supporters and to discuss the death threats against him. The SBU, successor to the Soviet-era KGB, is one of what Ukrainians call the three 'power' ministries – the army, interior ministry and intelligence services. Although the SBU could not behave with the impunity of the secret police in Soviet times, it still inspired respect, even fear, in most Ukrainians. The regime used the SBU, illegally, to intimidate and undermine domestic political opponents. Embarrassing evidence of that emerged in the summer of 2004 when an SBU general serving at the Ukrainian embassy in Germany caused a scandal by announcing that he and his SBU colleagues had been ordered to spy on opposition members when they travelled abroad.

There had never been a mass purge of the Ukrainian intelligence services and when the SBU was created, many of the same faces remained. During Soviet times the Ukrainian KGB had a reputation as one of the most zealous and repressive branches of the organisation. Many of those who were still serving in 2004 only thinly disguised their contempt for the notion of an independent Ukraine and felt greater loyalty to Moscow than to Kyiv; they yearned for the old days of 'discipline and order'. The SBU and Russia's new version of the KGB, the FSB and the foreign intelligence branch, the SVR, still maintained close contacts, exchanged information, and some Ukrainian personnel worked secretly for their Russian counterpart.

But Yushchenko also knew that many in the SBU were Ukrainian patriots and supported his political views; his task was to determine who had the upper hand. The SBU was bugging opposition politicians' and activists' telephones but it was doing the same to the regime's candidate and Yushchenko's people were receiving some interesting material from the secretly recorded conversations.

The opposition leader had arrived for the 9pm meeting forty minutes late and without Yevhen Chervonenko, the burly Nasha Ukrayina member of parliament who accompanied him everywhere and supervised his security. Chervonenko later lamented that he was not asked to attend the dinner and said he would have tasted each dish himself before allowing Yushchenko to eat.

At the dinner table that night were the SBU chief, General Ihor Smeshko, his deputy, Volodymyr Satsyuk, who sat together on one side, Yushchenko and another MP and close colleague, Davyd Zhvaniya. Dinner was crayfish, followed by a selection of traditional Ukrainian dishes, meat and salads, all accompanied by beer, vodka and, at the end, some cognac. Smeshko assured Yushchenko that the intelligence agency would do all in its power to maintain peace and see the election went fairly.

Appointed head of the SBU in September 2003, Smeshko was intelligent and regarded as pro-Western. He had served in the Soviet army from 1972 until the end of the USSR when he left with a general's rank. He speaks English and German, gained a doctorate in military cybernetics, and was an academic until 1991. The following year he was appointed Ukraine's first military attaché in Washington. Smeshko was an official liaison officer with Western intelligence agencies;

he impressed his CIA counterparts who thought that he was as honest as a spy could be, a genuine Ukrainian patriot, and genial company. The SBU chief at the time, however, suspected him of being a CIA turncoat. Some opposition figures, on the other hand, believed he was good at concealing his true nature and was a protégé of presidential administration chief Medvedchuk, with all that entailed. Smeshko, who had access to the regular opinion polls the government commissioned for its internal use, and which were not made known to the public, knew that Yushchenko would win in a fair poll. During the conversation that night he hinted that his heart was with the opposition.

Yushchenko left around two in the morning and returned to his own home. His wife said that when she kissed her husband there was a metallic taste and she asked him if he had taken medicine. The next day Yushchenko felt unwell. As the days passed he became more gravely ill and doctors in Kyiv were at a loss to explain what was ailing him. Pustules and cysts erupted on his face. Katya said: 'It became worse with each day and watching the change in his appearance was like something out of a bad horror novel. I was afraid that I would lose him and there was nothing I could do except pray.'

Finally, one of the opposition oligarchs working closely with the campaign staff became concerned that there was a sinister reason for the illness and insisted Yushchenko should be transported for treatment to a private clinic in Vienna.

Yushchenko arrived at the Rudolfinerhaus clinic on 10 September. In the days that followed information was patchy and contradictory. A doctor of Ukrainian descent, Mykola Korpan, who worked at the clinic, told the press Yushchenko had been poisoned. An international press agency reported that another senior doctor there had said there was no evidence of poisoning but it later emerged the clinic had not authorised such a statement. The discrepancies were seized upon by the Ukrainian government, which did everything to suggest it was all a story concocted by Yushchenko's camp. A TV station owned by Kuchma's son-in-law sent a crew to Vienna who worked intensely to debunk the poisoning accusation. The pro-Yanukovych staff suggested variously that Yushchenko had eaten bad sushi, contracted a sexual disease, or suffered a strong reaction after cosmetic surgery and injections to improve his looks went wrong. Vasyl Baziv, deputy head of the presidential administration, tried to laugh off the allegations and suggested Yushchenko's election campaign team leader Oleksandr Zinchenko should sample all of the opposition leader's food 'the way they did it in the Middle Ages'. Baziv also advised 'nothing would have happened if he had drunk 100 grams of vodka before eating'.

Yushchenko later told the press that he had come close to death and that the doctors had said he would have died had he delayed his arrival by a few more days. The clinic was able to say how he had been affected – 'acute pancreatitis with second-degree interstitial hydropic changes and numerous concurrent diagnoses, namely second-degree reflux-oesophagitis, acute left-sided proctocolitis, atypical polysegmentary viral skin disease, peripheral paresis, and left-sided otitis' – but not what caused it.

His family and friends, and Yushchenko himself, were convinced that he had been the victim of an assassination attempt, and that the poison had been administered at the dinner with the intelligence chiefs. But it was the end of the year before Dr Michael Zimpfer, director of the Rudolfinerhaus clinic, said: 'There is no doubt about the fact that Mr Yushchenko's disease has been caused by poisoning by dioxin.'

Exhaustive tests confirmed that Yushchenko had received between one thousand and six thousand times the 'safe' level of a dioxin called 2,3,7,8-TCDD Tetrachlorodibenzo-p-dioxin, which had probably been administered orally. It was the second largest dose that anyone had ever been known to survive. One source said his life may have been saved because Yushchenko vomited on the way home after the dinner. The disfigured and heavily pockmarked face was a recognised symptom of dioxin poisoning. With a hideous irony it emerged that dioxin was the active ingredient in the substance used by American forces in Vietnam called Agent Orange. It had been sprayed from aircraft to defoliate the jungles, hiding Vietnamese guerrillas. It was only much later that scientists discovered that the chemical was responsible for crippling diseases and an increased incidence of cancers that affected thousands of Vietnamese civilians and US servicemen who came into contact with it.

Yushchenko returned to Ukraine on 21 September looking haggard and weak, and when he appeared in parliament his ravaged face shocked MPs and television viewers. He warned other opponents of the government that similar fates awaited them if the regime was allowed to prolong its reign. Yushchenko was in such intense pain that during some of his public appearances he was wearing special apparatus that automatically injected painkilling drugs into his body.

Later he said: 'My conviction has only grown that what happened was a deliberate attempt against me as the leader of the political opposition. The poison was meant to kill me.' He said that usually an illness such as his demanded months of recuperation and that he had been lucky to be able to return to campaigning within a month, adding: 'I want to tell you that not many people return at all from the place I was at.'

The regime continued its efforts to discredit the poisoning allegations. A parliamentary committee headed by an MP regarded as a Kuchma loyalist produced initial findings which did not accept Yushchenko's claims and accused him of unwillingness to cooperate in their investigation. The pro-government TV channels gave great prominence to these comments but ignored contradictory conclusions by other members of the investigation – including those of an MP who was a doctor – that a cocktail of very toxic substances had been introduced into Yushchenko's body. The weekly *temnyk* directives sent by the presidential administration to the media gave instructions how to play the story to undermine the poisoning allegations. 'We know that this poisoning is a fake,' announced Dmitriy Kiselev, a notoriously sycophantic government mouthpiece on the ICTV channel owned by Kuchma's son-in-law.

There were many theories about who was responsible. Greatest suspicion fell on the deputy intelligence chief, Satsyuk, but he and his boss, Smeshko, indignantly refuted the accusations. Some toxicologists backed them up saying that dioxin needed between three days and two weeks to take effect and could not have been administered at the dinner since Yushchenko fell ill the next day. But others have said that the normal time lag before the poison became obvious was shortened because of the huge dose used. One of the Vienna doctors, Korpan, believes the dioxin was administered in combination with a protein called Alpha-Fetoprotein that allows the body to ingest the poison almost immediately.

Many of Yushchenko's closest colleagues suspected that Russian intelligence was involved, in collaboration with Ukrainian intelligence and those working for the regime. Yuriy Pavlenko, who became a minister in the new government, said: 'This was done by people who wanted to kill him or to effectively knock him out of the presidential race. The fact that it happened in September when Yushchenko's poll ratings gave him what looked like an untouchable lead over any other candidate is significant. There were forces that were not interested in Ukraine becoming a strong, truly independent European power and having close ties with the West. These were internal forces as well as external forces. Russia has campaigned against Yushchenko and interfered in a shameless way in the Ukrainian election and its intelligence forces cannot be excluded from the top suspects.'

Yuriy Kostenko, the leader of one opposition coalition member, the People's Party, said: 'The Russian government sees Yushchenko as a danger because they believe he will wrench Ukraine from their control. We are convinced that Russia was behind the poisoning but tension is so high with Moscow there is no telling what they might do if we publicly accused them of trying to murder Yushchenko.'

Yushchenko had promised that if he won, his first visit abroad as president would be to Moscow and the decision was taken not to level such grave accusations at Putin before their first meeting.

Suspicion fell on Russian intelligence services, not only given Moscow's hostility towards Yushchenko, but also because the poison was manufactured in relatively few facilities, one of them being the former KGB laboratory now under the control of the FSB. The Kremlin also had a long tradition of murdering Ukrainian independence leaders and activists, quite apart from the hundreds of thousands of ordinary people who were killed in Soviet purges, particularly in the thirties. In a Paris church in 1924, a Soviet agent shot dead the leader of the short-lived Ukrainian state after World War One, Symon Petliura; another Soviet agent, who befriended nationalist leader Yevhen Konovalets, killed him with a bomb hidden in a box of chocolates in Amsterdam in 1938; and in Munich in 1959, the KGB assassinated Ukraine's most prominent wartime nationalist leader, Stepan Bandera, whose guerrilla forces fought on against Soviet rule into the fifties. He was killed by a pistol firing a poisonous mist which made death appear to have been caused by a heart attack. The method was revealed only after the KGB agent responsible, a Ukrainian called Bohdan Stashynsky, who had killed another Ukrainian leader in exile by the same method, defected to the West. Autopsies on the exhumed bodies proved he was telling the truth. Stashynsky was tried and convicted of murder but because of his cooperation was given a lenient sentence of eight years which he served in a German prison. He was then spirited out to the US where he was given a new identity and was still living at a secret location when this book was written.

Soviet intelligence devoted resources to developing discreet and untraceable ways of eliminating enemies from the earliest days of Soviet intelligence. Former KGB spies have confirmed the continuing existence of 'Laboratory Number 12' or 'Lab X', also known by the Russian word *kamera* meaning chamber, where research on stealth murder methods took place from 1921 onwards. The Kamera fell under the KGB's 'Technical Operations Directorate' and was housed in a building on Varsonofyevsky Lane, close to the Moscow headquarters of the KGB, and now the FSB, at 2 Lubyanka Street. The former KGB general, Oleg Kalugin, who defected to the United States during the Cold War, said he knew of a deadly gel designed at the Kamera to be applied to objects that would be handled by the target, such as car door handles and telephones. Russian banker Ivan Kivelidi died in 1995 after using a telephone smeared with a poison. In 2002 the FSB did not disguise the fact that they had killed a

Chechen warlord, the Saudi-born Khattab – real name Saleh Abdullah Al-Suwailem – by doping a letter with poison he absorbed through the skin.

General Kalugin supervised an assassination operation in 1978 where the Kamera provided another deadly poison, ricin, which was used to kill an anti-Communist Bulgarian journalist, Georgi Markov, who worked for the BBC and Radio Free Europe/Radio Liberty in London. A microscopic pellet containing ricin was injected into him from a mechanism hidden in an umbrella as he waited at a bus stop.

In Soviet days the laboratory's inventions were tested on prisoners who had been condemned to death. This may not happen any more, but according to former Russian military intelligence officer Boris Volodarsky, writing in the *Wall Street Journal* in 2005, the old KGB facilities are still being used by Russia's new intelligence agencies. That has been confirmed by Alexander Litvinenko who served in both the KGB and its post-Communist successor, the FSB. He defected to Britain in 2000 and said the Russian government has continued to sanction assassinations against political opponents and that the old Kamera was still in business producing designer poisons.

In recent years there has been a spate of incidents in which these long-trusted techniques have been employed. After Chechen terrorists seized a Moscow theatre in October 2002, FSB Spetsnaz special forces pumped an aerosol version of a powerful, fast-acting opiate named fentanyl into the theatre that swiftly made both the terrorists and hostages unconscious. The Spetsnaz swept into the theatre killing all forty-one terrorists. But the gas, developed by the Kamera, made the hostages seriously ill. The FSB, trying to keep its fentanyl spray secret, refused to tell doctors how to treat their patients appropriately, and 129 hostages died.

POISON AND THE MARK OF THE BEAST   243

In 2004 two Russian journalists known for their opposition to the Putin administration and for the defence of human rights in Chechnya, Anna Politkovskaya and Andrei Babitsky, were poisoned on their way to cover the Beslan siege. Politkovskaya suffered severe illness when she was drugged on a plane. Babitsky was drugged after being picked up by police at a Moscow airport. And in an echo of Yushchenko's fate, friends and family of Yury Shchekochikin, a member of the Russian parliament and deputy editor of the opposition newspaper *Novaya Gazeta* in Moscow, believe that his death was caused by dioxin poisoning. Shchekochikin was investigating a company owned by a former senior KGB official for corruption, and he died in July 2003 after developing a mysterious skin disorder similar to Yushchenko's.

Several weeks later, the storm surrounding Yushchenko's poisoning intensified when Channel Five received, probably from the Ukrainian SBU but possibly from dissident Russian intelligence personnel, what purported to be a secretly recorded telephone conversation between two Russian agents, one in Kyiv, the other in Moscow. On it they talk about a poisoning attempt being prepared and one of them says the intention is not to kill Yushchenko but to give him 'the face of a beast', presumably because someone thought that would repel voters. The recording mentioned the name of a prominent Russian helping the Yanukovych campaign as involved in the plot. He denied involvement, as did the senior spokesman of the SVR, Russia's foreign intelligence service, Boris Labusov. When asked whether his colleagues had played a role, he primly snapped, 'I consider it below my dignity to comment on that.'

Former Russian military intelligence officer Volodarsky said that even the Ukrainian regime's reactions after the poisoning smacked of Soviet-style 'active measures' to sow confusion. He said: 'One thing in their design is constant. They must make the victim's death or illness appear natural or at least produce symptoms that will baffle doctors and forensic investigators. Yushchenko's case produced just the kind of confusing symptoms that would characterise a poison produced by the Kamera.' Someone was certainly putting a lot of effort into clouding the truth about who was responsible for the poisoning. In November 2004 a Ukrainian claiming to work for his country's intelligence services approached a Western intelligence agency saying he knew who was behind the assassination attempt. He was spirited out of Ukraine to neighbouring Romania, then to Hungary, and was promised refuge and a new identity in north America. I was offered the opportunity to meet him before he was flown to his new home. However, the day I was to fly to Budapest, I was told that his handlers had concluded he had been sent to spread disinformation. He was claiming that Yulia Tymoshenko masterminded the poisoning – an obvious ploy to split the opposition. When he realised he was not being believed, the man then returned to Ukraine – something a defector was unlikely to have done – and dropped out of sight.

Many do believe that the poisoning was supposed only to neutralise Yushchenko as a presidential candidate, either by incapacitating him or by disfiguring him. As election spin doctors the world over know, a candidate's appearance has a tremendous influence on the way electorates vote. But if his enemies' intention was to brand him with the mark of the beast – as suggested in the secret recordings of the two Russians – it was a spectacular miscalculation because Yushchenko's popularity rose as people's hearts went out to him. Even without any firm proof, many ordinary Ukrainians and most of Yushchenko's supporters assumed the authorities were behind the poisoning. One Nasha Ukrayina supporter, Yuriy Matsiuk, said at a rally in Kyiv: 'We knew from the beginning it was poisoning. The government knew they couldn't beat Yushchenko fairly so they wanted to kill him or prevent him campaigning. Lots of people are influenced by how a person looks and the authorities thought if they made him look dreadful that would stop people voting for him. That's stupid, but that's how they think.' The scarring had become a badge of courage and honour. Throughout the rest of the campaign, at rallies all over Ukraine, people pressed up close to Yushchenko and wanted to touch him and kiss him on his cheeks.

The damage to Yushchenko's face only provided irrefutable evidence of an evil abroad in the country. His stalwart response to what had been inflicted on him impressed Ukrainians and it seemed to strengthen Yushchenko's resolve. Most strikingly, his previously languid speeches underwent an inspiring transformation. Yushchenko admitted that he sometimes found it difficult to look at his own reflection in the mirror and lived in hope that the poisoning effects would eventually wear off. His wife said she took encouragement from doctors who predicted there would be a full recovery. She said: 'The children were not frightened or repelled by the transformations and that's because they love him and he's still their dad whatever he looks like. I think we all became stronger because of that experience. Viktor became more determined than ever to win the election, not for himself, but to rid the country of the kind of people who use such methods.'

A few weeks after Yushchenko was poisoned, prime minister and regime presidential candidate Viktor Yanukovych visited the western city of Ivano-Frankivsk. The large city is one of the most enthusiastically patriotic places in Ukraine. Like the rest of West Ukraine, it had never been under Moscow's rule until World War Two, and most people there associate the calamities that befell them when they were incorporated into the Soviet Union with Russian imperialism as much as with Communism. Yanukovych's desire to get closer to Russia and to make Russian a state language were a red rag to West Ukrainians. As his campaign bus entered the pretty city, the streets were lined with people jeering the government candidate.

The bus drew up in front of a crowd shouting anti-government slogans, the doors opened and Yanukovych stepped out. A few seconds later something flew through the air, Yanukovych clutched at his right side, then fell to the ground where he remained. Security men swarmed around the prone figure and dragged him to an accompanying van which sped the stricken prime minister to the emergency ward of a local hospital. Later the nation was relieved to see, on its television screens, that Yanukovych had survived, although, as he spoke haltingly from his hospital bed, he appeared extremely weary and there was a near-death-experience look in the eyes staring at the camera. In a grave voice Yanukovych bemoaned the wickedness that had landed him in hospital. He said he now understood that 'nationalism is a disease', sighed that he did not hold the perpetrators responsible but blamed Yushchenko and the maleficent opposition that had twisted his assailant's mind.

What had happened that had so rattled the tough Yanukovych? When people discovered he had been hit by an egg there were howls of laughter that echoed until the end of the elections. The incident spawned scores of jokes which were retold by Yushchenko, Tymoshenko and other opposition speakers addressing rallies, leavening the otherwise serious subjects under discussion. Internet sites carried video clips of the episode with slow motion used to show the egg splattering into Yanukovych and his subsequent collapse. The Internet also posted a photograph of a proud chicken sitting above the caption: 'The hero chicken that laid the egg that hit the prime minister'.

But people could not understand why Yanukovych made such a drama out of being felled by what was, after all, just an egg. It was obvious he could not have been hurt and there was no dividend in showing a politician who wanted to project a tough image buckling under such an onslaught. It did not add up.

Over the following weeks, a remarkable story trickled piece by piece out of the Yanukovych camp, which proved itself far from leakproof during the long months of the campaign. The explanation that emerged was that after the swell of support for Yushchenko following his poisoning, the Yanukovych team had searched for something to provoke a similar outpouring of sympathy for their man. They had whipped up a climate of fear by warning of terrorism and violence and had already planted weapons and explosives to besmirch the opposition. Now they hatched a plan to fake an assasination attempt by having someone shoot Yanukovych, who would be wearing a bulletproof vest under his clothes. The weapon to be used would be a modified pneumatic pistol, readily available in Ukraine, which used a .22 cartridge to fire a tiny calibre air-gun pellet. The report of the gun sounds like the real thing but the pellet would cause very little damage even if it hit an unprotected part of Yanukovych's body. The prime minister, according to the information, was psyched up to take a small impact after getting off the bus and collapse as if shot. But the plan became scrambled when, by complete coincidence, a student who genuinely hated him, hurled an egg before the 'assassination' shot could be fired by the Yanukovych campaign's plant.

Viewed with this in mind, the film of the incident does indeed show an unnatural moment of hestitation between the egg hitting Yanukovych and his face registering a decision to fall. It is as if he realises something is not going according to the script but there is too little time to process all the information and so he continues with the pre-arranged plan to collapse. It is this version of the egg episode which became popularly accepted and was one of Yanukovych's greatest PR blunders, though not the last, and they were all mercilessly exploited by the opposition.

During his hospital broadcast Yanukovych piously claimed that he never insulted his opponents – something that everyone knew was not true. He demonstrated how untrue in a number of unforgettable public appearances that also quickly became staples on the Internet. In the most infamous, Yanukovych addressed a large rally of his supporters in Donetsk and described anyone voting against him with a Russian word *kozli* that literally means 'goats' but has the insult value of 'wanker' or 'arsehole'. It was a moment he would come to rue.

Whether or not Moscow had anything to do with the poisoning, there was no doubt that Putin did his utmost to undermine the opposition and ensure victory for Yanukovych, and the Kremlin maintained a pattern of interference.

Putin sent one of his top advisors, a political strategist and spin doctor called Gleb Pavlovsky, to assist Yanukovych's campaign team. Pavlovsky had been credited with helping Putin's own election victory by suppressing opposition views in television coverage and by using 'black technology' to discredit opponents. The Kremlin also earmarked around three hundred million dollars to be spent on Yanukovych's campaign.

On the eve of what turned out to be the first two rounds of the election, Putin twice visited Ukraine to bolster Yanukovych's chances. On the first occasion the pretext was to take part in the sixtieth anniversary commemorations of the liberation of Kyiv from the Nazis. But the date for the commemoration was brought forward by a week and the military parade, complete with old Communist flags, was seen as a crude warning that force would be used, if necessary, to decide the election.

On that trip Putin was also broadcast live on three television channels across the country giving plugs for Yanukovych and pledging that he would work to introduce dual nationality. He also advocated travel between the two countries using domestic ID documents instead of passports, something that appealed to the many Ukrainian citizens who worked in Russia and ethnic Russians living in Ukraine who wanted to visit relatives in Russia without elaborate border formalities. Putin praised Yanukovych's economic successes and explicity linked the two countries' destinies, extolling the merits of the planned Single Economic Zone, the most important building block of his dreams for a revived empire.

The trip outraged many Ukrainians who thought it was a scurrilous intrusion. Yushchenko wrote to Putin saying that the visit would be viewed as interference in Ukraine's affairs whether the Russian president intended this or not. On his own visit to Ukraine, the deputy president of the European Parliament Janusz Onyskewiecz criticised what he called Russia's interference in the election. 'The level of the interference of some circles in Russia in the Ukrainian elections is something deplorable,' he said. 'This is a problem and I think it is up to the Ukrainian people to decide who should be their next president. It is not for other countries to indicate which candidate would be better.'

There were clear precedents for Putin's behaviour. At his birthday party near Moscow earlier that year, the news had shown the Russian president kissing Kuchma and Yanukovych whilst declaring, 'Russia is not indifferent to the choice that the people of Ukraine will make . . . The future of relations depends on how Ukraine's leadership will build its policy toward Russia.'

Putin was putting a lot of misplaced trust on how to behave in Ukraine in his swaggering spin doctor, Pavlovsky, who had failed to grasp what was happening. Yet it still puzzled observers that the Russian leader blundered so badly in Ukraine, shredding any residual belief that the post-Communist Kremlin and the West now shared common values of democracy and political behaviour. Serge Schmemann, writing in the *New York Times*, asked why Putin would squander his dwindling standing in the West by interfering so openly in Ukraine's election. He thought there was something to speculation that Putin had 'fallen under the sway of anti-Western fellow alumni of the KGB, who dominate his entourage'. He continued: 'Many of the men and women who wield power in Russia – especially former KGB operatives like Mr Putin – have inherited a Soviet mentality that considers politics to be a naked struggle for power. The notion that Ukrainians might actually want a say in who rules them would not dawn on this group; it presumes that no Ukrainians would be so insubordinate unless anti-Soviet (make that anti-Russian) forces were behind them.'

Vyacheslav Nikonov, president of Moscow's Politika Foundation, a pro-Kremlin think tank, said, 'Russia is not really enraptured with Mr Yanukovych. It simply cannot accept Viktor Yushchenko . . . he is a vocal advocate of Ukraine's withdrawal from the so-called Single Economic Zone.' And he went on to say: 'A Yushchenko victory would mean Ukraine's accession to NATO in the next two to three years. Washington and the Ukrainian opposition leader have already exchanged promises.' He warned that if that happened 'we would have to forget about friendship with Ukraine, and Ukrainians would have to forget about their sovereignty'. From Moscow, Russia's Communist Party leader Gennady Zyuganov echoed those views and called on Ukrainian Communists to vote for Yanukovych so as not to allow the victory of a 'representative of pro-Western forces' which, he said, would 'put off prospects for the reunification of our people for a long time'.

Millions of ethnic Ukrainians live in Russia permanently and have citizenship, and a much smaller number of Ukrainian citizens reside there as temporary workers. In the months before the election, Yanukovych appeared on huge billboards in Moscow, and Russian television programmes, which are broadcast into much of Ukraine, also did their best to boost his image. The Ukrainian government even announced it was going to set up 420 polling stations across Russia for the presidential election. The opposition quickly recognised it would be almost impossible to mount proper scrutiny at these places, which would provide a terrific opportunity to generate a huge number of false votes for Yanukovych. Kuchma immediately came under pressure to slash the number of polling stations in Russia, which he did, to forty-one – still a number that could produce a lot of mischief. Then Nasha Ukrayina referred the matter, on a technicality, to the country's supreme court which ruled that four polling stations would be sufficient. The decision foreshadowed the momentous role the legal body would play later.

Volodymyr Polokhalo, director of a Ukrainian political think tank, the Centre for Political Analysis, called the approaching election 'the dirtiest, most immoral and dishonest of all post-Soviet campaigns in Ukraine'. He said: 'The Russian factor is present everywhere . . . This has turned into Russia's election for Ukraine's next president.' He believed the Kremlin wanted to prevent Yushchenko becoming president because, apart from the desire to keep Ukraine in its orbit, and the concomitant foreign policy implications of a failure to do so, it also feared that ordinary Russians might be inspired to clamour for change in their country.

Some Russians were unhappy with their country's interference. Grigory Yavlinsky, head of Russia's liberal Yabloko Party, said: 'Russian authorities are defending not only a bankrupt nomenklatura-oligarch regime in Ukraine, but also themselves.' From further abroad, there was a growing chorus of concern. International bodies like the Organisation for Security and Cooperation in Europe (OSCE), the EU and the Council of Europe, urged the Ukrainian government to hold fair elections and again hinted at sanctions if they did not. The opposition took heart from the election observers sent by many of these bodies, including six hundred in the first round from the OSCE. The US too backed up its plea for fair elections by announcing it had placed on a visa black list oligarch Hryhoriy Surkis. It was a clear signal aimed at the heart of the government because Surkis was the business partner and political associate of presidential administration chief Viktor Medvedchuk.

Two weeks before the first round of the Ukrainian elections, the Belarusian president, Alexander Lukashenko, won a referendum entitling him to tear up his country's constitution and ensure his continued reign as a Stalinist dictator. The rigged referendum, in tandem with equally fraudulent parliamentary elections, was followed by opposition demonstrations. But the Belarusian opposition was much smaller and more weakly organised than anti-government groups in Ukraine, and the protests were swiftly crushed by the security forces. The Kremlin immediately approved the voting outcome as free and fair. Kuchma and Yanukovych congratulated Lukashenko, a man who had once publicly praised Hitler's statecraft, and invited him to the premature liberation celebration in Kyiv.

In Ukraine the atmosphere had become ugly in the final days before the election. Most independent observers agreed Yushchenko would win easily in a fair contest and the government seemed panicked by the large opposition rallies. The presidential administration was also disturbed by the large number of election monitors that had turned up. The *temnyk* directive it sent to the media for the week 17–23 October included instructions to discredit foreign election observers by linking them to Western intelligence agencies.

Security forces once again raided the offices of the largest pro-opposition support group, Pora, and detained its leaders. On the night of 25 October camouflaged assailants ambushed the car of parliament member Volodymyr Bondarenko, one of Yushchenko's key campaign staff, throwing Molotov cocktails that set alight his vehicle on a highway outside Kyiv. Bondarenko had uncovered the huge cache of denigrating anti-Yushchenko black propaganda materials which had embarrassed the government so much, and had repeatedly accused the police of acting as the regime's storm troopers.

He believed he and his driver were lucky to escape with their lives and that the assailants intended to shoot them had they been caught. He said: 'I'm convinced one hundred per cent that this was an assassination attempt, punishment for my criticism of the police. I have said it before and I am saying it again: criminals have become completely amalgamated with law-enforcement agencies.'

The scene was set. The opposition warned there would be massive fraud and that the regime could use force. Yushchenko said: 'We believe there is a colossal threat to Ukraine's election being held in a free, democratic fashion. Knowing our authorities, we can only expect that they will resort to cheating and brutality towards voters.'

Chapter Ten

ELECTION STEALING

Balloting in the presidential election on 31 October should have been a very transparent matter in Ukraine; the tall boxes, sporting the nation's trident symbol on the front, were constructed of thick sheets of clear plastic. At ballot stations set up in schools, colleges, libraries and other government buildings, voters first walked up to a table and presented their 'internal passport', an ID document that is a hangover from Soviet times and contains name, date of birth and address. After an election official had checked that the name corresponded to an address on the electoral roll, the voter was handed a ballot paper torn from a book. The voter signed in a space on the electoral list and then again on the portion of the ballot paper that remained in the book. That remaining portion was countersigned by the election official to record that it had been issued for use. The information in the book could not be linked with the cast ballot.

The ballot paper was a large one because there were twenty-four candidates taking part in the first round. Voters marked their choice in a curtained booth and then deposited the paper, folded or unfolded, through a slot at the top of the transparent ballot boxes.

Opinion polls showed that most people expected there would be cheating at the election but as people went to vote there was an atmosphere of optimism that matched the glorious weather of a perfect, sunny autumn day. Many people came in family groups, parents bringing along their children. No political lobbying was allowed on the day of the election and the various party symbols were supposed to have been removed. But still many voters came wearing an orange tie, scarf or ribbon. Women wore orange dresses, blouses and even tights. In many villages there was a festive atmosphere and it seemed essential to have a sound system at the entrance to the polling station blasting out disco music.

But at some of the voting stations observers noticed less cheerful things. Towards the end of the day, the boxes would suddenly be loaded with thick clumps of ballot papers, folded over together: obvious signs of crude ballot stuffing. This widespread practice involved ballot papers that had not been officially distributed to the polling stations and had been pre-marked somewhere else in favour of Yanukovych. At a ballot station in the northern Sumy region, opposition observers called in the police to investigate. A video camera caught the police, backed up by special interior ministry troops, pulling out their truncheons and attacking the small group of observers, spraying some of them in the eyes with tear gas. Opposition observers were attacked at scores of polling stations around Ukraine, either by groups of well-organised thugs while the police stood by, or by the police themselves.

In the following days, several thousand people from Sumy protested after six of the election observers were sentenced to ten days' detention for 'disrupting the peace'. That protest, like the one on 31 October, was brutally dispersed by police with tear gas and batons.

Ballot stuffing was predominantly used in the eastern and southern regions where the regime felt most confident it could rely on local officials not actually perpetrating the fraud to turn a blind eye. In Central and West Ukraine, where this compliance could not be relied upon, the result was distorted by exploiting the right of voters to cast their ballot elsewhere than their normal place of residence. This 'absentee' voting right was intended for people who were away from home because of work. In the autumn and winter of 2004, hundreds of thousands, if not millions, of Ukrainians were apparently away on business on the Sundays voting took place. A few days before the 31 October vote, and again prior to the 21 November run-off, large groups, mostly young men, arrived at deserted sanatoriums and holiday camps around the country. Locals who asked them who they were and what they were doing received evasive answers or no replies at all. Other such groups would arrive by special train or bus on the day of the vote. Armed with the absentee voter documents they were bussed to polling stations where they cast their votes. All that effort would have been pointless, however, had they only voted once, so the sullen voters were bussed around on an odyssey that took them to innumerable rural polling stations. The opposition, and some of those taking part in the fraud, called the method 'the carousel' or 'merry-go-round'. Nasha Ukrayina estimated some of the carousel riders voted twenty times and that Yanukovych might well have gained several million votes that way.

The scheme had been prepared meticulously in advance. The interior minister, Mykola Bilokon, made it possible by issuing a seemingly innocuous instruction – Number 571 – on 26 May 2004, which cancelled the requirement for police to record in people's internal passports their temporary place of stay. Such registration would have allowed the absentee voter to cast their ballot at only one location because it would have been checked by the official issuing the ballot paper. Without any temporary address logged in their internal passport, the merry-go-round was unrestricted and the groups could criss-cross the regions, voting at polling stations miles apart to lessen the chance of detection.

Every opportunity for distorting the result was used. The bogus presidential 'technical candidates' enabled the regime to pack local election commissions with Yanukovych supporters. Some opposition representatives were either bribed or intimidated to secure their cooperation, while others were excluded by spurious or illegal means from the polling stations during the count. Under these circumstances those counting the votes simply ignored ballots cast for the opposition or added them to the pile containing votes for Yanukovych, instances of which were captured on video.

The officials at the polling stations would then sign a protocol listing how many votes each candidate received and this document and the ballots were then supposed to be transported, under police escort, to the territorial headquarters. But en route a Yanukovych operative would meet the vehicle and protocols with an unsatisfactory result would be substituted by a more agreeable version, with or without the cooperation of the official from the polling station.

The official protocol tallies from Ukraine's thirty-three thousand polling stations were reckoned at the country's 250 territorial voting headquarters, which then transmitted the results by computer to the election commission in Kyiv. Or at least that is where they thought they were sending them. The presidential administration had surreptitiously introduced a technique for intercepting the results and secretly massaging them before sending them on to their final destination. The opposition became suspicious that the computer system was being manipulated because of the inexplicably long intervals between the results being transmitted by territorial commissions and the CEC receiving them in Kyiv. Their suspicions that the results were first going to a computer controlled by the government camp were borne out a few weeks later.

Clandestine recordings, provided by the SBU intelligence services, provided other evidence of dirty tricks. One revealed a senior Yanukovych election aide calling someone in Moscow to complain about the low quality of counterfeit ballot papers printed there for the ballot-stuffing operation and a request that better ones be prepared for the next round. Also caught on the recordings was an official of the pro-Moscow Orthodox Church eliciting subsidies from the Yanukovych staff for the expenses of clergy whipping up support for the regime candidate. These and other voice and video recordings which emerged after the first and second rounds of the election were ignored by the prosecutor-general, Hennadiy Vasilyev, who was a close ally of Yanukovych and a leading member of the Donetsk oligarch clan.

As voting ceased the first exit polls conducted by the opposition and independent groups indicated that Yushchenko had gathered most votes, forty-five per cent to Yanukovych's thirty-seven per cent. The first results published by the CEC, though, some six per cent of the total and overwhelmingly from East Ukraine, put Yanukovych far ahead with fifty-four per cent of the vote compared to Yushchenko's twenty-nine per cent. But as more results flowed in, the gap between the two front-runners steadily narrowed. There was dismay at the presidential administration because the vote for Yushchenko was so enormous it was proving difficult to distort the results without making the fraud ridiculously obvious.

On 1 November, the day after the election, the CEC suspended completion of the tallies and said it might not have the official result for another week. The results were frozen at 39.88 per cent of the vote for Yanukovych and 39.22 per cent for Yushchenko. Taken together with the ballots cast for the other candidates, ninety-four per cent of the vote had been counted. By law the CEC had to declare the full result within ten days of the vote. Yushchenko's campaign manager, Oleksandr Zinchenko, said: 'It is with good cause that the CEC stopped announcing the election results. They simply do not have the courage to declare Victor Yushchenko the winner.'

The remaining six per cent of uncounted votes were overwhelmingly from Yushchenko strongholds. If added to his declared share, they would put him ahead but without enough votes for an outright victory, which required more than fifty per cent of the ballots in the first round. But the psychological advantage of winning the first round would provide an immense propaganda boost ahead of the run-off on 21 November. Battle commenced for this valuable prize.

The day after the election, the regime took another blow when international observers reported serious infringements. The leader of the OSCE election observers, Bruce George, said it was a step backwards from Ukraine's parliamentary polls in 2002: 'With a heavy heart, we have to conclude that this election did not meet a considerable number of the OSCE, Council of Europe and other European standards for democratic elections.' The monitors focused on the use of the state apparatus, admin-resource, to disrupt Yushchenko's campaign. George said: 'We found overwhelming bias in favour of the incumbent prime minister in the state media and interference in his favour by the state administration. Mr Yanukovych's campaign failed to make a clear separation between resources owned or managed by the incumbent political forces and the property of the state.'

The Western-funded Committee of Ukrainian Voters (CVU)

estimated a week after the ballot that some 2.8 million ballots were rigged in favour of Yanukovych. It said the cheating was 'the biggest election fraud in Ukraine's history' and involved at least eighty-five thousand local government officials. The group named Donetsk, Luhansk, Zaporizhya and Mykolaiv as the most fraudulent regions, with Crimea, Sumy and Kharkiv not far behind. It said there were extensive flaws in preparing the protocol tallies of voting.

The CVU confirmed anecdotal evidence that the most serious infringements were in organised mass voting with absentee ballot documents and criminal interference in the electoral process. It said opposition members of many local supervising committees were illegally excluded, while intimidation and violence was used against election officials, observers and journalists at many places. Gunmen burst into one polling station in Kirovohrad where the vote favoured Yushchenko and fired shots before stealing the ballots. Elsewhere, a Georgian member of parliament, Gregor Materadze, an accredited international observer, was beaten up by regime thugs.

The watchdog group said tens of thousands of voters were left off the electoral list and an unusually high percentage of voters cast their ballots at home. Ukraine makes special provision for people who are handicapped or ill to vote at home. Hospital patients and prison inmates are also allowed to vote at their place of 'residence' rather than the local polling station. But the opposition had not foreseen how the regime would exploit these captive voters, far from the prying eyes of observers. The privilege of voting at home was supposed to extend only to 'Category One' severely disabled people yet ostensibly Ukraine had a distressingly high proportion of these – thirty per cent, for instance, of the entire population in the southern Mykolaiv region alone. It seemed too that the jailbirds were voting for one of their own: all 2,139 inmates in the eastern city of Luhansk cast their ballots for Yanukovych, according to the official results. An inmate who was released between the first and second rounds of voting said prison authorities warned convicts their conditions would worsen and their sentences might be increased if they did not vote for Yanukovych, though some prisoners refused to vote for him despite the threats.

Against this emerging backdrop of fraud on a giant scale, the political rivals each put on a show of confidence. Parliament was in boisterous mood with deputies from the opposition wearing orange bandanas and ribbons while Yanukovych's supporters from his Regions of Ukraine Party wore scarves in his blue and white campaign colours.

When Yulia Tymoshenko addressed parliament she cited final opposition exit polls showing that Yushchenko had garnered 53.4 per cent of the vote while Yanukovych received only 27.86 per cent. She accused the government of widespread cheating. Nasha Ukrayina lodged seventy formal complaints with the CEC about gross election abuses within the first day, and the number grew over the following days. Yanukovych's campaign team immediately denied the accusations and retorted Nasha Ukrayina had faked more than a million votes for Yushchenko in West Ukraine and bribed election officials in at least one district.

Former president Kravchuk entered the debate, counselling that it was unnecessary to count the rest of the votes because 'it's not important who got ten or fifteen more votes – the important thing is who goes into the second round'. He reacted tetchily when I asked him in the parliamentary lobby about the OSCE's negative assessment. Kravchuk said the OSCE had not been critical and then became angry when I told him I had their report with me and could demonstrate it showed international monitors were dissatisfied with the way the election had been conducted. Red with anger, he lectured me about how George Bush's 2000 election had been disputed. 'Nobody in the world has seen elections where there have been no infringements,' said Kravchuk, former statesman and now Medvedchuk's lieutenant in the Ukrainian parliament. The next day some of the press reported light-heartedly that I had nearly given Kravchuk a heart attack and it would have been sad indeed if Ukraine's 'founding father' expired while defending those engaged in a shameful crime against the country.

Days later there was still no final result. CEC chairman Serhiy Kivalov, trusted by the regime, attributed the delay to missing protocols and to waiting for local courts to rule on complaints about election law violations. The protocols were a vital ingredient of the government fraud. A week before the election Yushchenko produced at a rally a blank protocol from the Cherkasy region that he said had already been signed and stamped by the members of the local electoral commission, ready to be filled in with whatever results the government wanted.

The day after the vote, opposition activists from Pora flexed their muscles by holding a large protest rally against falsification. They had originally planned to stage the action outside the CEC building, but switched venue after receiving information that the regime intended to provoke bloodshed in order to soften up the country for fraudulent results by portraying the opposition as dangerous extremists, hell-bent on violence. The interior ministry had deployed special forces and armoured personnel carriers around the building, and Pora learned that hundreds of young men wearing Yanukovych's blue and white election paraphernalia had been transported into the capital. The plan, said the opposition, was for these Yanukovych 'supporters' – probably minor criminals and police college students – to provoke a fight with Pora members after which the troops would step in to restore calm as brutally as possible. On 4 November, though, Pora did turn up at the CEC and deposited a washing machine dressed up as a ballot box outside the building. They filled it with ballot papers which, having been laundered, yielded a unanimous vote for Yanukovych.

As time passed, the CEC downplayed the allegations of widespread fraud. Whilst regime supporters controlled the commission, there were a small number of its members who wanted to assist in the exposure of the vote-rigging. The CEC was sheepishly forced to admit that on 31 October nearly 130,000 more votes had been cast than legitimate ballot papers had been issued. This from just seven of Ukraine's twenty-five provinces. The CEC did not announce the national figure for excess ballots. In most Western countries such an admission would itself have been enough to cast doubt on the entire election process. In Ukraine, however, the CEC said that although there were some defects, the country should continue to trust the commission. No attempt was made to give a plausible explanation for the provenance of the extra ballot forms.

A friend of mine, who worked for the government candidate's propaganda team, said at the time that behind the scenes the Yanukovych camp had been severely shaken by the high showing for Yushchenko. 'The Yanukovych team have been traumatised. The real results show that Yushchenko probably got more than fifty-four per cent.' Yanukovych's staff, he said, were desperately trying to court the Communist and Socialist candidates who secured ten per cent of the vote between them. They had, astonishingly, also considered offering a compromise to the opposition involving a Yushchenko presidency with Yanukovych remaining prime minister.

On the tenth day after the first round, the CEC finally announced the results, which confirmed that the decisive second round would be between Yushchenko and Yanukovych. The previous results were reversed and now the CEC put Yushchenko slightly ahead with 39.87 per cent of the vote compared to Yanukovych's 39.22 per cent. It was very unlikely that these represented the true vote share, but it was certainly a morale booster for the opposition that their candidate was going into the second round as leader.

An opposition sympathiser on the CEC, Andriy Mahera, conceded that the delay had planted doubts in many people's minds about the commission's integrity. He said: 'The very fact that the Central Election Commission is announcing the results only on the final, tenth day, is undoubtedly a reason which gives birth to rumours of certain political interference.'

Yushchenko celebrated the fact that, despite all the underhand methods used against Nasha Ukrayina, the government had been denied a first-round victory. One of the opposition coalition leaders, Yuriy Kostenko, said: 'Voters today will be singing with happiness because it's their victory and they have gained faith in their own strength.'

After the results were announced there was intense horse-trading by both sides to forge alliances with the legitimate losing candidates – as opposed to the 'technical candidates' – in the hope of gaining not only their new supporters' votes but also their valuable networks of local party activists. The most important deal was sealed with the fickle Socialist Oleksandr Moroz. He said he was willing to support Nasha Ukrayina, although not actually to join the coalition, if it agreed to some of his party's demands such as implementing constitutional reforms to give the prime minister increased powers, refusing to grant the outgoing president Leonid Kuchma immunity from criminal proceedings, and withdrawal of Ukrainian troops from Iraq.

Moroz never completely shed the dour style he acquired in his political apprenticeship as a Communist Party member, and his drab speeches rarely had audiences dancing in the aisles. But when the Socialist Party turned to the coalition, it brought with it a figure whose panache quickly made him one of the opposition's stars – Yuriy Lutsenko. Young, energetic, and benignly tough-looking, Lutsenko's blunt, upbeat speeches and sense of humour left no room for despair, however grim the situation was to become. Also coming over to the Yushchenko camp was Anatoly Kinakh, who had briefly been prime minister after Yushchenko was removed from the job in 2001. He had gained just under one per cent of the vote, but was generally well regarded.

The realigned forces resumed the campaign with a full programme of political rallies around the country for the three weeks until the second, and supposedly final, round of the election. Cracks had been revealed in the regime's fraud strategy and some honest officials, like the CEC's Mahera, were beginning to emerge through these fissures. They gave dramatic descriptions of what was happening from an insider vantage point, and their actions were to inspire others.

One such group were police officers from the eastern city of Kharkiv. Disgusted that the police force was being used to undermine the election, they wrote an unsigned letter to the speaker of the Ukrainian parliament, Volodymyr Lytvyn, detailing vote-rigging in their city and warning that similar methods were going to be used during the second round.

I managed to make contact with the men through a member of the Nasha Ukrayina campaign in Kharkiv, and arranged to meet them two days later, on a Saturday when Yushchenko by happy coincidence would be addressing a rally in the city. I assumed the Nasha Ukrayina activist was not blind to the possibility that it might be some sort of trap to discredit me, a Western journalist who had already upset the government earlier that year with revelations about the Gongadze murder. I had become friends with a Canadian election observer, John Mraz, who I met during the first round of voting. He had returned for the second round and I was pleased when he said he would like to come along. It was good to have John as my companion as the small plane took off for the bumpy ride from Kyiv to Kharkiv. Even though John has an impressive physical presence – he looks as powerful as a Canadian moose and has managed to survive in some dangerous places – I was primarily glad he was with me to act as a witness in case a set-up had indeed been planned.

We were due to meet the officers in the evening, after the Yushchenko rally. Kharkiv, the country's second largest city with around 1.5 million people, gives the lie to 'east is pro-Russian' generalisations and this was borne out by the large crowds that turned out for Yushchenko. The people here use Russian routinely, but they know how to speak Ukrainian and they are certainly not confused about their nationality. Whenever he appeared for a rally in the east or south of the country, Yushchenko always asked at the start of the meeting 'Which language shall we speak in today?' If the audience shouted 'Russian' then he spoke in that language. In Kharkiv, the crowd, which I could hear talking among themselves in Russian, asked him to speak in Ukrainian.

The local pro-regime authorities had twice altered the venue for the meeting in the hope of sabotaging it. That very morning, when local Nasha Ukrayina members arrived to prepare the space for the rally, they found it filled with tractors. The city authorities glibly announced that an exhibition of farm machinery had been scheduled for that day. Only after bitter wrangling was permission given for the meeting to go ahead at another spot, and the organisers had to rush to erect the stage for the speakers and set up the sound system. The opposition, however, had become accustomed to such bureaucratic attempts to sabotage its meetings. If the authorities could not prevent Nasha Ukrayina holding its rallies, they sometimes tried to prevent Yushchenko reaching them. In the weeks before and after the first round, his planes had been refused permission to land at airports and forced on lengthy diversions. The reasons given for the diversions, usually bad weather, were concocted.

Kharkiv was founded in the seventeenth century by Cossacks and swiftly became a rich and important centre famed for its splendid baroque buildings. It also acquired a reputation for culture and education. In the twenties, it became one of the main founts of the brief but dazzling cultural revival granted Ukrainians before the purges and mass killings. The Comminists even made it Ukraine's capital for fifteen years from 1919. It still has a reputation for being home to the intelligentsia, and I imagined academics and blue-collar workers side by side on the Metro in the morning rush hour, all completing their crosswords well before reaching their destinations. World War Two saw much of the city destroyed, but one of its magnificent surviving landmarks, Uspensky Cathedral and the adjacent imposing bell tower next to it, formed the graceful backdrop to the crowd of thousands of supporters spread out before the stage.

Yushchenko's confidence had grown rapidly in the hectic months of the campaign, surviving everything the regime had thrown at him, including the assassination attempt. One of his characteristic phrases was 'Dear friends', and he began his speech with an appeal to any who wanted to throw an egg to delay doing so until the end of the speech, because he understood 'that you have to spend a few days on life support' after such an attack and he did not want to keep his audience waiting that long.

Yushchenko addressed the local government's attempts to scupper the rally and he told his audience with a mixture of humour and affection: 'You are strange people. They drive you from one place to another, yet you come. They eject you from Constitution Square and you come, they eject you from Freedom Square yet you come here. We will not give away our constitution or our freedom.' He said that people had demonstrated they were no longer prepared to live according to *ponyatia*, the street slang for the Ukrainian underworld's esoteric gangster lore. He said: 'I want to say, dear friends, that what we can feel today is that the fate of our country is no longer in the hands of criminals and convicts. They are not going to dictate the fate of my children or your children.' He reminded everyone to check before the second round that they were on the electoral roll and all the details were correct so that they could not be refused the chance to cast their ballot. 'Remember that without you, not only will there be no elections, there will be no Ukraine,' he exhorted.

After Yushchenko and the other speakers had finished, a popular rap band called Tartak appeared on the stage. The opposition had targeted younger voters, and rock bands often accompanied the politicians to make the rallies more interesting. I liked Tartak and their clever lyrics that had a political edge, but as they started thumping out the notes to their most famous song of the election season, John and I walked off to meet the rebel police officers.

The men were obviously concerned to conceal their

identity and had not only agreed to speak to me on condition of anonymity. They had also insisted on elaborate precautions to ensure that John and I were not followed by government agents. We met my Nasha Ukrayina contact, Anatoly, outside Kharkiv's largest store and waited for instructions he was expecting to receive at 7pm. The call came precisely on time and instructed us to walk by a certain route to another street and to be ready for a second call. Before we got there, Anatoly received another call and we were told to walk to a busy intersection. We arrived at the place they had stipulated and there was a third call. Anatoly was told that a van would arrive at the intersection and we were to get in. Almost immediately a minibus drew up close to us and its door slid open. A middle-aged man beckoned us in. There was no time for an appraisal of the people inside. The face that peered out at John and me was weighing us up and I knew that if we hesitated even for a few seconds the van was likely to speed off.

We got in and drove along one of Kharkiv's main roads. We shook hands with the four men inside the van and were asked to show some form of identification. The men were all dressed casually but everything about their appearance still proclaimed 'police'. They were polite, friendly and apologised for leading us around the city but hoped we understood that they had to take precautions. There was excitement but no tension, and something reassuring about their manner that allayed my concerns about a possible set-up or worse.

We drove for around fifteen minutes and were told that another two police officers would meet us at our destination. We went further out of Kharkiv, the traffic thinned and there was less street lighting. As we drove along the edge of a park, the darkness of the November night was interrupted by a flash from a vehicle's headlights. We pulled in close to it, parked and our driver switched off the lights. Another two men walked up to our vehicle and shook hands with everyone. The new arrivals were also friendly but asked us to leave our mobile phones, and any recording devices or cameras, in the van with one of their number. We would hold our conversation in the park. I was expecting to be searched, but we weren't. We had placed ourselves in the hands of these total strangers and perhaps they wanted to demonstrate a reciprocal trust.

It turned out we were at the city's large war memorial park and we walked deeper inside away from the road along a path that took us past monuments to Soviet war heroes. It was pitch black and the park was deserted. We came to a halt slightly off the path and I scribbled notes on a pad I could hardly see as they began to tell me their story.

There were five men, aged between their late twenties and early fifties, including majors and a colonel. They said their motive for writing the letter to the parliamentary speaker was disgust at the interior ministry's involvement in election fraud in the previous month's first round of voting, and in thuggery directed at opposition activists in the weeks before and since. The men said the police force had become an adjunct of organised crime and they wanted Yushchenko to win because things would deteriorate further under Yanukovych, whom they held in immense contempt because of his criminal convictions. They believed that apart from the two known convictions, Yanukovych had been involved in other criminal matters.

The colonel said that on the eve of the first round, police had guarded a room in a local authority building where he estimated around five hundred thousand ballots, pre-marked for Yanukovych, were kept hidden. Police escorts were ordered to supervise their dispersal among local polling stations on election day. While the Central Election Commission had been forced to admit that some 130,000 more votes had been cast than there were official ballot papers, the information from these officers showed the use of fake ballot papers had been much more widespread.

All the police, they said, had been forced to sign a document agreeing to vote for Yanukovych as well as pledging to get their family and up to fifteen other people to do the same. Police academy students, they said, had been dispatched in organised groups around Ukraine to vote up to ten times each with fraudulent absentee voter documents. A special undercover police unit had also been formed to intimidate opposition workers and destroy campaign materials. They said the group had planted a bomb in a Yushchenko campaign office and explosive materials in the car boot of opposition activist Yuriy Potykun who was subsequently arrested with great fanfare. A group of around a hundred petty criminals and vagrants had also been paid to masquerade at Yushchenko rallies as supporters, and to cause trouble to give him a bad name.

Speaking more generally about the culture of corruption, the colonel claimed that most of the upper echelons of Ukraine's police were controlled by officers who had paid the administration big money for their commissions: 'The man in charge of our region paid seven hundred thousand dollars for his position. They get the money back through corrupt schemes of their own. Kuchma, Yanukovych, organised crime – they are all intermeshed.' The cost of a colonel's epaulettes was between $50,000 and $150,000 and even a sergeant had to pay five hundred dollars.

One of the men said: 'We all joined the police to fight crime, not to be part of a criminal gang. But that is what police forces have become. We are organised crime.' They believed that most of their colleagues, like them, wanted to do an honest job and were ashamed of taking part in the vote-rigging, but most were too scared to prevent it. Another added: 'The men are told their job is to make sure nobody pees in the voting boxes and that nobody kills anyone else at the polling station. But as to tampering with the voting, well, we are told to turn a blind eye. Who are honest police going to turn to when we know most of our superiors are criminals themselves?'

An intensive internal investigation was under way at police headquarters to discover who had sent the unsigned letter to the parliamentary speaker, and they knew some of them were already suspects. When asked what the consequences would be for them if their identities were revealed, the men made gestures denoting shooting. The completely matter-of-fact response was chilling because it was an insider view. Police officers, they said, had carried out murders at the behest of senior commanders; some of them had sons working in the police or wives who were teachers who would also be dismissed or punished.

I was in no doubt they were telling the truth and were who they said they were, but unbidden, they produced their MVS identity cards. Some had covered their names and only revealed their photographs, but two showed us the entire card, complete with names. They drove John and I back into the city. As we parted and shook hands, these brave and modest men thanked me for taking the trouble to see them. I can find words for most occasions, but this time I was speechless.

A few days after my piece about the police officers appeared in the British press and had been translated by Ukrainian news outlets, I went to a Kuchma press conference in the presidential administration. A spokeswoman for the interior ministry in the Kharkiv region had already called the men's allegations lies, but said the officers would be 'guaranteed safety if they have the courage to give their names'. There was no reason to believe any government guarantees of safety, especially when the official line was that the officers were lying. Scores of journalists were packed into the hall for the press conference and there was standing-room only. A journalist asked the president about my story. Sitting at an elevated rostrum, Kuchma dismissed the piece in 'a foreign newspaper' and 'felt sorry' for the journalist who he said had obviously written it to order. Kuchma did not know I was sitting a few rows in front of him and was taken aback when I interrupted to say I had written the article and certainly not at somebody's instruction. There followed a short exchange and Kuchma called my piece a 'political provocation' and hastily changed the subject to alleged opposition intimidation of Yanukovych supporters.

As accusations were traded between the two camps, other forces in Ukraine wondered whether they could exploit the situation. For two years before the elections, a group of people who had prospered in the Soviet era intelligence agencies and the army had nostalgically hoped that they could come to supreme power in Ukraine in the way Putin, a former KGB colonel, had restored the power of the secret police in Russia. The focus for the designs of the Ukrainian Soviet sentimentalists was former head of the Ukrainian intelligence forces, General Volodymyr Radchenko.

On 17 November the All-Russian Officers' Conference issued a curious statement addressed to Ukrainian officers and the Ukrainian people. It said that someone with a criminal past – Yanukovych – could not be president, but that they could not trust Yushchenko either. In order to ensure relations between the two countries did not deteriorate, they advocated Ukrainians elect as their leader either Radchenko or Socialist Party chief Moroz. Moroz could have, in theory, stood in the second round if Yanukovych dropped out, because under Ukrainian regulations the run-off would then have been between the leader of the first round and the person with the next largest share of votes who wanted to stand (Moroz had come third in the first round). But how Radchenko could have been a candidate remained a mystery.

Yanukovych had never been a very elegant public speaker and when he did talk he often put his foot in his mouth, as with the infamously ill-judged reference to anyone who did not vote for him as *kozel*, roughly meaning 'arsehole' or 'wanker'. He had baulked at taking part in televised political debates saying he preferred his actions to speak for him. But that lofty strategy had been imperilled by the revelations about electoral abuse and under Ukrainian election rules the two candidates in the run-off were to take part in a TV debate. If one of them refused, the other was allowed to appear on national TV using the entire time allotted for the debate. Yushchenko's camp was eager for the debate to go ahead because it would be the first time in the election campaign that he would have a chance to explain his policies on nationwide TV. Reluctantly Yanukovych agreed to the encounter, which was broadcast live throughout Ukraine on the evening of 15 November.

To limit their candidate's scope for embarrasing himself, the Yanukovych camp insisted on a bland format that virtually excluded real debate. Each candidate was to make statements and ask questions that had previously been supplied to his rival.

They faced each other standing behind separate rostrums with a moderator telling them what subject was next on the agenda and how long they could speak for.

Yanukovych opened by saying that he had been reluctant to take part in the debate but had relented after many of his supporters had pleaded with him. 'I will speak in the way that I believe an honest citizen should speak, looking you straight in the eyes, with respect towards people in a principled and honest way.' He pointed to economic improvement during his time at the helm and said that Yushchenko, during his nineteen months as prime minister and earlier as head of the national bank, had brought Ukraine to economic ruin. He did not mention that throughout the last ten years of that time of economic ruin, the man in charge of the country was his patron, President Kuchma. He promised closer relations with Russia through dual nationality and the Single Economic Zone agreement. Yanukovych appeared more aggressive than Yushchenko, but often spoke haltingly, with long pauses between words. Yushchenko spoke more articulately, promising to improve the economy and stamp out corruption. But his statements were so packed with dry information, especially statistics, that they left many viewers with glazed eyes.

Yushchenko stressed that he was not hostile to Russia, which he regarded as a strategic partner, but he said Ukraine needed closer relations with the EU and that membership was only possible if there was a change of government. 'This government tells us that Europe doesn't want us. My friends, I ask you, would you want as a partner a corrupt government . . . a country where the law does not function, where your rights mean nothing, where a telephone call from the presidential administration or from a government office in Kyiv is far more important than the whole body of Ukrainian laws?'

Both men accused each other of lying and Yanukovych said that he hoped God would forgive Yushchenko. Neither candidate struck a knockout blow, but the exchange had been a great success for Yushchenko because it was the first time millions of Ukrainians had seen him perform during the election period, and many were amazed that he was not the Nazi devil portrayed in the regime's propaganda.

Most independent commentators agreed that Yushchenko had appeared more honest than Yanukovych, but that overall their performances had been pretty equal. Quick as a flash after the debate, though, the Russian news agency Itar-Tass, a Kremlin mouthpiece locked in a perpetual wrestling match with the truth, reported a poll by the French Bordeille Fund which, they said, showed sixty-eight per cent of those questioned thought Yanukovych had won the debate, versus twenty-three per cent for Yushchenko. Other media picked up the piece. However, all inquiries by journalists wanting to contact the Fund for comment failed, and it turned out not to exist. Or, more likely, it existed in the imagination of Putin's spin doctor, Gleb Pavlovsky, on loan to the Yanukovych team.

Before the first round, Yulia Tymoshenko had urged opposition supporters to turn their country into 'an orange nightmare' for Kuchma and the regime. In the weeks before the second round, Kyiv and many other cities and towns were festooned with orange ribbons and flags tied to fences, lamp posts, trees and car aerials, and worn by people as armbands or wound round hats and rucksacks. Yanukovych's blue and white campaign colours were almost nowhere to be seen in the capital. At night his thugs often slashed the tyres of cars decorated with orange ribbons or flags.

Intimidation was rife with the regime using undercover security services to threaten people. The Yushchenko campaign chief in the Poltava province east of Kyiv, Ivan

Baryliaka, was threatened by three gunmen in civilian dress who surrounded him as he arrived at the hotel used as the opposition HQ. They held a pistol to his head and then smashed his car windscreen, but not before Baryliaka and his son noted the number plate of the gunmen's car. It had the prefix 'MI' which designated a militia (police) vehicle. They called the police who arrived at the hotel as the three gunmen pulled up for a second time, only to see them show their official IDs to the police, who then left. The Baryliakas escaped without waiting to see what the gunmen would do next. There was no police investigation and the hotel refused to allow the opposition to continue using it.

Despite the overwhelming evidence of electoral fraud and the domestic and international criticism, the regime decided to brazen it out. It had never countenanced handing over power. But neither had it expected such a groundswell of support for Yushchenko. The government had no alternative to its strategy of cheating and its only option was to carry out fraud on a still grander scale. Putin also emphasised his support with another visit to Ukraine to meet with Kuchma, Yanukovych and Medvedchuk ahead of the second round.

As the vote approached, Yushchenko told his supporters: 'Don't be in a hurry to leave the polling station. Be at the polling station the entire day, particularly after 8pm, when the voting stops and the counting starts. We want the first ones to know the result of the election in your polling station to be yourselves.' The opposition said it was fielding tens of thousands of election monitors and Yushchenko pledged that hundreds of thousands of his supporters would take to the streets if the government tried to steal the election.

On the eve of the second round, Yanukovych and the man who nominated him as his successor, President Kuchma, went on television to warn that the opposition was planning to overturn a Yanukovych victory by violent revolution. Kuchma said: 'We all know that revolutions are planned by dreamers, are accomplished by fanatics, and the resulting situation is exploited by dishonourable people. There will be no revolution.' He said the opposition was endangering democracy. Yanukovych also warned Yushchenko he was determined to remain: 'New authorities are in power. You simply haven't noticed. They are already at work. You must understand that they are here to stay and you cannot dislodge them.'

Yanukovych was confident of Russian spiritual as well as temporal support, and the Russian Orthodox Church openly backed him. While repeatedly saying they were neutral, priests of the pro-Moscow Orthodox Church in Ukraine distributed pro-Yanukovych literature and called the prime minister a man of peace and unity, while condemning Yushchenko as an extreme nationalist. The independent Ukrainian Orthodox churches and the Catholic Church declared that taking part in election cheating was sinful, but did not engage in overt lobbying. However, they did not need to. If a person was a member of these Ukrainian churches it meant *ipso facto* they were inclined to cherish their country's independence much more than any Yanukovych.

The interior minister, Mykola Bilokon, warned that his police and special troops would swiftly crack down on any protestors challenging the result of the second-round election. He boasted that after the result – by which he meant a Yanukovych victory – he and his senior colleagues would spend three days drinking to celebrate. The binge was probably scheduled at the new luxury home set in two acres of the Kyiv region's most beautiful countryside that Bilokon had received for his work. Others in the regime's ignoble aristocracy were also given luxury properties.

One of Bilokon's neighbours was the transport minister, Heorhiy Kyrpa, whose own mansion stood amidst fourteen acres. Kyrpa controlled hundreds of millions of dollars from the railway's vastly lucrative freight services, and from international loans to improve the country's communications. The minister was also deeply involved in the regime's election effort, and during the first and second rounds of the election, unscheduled trains packed with thousands of people involved in the absentee voting scam travelled around the country. Most significantly, he had diverted hundreds of millions of dollars into the campaign coffers. When Kyrpa did this, he, like his colleagues, could not imagine the regime losing, and thought the missing money could be concealed by a friendly audit or replaced from fresh embezzlements. It was to prove a fatal mistake.

One student from Pora, Oleh Mirchuk, summed up the prevailing mood of readiness and defiance: 'Of course there is apprehension. But we are not going to lie down and accept fake results as has happened for the past thirteen years since independence. We want democracy and to have lives where we are not controlled by the whims of criminals. People will stand up this time.'

The night before the run-off election between Yushchenko and Yanukovych, 20 November, brought storms and blizzards to large parts of the country and many places began election day without electricity. Crude ballot stuffing and widespread multiple absentee voting were again the biggest scams. There was also more violence. A Nasha Ukrayina member of parliament, Yuriy Orobets, was beaten up in Mukachevo by thugs linked to the provincial governor. In all the reported cases of violence the victims were opposition supporters. The government would have loved to publicise incidents of violence against their supporters by

Yushchenko activists – witness the egg episode – but they failed to find any such examples. In Kyiv, activists from Pora lay down in front of buses carrying employees from the state energy company, Naftohaz, who had leaked information that they were being forced, under threat of losing their jobs, to take part in the absentee voter scams. The person in charge of one bus suggested unpersuasively: 'These people are going out for a picnic. The weather is bad in Kyiv so they are off for a picnic.'

While some people were leaving Kyiv to vote, others were arriving to vote repeatedly in the capital. At least seven buses came from Cherkasy south-east of Kyiv. Most of the voters, who cast ballots five times at different polling stations, were students pressured to take part in the cheating. Yushchenko supporters tried to stop the buses leaving but police vehicles escorted them out of Cherkasy. Apparently some hundred and fifty thousand people had used absentee ballots in Kyiv – although the true number had to be divided by five or ten or fifteen depending on the enthusiasm of those voting.

The mood was sombre among Nasha Ukrayina supporters when the polling stations closed at 8pm. Everyone knew that the government was determined to hang on to power and was prepared to use every underhand technique available to do so. Exit polls indicated Yushchenko had beaten Yanukovych by a margin of up to eleven per cent. When the polling stations first closed, the CEC had reported voter turnout in East Ukraine similar to the nationwide average of around eighty per cent. But as the voting results became known, the architects of the cheating schemes realised they would need to show many more votes for Yanukovych than they had predicted in order to cancel out the high pro-Yushchenko vote in districts they could not control. Some hours later the CEC's voter turnout figures inexplicably rocketed. In Yanukovych's Donetsk stronghold it soared from seventy-eight to 96.2 per cent, and in neighbouring Luhansk the turnout was adjusted from eighty per cent to 89.5 per cent. In several eastern districts, turnout was apparently forty per cent greater than during the first round. The adjustment in turnout figures was later estimated to have added 1.2 million votes to the total for Yanukovych.

The opposition realised that the regime was pressing ahead with mass falsification. The CEC announced figures that stretched credibility to insane degrees, claiming that ninety-seven per cent of the Donetsk electorate which voted for Yanukovych. In the early hours of Monday morning, Yushchenko defiantly announced the opposition would not accept the government's attempt to steal the election and the population braced itself for a fight.

The place where they were to make their stand and which was to become familiar to TV audiences all over the world was at the point where Kyiv's main boulevard, Khreschatyk, meets Independence Square – the Maidan. There in the early hours of Monday morning, Yushchenko had asked his supporters to meet at 9am. Opposition activists from Pora had started to pitch tents near the Maidan at 2.30am that morning. Independence Square had been refurbished since its drabber Soviet days when its central features were two large fountains. In the last years of Soviet rule, under the freer regime initiated by Gorbachev, the Maidan had become a public meeting place for pro-democracy and pro-independence activists. There were often political speeches and busy knots of men and women in intense discussions at Kyiv's Forum.

Khreschatyk, like much of the rest of old Kyiv on the west bank – called the right bank by Ukrainians – of the river Dnipro, had been obliterated during World War Two. As the

Germans advanced in 1941, retreating Soviet forces planted timed bombs in buildings along Khreschatyk without warning the civilians who remained in Kyiv, many of whom were killed – far more than the handful of Germans who died. The city was again devastated in fighting when the Germans retreated. After the war much of Khreschatyk was rebuilt in its handsome pre-Revolution style, using old architectural blueprints and new German prisoners of war. The prisoners, many of them captured at Stalingrad, worked for a decade before the few thousand who survived were allowed to return home. Their meticulous handiwork, carried out with characteristic German diligence, is far superior to the shoddy Soviet-built high-rise apartment blocks on the outskirts of the capital and on the left bank of the Dnipro that were constructed later.

In the mid-nineties the Kyiv mayor embarked on a thorough refurbishment of the capital's centre and the potholed road, lined with chestnut trees, and the broken pavements were renewed; the grey, bleak state-owned shops selling sausage, vodka, cheap clothes and shoddy shoes, were privatised, and goods with designer labels appeared in glitzy new store fronts. Replicas of ancient churches that were blown up by Stalin in the thirties or by retreating Soviet forces in 1941 have also been reconstructed as faithfully as possible.

The square was also renovated, although its centre is still taken up by a fountain. Some works of art sprang up which seemed a pixilated hybrid of influences from ancient Rome and Walt Disney. Two large underground shopping malls were constructed on both sides of Khreschatyk below Independence Square. The malls are entered from a network of old pedestrian subways which run beneath much of Khreschatyk and Metro stations near the square. Drab and unlit during the Soviet era, after independence these labyrinths rapidly became lively showrooms for the entrepreneurial spirit, crammed with stalls and kiosks selling fruit, vegetables, canned goods, cheap clothes imported from Turkey and China, electronic goods, booze and flowers. Scores of buskers sing and play, and beggars beg.

Leading off Khreschatyk are steep, cobbled streets that lead to the parliament and the presidential administration buildings, both around a quarter of a mile away. Kyiv is built on many hills, and old cobbled tree-lined streets snake up and down the city, through the many parks and past baroque churches. Unexpected places provide vistas of the Dnipro, around a mile wide in places and speckled with sandy-beached islands. The river winds through the capital from the north down to the Black Sea, the route that attracted Viking traders more than a millennium ago and gave Ukraine its few centuries of forgotten glory.

Pora had asked the city authorities in advance, and had been granted permission, to hold a meeting at the Maidan on the evening of the election. Until then Pora activists had held gatherings in the riverside old town area of Podil and some of their number had already been living in tents there. On Monday morning, several thousand, mostly young people, carrying banners in Pora's distinctive yellow and black colours, marched up to the Maidan. They shouted 'Yush-chen-ko, pres-i-dent' and passing cars mimicked the slogans with their horns. Drivers shouted out an old greeting sometimes used as a battle cry: *Slava Ukrayini* – glory to Ukraine.

Pora leader Vladyslav Kaskiv said he was initially concerned that few people would come to the demonstration and, as he led the marchers up towards the Maidan, that the authorities would try to stop them reaching their destination. But nobody hindered them. The city authorities knew that the overwhelming majority of Kyivites supported Yushchenko and were not disposed to go against their own voters' wishes. The regime was still fixated on keeping the protestors away from the Central Electoral Commission building that had been the opposition's intended focus for demonstrations after the first round.

Perhaps the officials at the presidential administration who masterminded the election fraud plans thought that it was too unseemly to announce their man as winner first thing Monday. But just after 11pm that evening, the CEC declared that, with ninety-nine per cent of the vote counted, Yanukovych had a thin, but unassailable, lead of 49.4 per cent to Yushchenko's 46.7 per cent.

Putin had nevertheless congratulated Yanukovych on his 'victory' on Monday even before the provisional result was announced by the CEC, and long before the official result. The Russian election monitors in Ukraine issued a report saying the poll had been 'transparent, legitimate and free'. Others, though, disagreed. The EU, the US, the OSCE, the Council of Europe and Ukrainian election monitors condemned the elections and called on the government to conduct new polls. In Brussels, the European parliament's chief observer said the election result defied common sense and had more in common with a North Korean election.

Over the following days more and more reports emerged about the breathtaking scale of cheating, and it became clear that the level of electoral abuse far exceeded that in the first round. The regime had staked everything on winning regardless of how obvious the falsification methods. But ahead of the second round the opposition had again urged people to gather with video, stills cameras and tape recorders evidence of the cheating and much of this was aired on sympathetic local radio and television stations, especially Channel Five, and published on the Internet.

SBU intelligence forces were, secretly and unofficially, furnishing the opposition with excerpts from conversations they claimed were recorded between key Yanukovych campaign staff which seemed to bear out suspicions that results from regional election centres that were supposedly being transmitted directly to CEC headquarters were, in fact, first going to a computer terminal controlled by one of presidential administration chief Medvedchuk's underlings. There the result was adjusted in Yanukovych's favour before being sent on to the CEC. One recording of conversations between senior Yanukovych campaign staff and important election commission figures concerned the access codes needed to tap into the election computer system.

Another, shortly before the result was announced, contained what were identified as the voices of Medvedchuk and Yuriy Levenets, a Yanukovych campaign staffer, discussing CEC chairman Serhiy Kivalov's failing nerve:

Levenets: Greetings on democracy's holiday!
Medvedchuk: The same to you, Yura. [Kivalov] is panicking. He says he's not getting anything.
Levenets: He can't be getting anything. The boys are finishing up now; he'll have it all momentarily – literally in fifteen to twenty minutes.
Medvedchuk: But he says that something's broken down.
Levenets: No, it's all fine. He can't have anything right now. He doesn't have any information at all over there. It's all under my control.

Apart from Medvedchuk and Levenets, the telephone intercepts contained voices identified as those of Eduard Prutnyk and Serhiy Klyuyev, both important Yanukovych aides, as well as CEC chairman Kivalov.

The recordings showed that the real controls were at a secret location and the person operating the computer at CEC headquarters was like one of the monkeys in the early space programmes – the chimp rode at the pinnacle of some very sophisticated technology but, despite the illusion, controlled nothing. This was a high-tech interpretation of Stalin's maxim that it was irrelevant who people voted for; the important thing was who counted the vote.

The evidence of abuse that had been slowly growing since before the first round had by now become an avalanche that outraged people's pride and pressed them out on to the streets of Kyiv and other cities. Over the following days the crowds in the Maidan grew as people arrived by car, bus, train and plane from around the country. The demonstration became like a huge living organism which always grew larger at night after people left work, so that at times it was half a million or even a million strong. It was impossible to see the entire mass of people from any single vantage point on the ground.

On the Tuesday, as snowflakes fluttered against his face and settled on his hair, Yushchenko told the crowd: 'I am even more convinced than before that what we are doing in this freezing cold now should have been done in 1991. Because this world is always fair, you always have to pay a price. Perhaps today we are paying for the fact that thirteen years ago this was not done. I am sure, dear friends, that today, every minute, we are changing Ukrainian society.'

Yushchenko called on demonstrators to go to the Ukrainian parliament where an extraordinary session was scheduled. The opposition wanted to pass a motion of no confidence in the election results, but the government MPs failed to turn up so that there would be no quorum. Instead Yushchenko was abruptly declared president at an emergency session of parliament and symbolically took an oath of office on a sixteenth-century bible as hundreds of thousands of people cheered him outside. After accepting the title of president he appealed to law-enforcement officials and the military 'never to turn your guns against your own people'.

Yushchenko was criticised by a haughty Kuchma for turning the parliament into a circus by the impromptu inauguration. But Yushchenko later explained: 'We believed that we had to send a signal to society and voters that the declaration of the results in favour of Yanukovych was false. There were not yet that many people on the Maidan and we had to demonstrate to millions of people that we had enough strength, power and faith to do everything possible to overturn the falsifications and win elections fairly. Taking the oath in parliament was a political and moral act. Undoubtedly from the legal standpoint it was incomplete. But it was necessary to show that the fraud and the lying was far from the end of the story.'

What Yushchenko had done was to force both individuals and organisations to side either with him or against him. Some city and regional governments, as well as army and police units, now pledged allegiance to Yushchenko, raising the spectre of civil conflict. A former army general and an admiral, as well as serving police officers, appeared alongside Yushchenko or on Channel Five to condemn the falsifications and appeal to their fellow servicemen not to use force against the demonstrators. Three of Ukraine's biggest cities declared that they recognised Yushchenko as president and Kyiv said it too disputed the official result. Soon its local government would throw its weight behind the opposition and provide vital services like rubbish clearance, emergency medical services and ambulances on standby close to the Maidan, clean water and portable toilets.

Late on Tuesday night two members of the CEC, Andriy Mahera and Ruslan Knyazevych, said the commission was preparing to issue final results on Wednesday but that there was so much evidence of misdoing they would not endorse the results with their signatures. They urged others on the commission to do likewise. Despite these two and the deputy head of the CEC, Yaroslav Davydovych, refusing to sign, the majority said the result was correct and the CEC pronounced Yanukovych winner of the second round during a rowdy meeting. It declared that he had gained 49.46 per cent of the vote and Yushchenko 46.61 per cent.

Opposition supporters greeted the announcement defiantly. Yushchenko addressed them from the snow-swept stage on the Maidan and said: 'They want to put us on our knees to show that we are nothing but a rabble to them and that they can manipulate us. But I beg you not to be depressed by the election commission announcement. This government has done what we expected it would. It was always their plan to remain in power at any cost. But I want to pledge to you that my fight against the regime will only become more effective and stronger.' The opposition said it was challenging the results in the supreme court and thus the CEC's declaration was not final until the coalition's complaints about electoral abuses had been reviewed.

The tug in loyalties among the security services was increasing tension, and one way or another the situation had to be resolved soon. The opposition was getting stronger and the regime could not afford to wait much longer if it was going to use force. Yanukovych went on television to condemn the opposition saying 'a group of radicals has set itself the aim of splitting Ukraine by violence and illegal methods. They are following a previously prepared scenario.' The head of his campaign staff and governor of the national bank, Serhiy Tyhypko, announced that Yanukovych was preparing to be inaugurated as president.

In a move that indicated how the election was now becoming a story of global significance, 150 Ukrainian diplomats stationed around the world, risking their careers, issued a statement saying: 'We cannot remain silent and observe a situation which could call into doubt Ukraine's democratic development and destroy the efforts of many years to return our country to Europe.' Within days the number of diplomats condemning their own government had risen to 357. The election, they asserted, had been 'turned into a shameful war against our own people'.

Back in Kyiv, citizens debated whether the declarations by security service members would make an immediate violent crackdown on the opposition, which controlled the entire centre of the capital, more or less likely. Fears of possible violence increased when trains and scores of buses brought thousands of Yanukovych supporters sporting blue and white campaign colours into the capital from East Ukraine at the start of the weekend following the election. Yanukovych asked them to help him end demonstrations aimed at overturning his victory saying they amounted to 'an unconstitutional coup'.

Alarmed by the situation's potential for violence, which could spill beyond Ukraine's border, the international community started to become more closely involved. EU foreign policy chief Javier Solana told the European Parliament's foreign affairs committee that 'the country is now at the crossroads. We cannot rule out the outbreak of violence.' Washington announced that it did not recognise the results shortly after Yanukovych was declared winner. Secretary of State Colin Powell said: 'It is time for Ukrainian leaders to decide whether they are on the side of democracy or not, whether they respect the will of the people or not. If the Ukrainian government does not act immediately and responsibly, there will be consequences for our relationship, for Ukraine's hopes for Euro-Atlantic integration and for individuals responsible for perpetrating fraud.'

For the moment the security forces held back. The rapid pace of events had rattled the government and heated arguments broke out at meetings between Kuchma, Medvedchuk, Yanukovych and other top regime members about how to respond. The balance was tipping in favour of the opposition with more defections from the military and security services while the flood of demonstrators from all over Ukraine arriving in Kyiv continued unabated. Some, including Yanukovych, argued that force had to be used swiftly.

Chapter Eleven

ORANGE AGENTS

The demonstrations were gradually developing a routine. Those people staying in the tented city would breakfast early on meals prepared in field kitchens whose smoke, rising up to meet the descending snowflakes, lent a pleasant rustic odour to the camp. A mass, held jointly by Orthodox and Ukrainian Catholic priests on the stage, began the day officially. A Nasha Ukrayina deputy, Mykola Tomenko, would often be the first person to address the crowds with a summary of overnight events and an agenda for the day. Other politicians, usually including Yushchenko and Tymoshenko, would appear in the morning or later in the day. There would be visitors who would bring greetings from around the world: from student, human rights and political groups, and from Ukrainian diaspora communities. Foreign politicians came to show support including Poland's Solidarity leader and former president Lech Walesa. Estonia's youngest member of parliament stayed in one of the tents for weeks.

Ukraine's top rock musicians provided daily concerts and foreign musicians came to perform and show their support. But it was a song by previously unknown amateur musicians from West Ukraine that rapidly became the demonstrators' anthem. The group, called Greenjolly, composed a snappy tune to go with lyrics partly inspired by a Spanish revolutionary song but which also wove together slogans chanted at the demonstrations and phrases satirising the gangster *ponyatia* slang used by Ukrainian criminals and Yanukovych. The song's first defiant lines proclaimed: *Razom nas bahato, nas ne podalaty*! – 'Together we are many and we cannot be defeated!' Everyone quickly learned the words and recordings on cassettes and CDs were sold from stalls on the pavements and in the cavernous subway passages beneath the city's streets. The politicians danced to the tune on the stage and the crowds kept the chill at bay by dancing in the Maidan.

The song's composers, a local television presenter and a sound engineer, did not receive a penny from their hit, although they did not complain. In the spring of the following year, the song was voted by Ukrainians to represent their country at the 2005 Eurovision song contest. The 2004 contest had been won by Ukrainian singer Ruslana who was also a fervent Nasha Ukrayina supporter and who had begun a hunger strike to protest against the mass election cheating. Greenjolly's Orange Revolution hit failed in the international competition but it has continued to sell in enormous numbers in Ukraine since it was first heard on the Maidan.

The politicians commandeered a building nearby to hold their conferences, promising to keep their supporters informed about negotiations with the government and consult them about any important new steps. Some of the important proposals were in fact outlined to the demonstrators and put to a vote, inevitably receiving uproarious and unanimous assent. It was a morale-boosting glimpse of something that could be if the protests were successful. One bitterly cold evening Yulia Tymoshenko put forward a proposal that if Kuchma did not agree to some demands he should be blockaded in his official residence and put under effective house arrest. The proposal received a resounding endorsement.

Giant television screens showed close-ups of speakers on

the stage for those on the periphery of the crowd. Much of the time, events at the Maidan were broadcast live on Channel Five. The pictures showed people of all ages: young couples; middle-aged couples; elderly couples; parents with young children and babies; groups of teenagers; knots of people clustered around Georgian, Polish, Italian, Irish, British, French, Estonian, Lithuanian, Latvian, American, Canadian and a score of other nations' flags; family groups spanning three generations; young military cadets in uniforms; proud, elderly decorated veterans in Soviet uniforms and some in UPA guerrilla uniforms.

One young man, Mykola Hyrniak, brought his five-year-old daughter to the demonstrations. She had an orange bow in her hair and her father held her aloft on his shoulders so that she could see the stage. He said: 'I was a teenager when Ukraine became independent and we all hoped there would be a great future. We were disappointed and the governments cheated us and tried to fool us. We kept quiet and maybe they thought we would always keep quiet. They were wrong. We don't want a country run by bandits. We want a normal country where we can work and we can be free and have a government that works for us.'

Another young man, Oleh Krypko, joined the protestors with his St Bernard dog whose leash was adorned with orange ribbons. 'This is our unique chance to become better people, to preserve our dignity,' he said.

Banker Hennady Hamar, said, 'I am so tired of what has been going on in Ukraine. I want my son to have a different kind of life.'

Retired seventy-year-old schoolteacher Dmytro Schwartz arrived with his eleven-year-old grandson Davyd and told him: 'This is Ukraine's rebirth and you should remember that.'

A thirty-five-year-old carpenter, Oleh Kokot, said: 'We

need the new election to be filmed to prevent fraud and we need observers from Europe. It must be free and totally fair. The people can't be stopped now. They are like a horse that has been set free.'

Ihor Tokarivsky, a twenty-three-year-old lawyer from Lviv, said: 'When Yushchenko called on people to go to Kyiv, tens of thousands of people in Lviv immediately started making preparations to come here. In our family we knew it was our duty to come and everyone wanted to go to Kyiv so we had to decide on who would go and who had to stay to look after things in Lviv. So I'm here, my mother is here, my cousin, and my brother-in-law. If Yushchenko gives the word we will take these buildings by storm. If necessary we'll take them down brick by brick.'

Ihor's family is my family. His mother, Dara, is my cousin and they are the part of our family, on my mother's side, that I met for the first time when I visited Ukraine in 1990. Ihor and his sister, Iryna, had been children then and now he was a lawyer and she a doctor. Ihor's father stayed in Lviv because he was organising pro-Nasha Ukrayina activities there. Iryna could not come because she was heavily pregnant but her husband, also called Ihor, and also a doctor, had answered the call to go to Kyiv.

They had been in Kyiv several days before I received a message they were in the capital. I found them at a building a few hundred metres away from the Maidan called the Ukrainian Home, a large, relatively modern concert and exhibition centre which, when I first entered it in 1990, was still functioning in its original purpose as a Lenin museum. To the sound of wailing from Communist hardliners, the Lenin artefacts, along with a huge Lenin statue that stood in Independence Square, were carted off soon after the USSR fell apart.

When the demonstrations began, the Kyiv authorities gave permission for out-of-town demonstrators to rest, sleep and eat in the building. The floors were full of people, mostly young, asleep or sat on the floor chatting in excited groups. Volunteer doctors had organised medical bays and scores of people were queuing up to receive medicines for chills caught standing for hours in sub-zero temperatures. Volunteer cooks were producing a steady output of hearty dishes – meat, potatoes, and traditional, filling Ukrainian dishes of *holubtsi* and *varenyky*. Hot drinks were dispensed from canteen urns. The food and medicines had been donated both by ordinary Kyivites and businesses from the capital and elsewhere, who had also brought warm clothing and sleeping bags that now lay in huge piles for anyone to choose what they needed. One prominent gangster from the western city of Ivano-Frankivsk, where Yanukovych had suffered the egg attack, drove hundreds of miles to the capital in his swish four-wheel drive with a convoy of his gang members in other vehicles, to deliver warm clothing to the protestors. He told a friend of mine who travelled with him, 'Yes, I might be a criminal but that doesn't mean I want my country to be run by criminals. And certainly not Russian criminals.'

My wife, Iryna, and I were both working eighteen-hour days and staying in a rented apartment about fifteen minutes' walk from the Maidan. We invited my four family members to stay there so that it turned into a mini-Maidan with everyone coming in at different hours, sometimes to snatch some sleep or grab a bite to eat or just to take a hot shower before venturing out, in the case of Iryna and myself, to report on events and, for my relatives, to help create them.

Iryna's father, Stefan Chalupa, had been in the UPA Ukrainian guerrillas that fought against the Nazis and then against Soviet forces. He had been captured and given a life sentence by Communist authorities in Poland but released after eight years following Stalin's death. In the 1960s her family had emigrated to the US, and there in New Jersey were avidly following the unfolding drama. You could hear Stefan's old fighting spirit revived as he phoned us regularly and demanded blow-by-blow accounts of what was happening. He did not feel fit enough to fly to Ukraine but he was proud that his journalist daughter was now in the front ranks of a different type of struggle in the long battle for Ukraine's freedom.

Excitement at taking their fate into their own hands and the frisson of danger caused by the possibility of attack by the security forces generated an electric atmosphere among the demonstrators. With each day still more people turned up to join the demonstrations, and more army and intelligence service officers mounted the stage to declare they would refuse orders to attack peaceful protestors. Academics, artists, religious leaders, sports stars, musicians and other celebrities appeared on the stage to declare their support. In a country where most people had few things to be joyful about, there was immense pride in Ukraine's sporting heroes – the world heavyweight boxing champion, the world chess champion, Olympic medallists, soccer legends. These turned up at the Maidan and the government did its best to prevent news that they were joining Yushchenko on the stage to show their solidarity.

It seemed as if everyone in Kyiv was wearing something orange which as a political campaign colour was a complete innovation for Ukraine. Nasha Ukrayina had chosen orange because it was free of past political connotations such as red for the Communists, the blue and yellow of the flag which would put off ethnic Russians, and the red and black colours of Ukrainian nationalism. The fashion industry had decided on orange as the colour of the season for autumn 2004 long before, and Nasha Ukrayina organisers, aware of the choice, knew that orange clothes would be readily available for their supporters and that the streets, shop windows and television commercials would be a blaze of orange providing free advertising for the opposition. In the freezing cold the orange colour seemed to radiate a cheering and warming glow.

The nucleus of the Maidan was the tented city which Yanukovych supporters said was a den of iniquity and illness. Actually it was surprisingly clean and tidy, and the mood was cheerful. Alcohol and drugs were not allowed in the camp and their exclusion was enforced by uniformed personnel who were also on guard to prevent violence being stirred up by pro-government provocateurs. It was probably too cold for sex but romance, though, did flourish in the camp and more than a dozen couples who met at the Maidan eventually got married.

The uniformed groups also mounted patrols in Kyiv. In fact the crime rate in the capital during the period of demonstrations fell by a third, even though the police had all but disappeared from the streets.

Pora had been singled out for harassment by the authorities because they recognised that its excellent organisation and appeal to young people made it extremely dangerous. The government labelled it an extremist, radical group that promoted terrorism and said it was a creation of the US as part of Washington's plan to dominate the former Soviet space, accusations that were repeated almost verbatim by some Western commentators of the kind that, during Soviet times, had defended the USSR however atrocious its behaviour. The World Socialist website suggested that Pora had been developed largely by US organisations. In ponderous Socialist-speak, it declaimed that Pora's purpose was 'to implement a plan prepared well in advance to bring Ukraine more firmly under the control of the US and open up the country more fully to international capital'.

Pora leader Vladyslav Kaskiv freely admits that the group took foreign grants to help its organisation. Pora activists gathered at a tent camp in Crimea in the summer of 2004 to learn about the practical aspects of organising demonstrations. Russia and the pro-Yanukovych people called that evidence of a conspiracy to generate a 'Georgian scenario'. To me it sounded like smart forward thinking.

Did the grants to help build a civil society constitute interference in Ukraine's internal affairs? Of course they did – in the way penicillin is a flagrant violation of the rights of gangrene. But there has been no scrap of proof showing that Pora was taking instructions from the US or any other foreign country.

Kaskiv, a dark-haired affable man, was first involved in protests in the autumn of 1990 when he and other students set up tented protest camps in the centre of Kyiv and went on hunger strikes as they 'dreamt about freedom from the Soviet Union and a democratic Ukraine'.

He said he and his friends believed they had won when Ukraine became independent but realised they had been fooled by an old guard and new oligarchs who were both authoritarian and corrupt. He emphatically denied that the demonstrators were taking orders from abroad: 'People don't demonstrate for weeks in the middle of winter because they are being paid to. How much would it cost to pay hundreds of thousands of people each day to come out? You couldn't do it. A bunch of Yanukovych demonstrators really were paid to set up their own tents and they lasted a couple of days. The Orange Revolution happened because people believed passionately in the cause of freedom. It was all from the heart.'

Pora was especially adept at using new technology that its mostly young and well-educated members exploited expertly and imaginatively. Computers, the Internet and mobile phones were used for an effective information network that disseminated news and meant the organisation could mount protests rapidly and provide support for one another, as when the authorities raided local offices and arrested their members. The Internet was vital in an environment where all but one of the big television stations was controlled by the regime. Apart from posting straightforward information on the Internet, opposition supporters displayed a talent for wicked humour that satirised the regime in cartoons, video clips, photographs and songs. There was an Internet mini-series using cuts from a famous Soviet-era comedy movie about escaped convicts, with the dialogue transposed to events about the election and with Yanukovych as the main character. A real film clip featuring the prime minister collapsing after being struck by the famous egg was adapted in various cruel ways. Yanukovych's wife, Lyudmylla, addressing a crowd of her husband's supporters in Donetsk, said – in all seriousness – that the demonstrators in Kyiv had become addicted to drugged oranges being handed out in the Maidan and were thus zombified and incapable of quitting the protests. The clip of Mrs Yanukovych's voice was turned into a rap song. Pora reacted quickly and with humour to such developments. The day after Lyudmylla Yanukovych's allegations, oranges impaled upon syringes adorned the tented camp.

Uppermost in the minds of the opposition leaders was how to avoid a violent suppression of the protests by the authorities. But ordinary people, individuals and groups, began cooperating and coordinating their activities, sometimes as if by instinct. All had the same goal in mind – to show the government it could no longer dictate to them. There was no single, identifiable instant when it happened, but for everyone there came a moment when they realised that the protests had turned into a revolution.

Yushchenko had now become more than the leader of a party – he had become the focus of the hopes of millions of his people and despite the terrible toll taken by the poisoning, he now showed he had the strength to shoulder the heavy responsibilities that were piled upon him.

When he appeared at the Maidan he was flanked by an array of politicians and other prominent figures whose words and faces showed they were driven by the same sense of fervent commitment that had brought hundreds of thousands of people to the square. Somebody who from the beginning stood out through her ability to communicate in a spellbinding way that immediately lifted the spirit was Yulia Tymoshenko. Her firebrand, impassioned eloquence enthralled the crowds and provided a rousing complement to Yushchenko's more restrained style. She had been his deputy when he was prime minister and now she seized with both hands the opportunity to be his partner in shaping Ukraine's future. She was proud of her close working relationship with Yushchenko which she said was built 'on mutual trust, respect and a shared moral outlook on what needs to be done in Ukrainian society'.

She denied she was motivated by a personal hatred of Kuchma, although it is hard to accept that she could not bear a grudge against someone who had sent her, her husband, and some of her close associates to jail. She did say of

Kuchma, though, 'I know that nobody exists that has committed bigger crimes against Ukraine, her interests, and the Ukrainian people. If he is not made to answer before the law for what he has done then I think there is little justice in this life.'

If she had been given free rein, Tymoshenko would have led, like the heroine in Delacroix's stirring painting about the French Revolution, *Liberty Leading the People*, demonstrators to seize the presidential administration building and the parliament and hurl Kuchma and Yanukovych in jail. One night during the first week of demonstrations, she led thousands of protestors up from the Maidan to block off both ends of the street containing the presidential administration offices, which under Kuchma were the real seat of power. If not for Yushchenko's insistence on keeping as closely as possible within the constitution, Tymoshenko might have unleashed a charge and thousands in the crowd would have liked nothing better. It might have worked but it might also have given the government an excuse to order the use of force. Police troops that were reluctant to attack peaceful protestors might have felt differently if faced with a rampaging mob.

Tymoshenko seemed to have boundless reserves of energy despite only a few hours' sleep each night, and she told the protestors: 'I know you are cold. I know you are wet and want to go home. But we must never given in.' In the mornings she would appear on the stage with her blonde hair braided in a romantic peasant fashion and which some said looked like a halo. There is something of the mystic about her and she once told me: 'I do not separate my life and my faith. Because for me faith is simply faith in love, goodness, justice and, as in the fairytales, that good always triumphs.' Some indeed called her 'Goddess of the Revolution' or 'a Ukrainian

Joan of Arc' but most of the crowd affectionately called her 'Yulia' or 'Yulka'.

Tymoshenko showed she was willing to take the same, and perhaps greater, risks than the demonstrators. After the protestors surrounded the presidential administration she agreed to go inside the heavily defended building for a meeting with regime representatives. Many of her own supporters advised her not to go inside because they feared the regime would arrest her, or worse. She calmly walked in and everyone waited in the night as thick snowflakes fell. When a beaming Tymoshenko emerged she was greeted with a tremendous cheer. She had confronted the beast in its own lair and had returned triumphant. It was a breathtaking combination of showmanship and courage. On another occasion Tymoshenko approached the line of black-clad interior ministry troops with their large, grey shields propped on the ground in front of them like Roman legionaries, and attached an orange rose to one of the shields.

Months after the demonstrations she told me of her exhilaration during the revolution: 'If you can experience such times once in your life, then your life has been worth living.'

From the first days of protest there were rumours of an imminent crackdown by the security services. The regime had used its bullyboys during both rounds of polling and the interior minister had issued warnings that sounded as if he was spoiling for a fight. Thousands of interior ministry special troops were deployed during the week to form a heavily armed cordon between demonstrators and key government buildings housing the presidential adminis-tration and the cabinet of ministers and parliament. People walking around side streets and the courtyards of buildings in the centre of the city unexpectedly came across rows of buses and minivans, their exhausts belching smoke as engines ran to keep the occupants warm. Mostly the curtains of the vehicles were drawn to hide their occupants, but occasionally an unsmiling, expressionless face would stare back at passers-by. Knots of troops smoking outside would stop talking at the sight of strangers.

When the CEC pronounced Yanukovych the winner on Wednesday 24 November, Kuchma invited Yanukovych, Medvedchuk and the inner circle to toast their victory at his smart government villa at Koncha Zaspa, just outside the capital. But the celebrations were muted and nerves were frayed. The very fact that they had to knock back champagne and vodka at the villa was galling: the protestors in Kyiv had blocked off access to all the key buildings where such a reception would usually have taken place.

On Thursday 25 November, opposition coalition leader Yuriy Kostenko told me, after he attended a meeting of Nasha Ukrayina's top leaders, that, 'Some interesting things are happening: Ukraine's intelligence agency is coming over to our side and we're creating a national guard. There have been hundreds of soldiers and policemen asking who they should report to. They want Yushchenko as their commander-in-chief.'

The SBU also had their own armed forces and when the regime announced that the entire security establishment, including the SBU, was behind the government and ready to suppress disorder, the intelligence service quickly distanced itself from the statement.

It then transpired that the head of the SBU, General Ihor Smeshko, who despised Yanukovych because of his links to crime and corruption and also because the erudite spy chief thought him uncouth, had decided to send an even clearer message. In what Yanukovych took as a direct affront to him, two senior officers from the SBU, generals Oleksandr Skybynetsky and Oleksandr Skypalsky, had emerged on to the Maidan stage alongside Yushchenko. One of them was a reserve officer who advised Smeshko, the other retired, so Smeshko could take the position, if necessary, that they were not actually serving officers. However, it was clear to everyone the two generals were speaking for Smeshko when Skybynetsky addressed all security service personnel: 'We are calling on you to avoid any action which could bring you into confrontation with the people who you are sworn to protect.'

The regime was relying on special units of the MVS troops to spearhead any crackdown. The top MVS generals, including Interior Minister Mykola Bilokon, had been hand-picked as regime loyalists and were enthusiastic participants in the regime's culture of corruption. Yanukovych had invested considerable effort and money to get the security apparatus behind him, but now serious cracks were appearing in the government's attempt to assert absolute control. Army and police units and their officers in various parts of Ukraine had either declared they would disobey orders to move against the protestors, or – worse – had vowed to defend them. Many had turned up at the Maidan in their uniforms to show solidarity. General Mykhailo Kunitsyn, military commander for West Ukraine, promised that his soldiers would not 'act against their own people'. Police units from Ivano-Frankivsk escorted thousands of protestors the hundreds of miles from West Ukraine and through the police roadblocks around the capital that were designed to deter them.

On Friday 26 November, senior EU international mediators including the presidents of Poland and Lithuania flew into

Kyiv, and at round-table talks with all the parties secured an agreement that only peaceful methods should be used to resolve the crisis, a development that Yanukovych thought represented a retreat by the government.

The next day the same people who had prematurely toasted victory assembled again at the villa, and this time were joined by a clutch of generals from the MVS, the SBU and military intelligence. The atmosphere on this occasion was even more irascible than the earlier conference and Yanukovych was incensed by the humiliations he had suffered in the intervening days. The regime's election scenario had called for him to be ensconced safely as president elect by the weekend, and for the opposition to accept that it had once more been outmanoeuvred. But things had gone badly off script. The government had anticipated opposition protests, but nothing on the scale they now faced and they were taken aback by the intensity of the international criticism at the electoral fraud. The supreme court had ordered that Yanukovych could not officially be declared winner until they had investigated the opposition's allegations about election fixing, and that very day, parliament had voted not to accept the second-round results, passing a no-confidence resolution concerning the Central Election Commission.

Yanukovych was being prevented from entering his own office by demonstrators and now there were noisy protesters outside the villa.

SBU chief Smeshko was present at the meeting and said that Yanukovych and some of his political allies from East Ukraine were tense and wanted a crackdown on the protestors. They called on Kuchma to declare a state of emergency and for action by the security forces to break the protestors' siege of government buildings. Yanukovych, for his part, did not believe the supreme court had the authority to counter the CEC's declaration that he was the election winner, and insisted he be inaugurated. Smeshko said that Yanukovych became furious when Kuchma gave a lukewarm response to proposals for a crackdown, and asked the president if he was selling him down the river. Kuchma replied tartly that if Yanukovych felt so brave he should go to the Maidan and display his courage there.

Smeshko said that he warned the assembled group that most soldiers would refuse to attack peaceful protestors and the demonstrators would resist any aggression against them. He then challenged Yanukovych to order his faithful MVS minister, General Bilokon, to launch a crackdown if he was willing to take responsibility for what followed. A livid Yanukovych did not reply, which Smeshko took to mean he was not willing to risk bloodshed.

All this time, a TV journalist and camera crew were waiting in the lobby to produce footage for the evening news showing how the government was persevering unruffled by the anarchy of the orange revolutionaries. Kuchma summoned them in but Yanukovych could not contain his rage. Viewers saw him petulantly throw down his pen and stalk out.

These accounts of what happened at that meeting have emerged piecemeal from people who are, of course, disposed to portray their actions in the best possible light. Kuchma's own acount is that he believed a de facto decision had been taken to avert violence.

Tymoshenko, however, told me she understood that, on the contrary, a decision to use force had been taken. 'I think that, according to the information we have, all the significant players gathered at Kuchma's country house – Medvedchuk, Yanukovych, the generals of the SBU and the interior ministry,' she said. 'They came to an oral agreement to launch an attack. And who directly gave this oral command doesn't matter because this was a joint decision.'

On 28 November there were ominous troop movements and Yushchenko and Tymoshenko warned the demonstrators that an attack was expected that evening. Long columns of MVS troops had been spotted heading towards the capital. The order to deploy them had been given by an MVS general, Serhiy Popkov, and at around midnight there were between ten and fifteen thousand MVS troops, perhaps more, in or on the outskirts of Kyiv.

Yushchenko, Tymoshenko and other senior Nasha Ukrayina members were at this stage holding feverish meetings with representatives of the security services, some of whom were now firmly on their side. Scores, possibly hundreds, of armed SBU officers were in the crowds at the Maidan and Smeshko said they were going to do their best to defend the protestors. SBU snipers were on rooftops around the city centre and elsewhere.

One official at the presidential administration told me that the scale of the protests had startled his boss, Medvedchuk. He said Medvedchuk was advising Yanukovych, and both were unwilling to compromise. 'They are waiting to see what armed forces Yushchenko can muster to his side. If he really does have significant forces on his side, they will not use force, but if they feel he does not have a sufficient number of guns on his side they will use armed force against him.' The source said that Putin's envoy to Ukraine, Boris Gryzlov, had made an initial promise that if there was an attack on the protestors, Russia would support the Ukrainian government diplomatically against the inevitable storm of international criticism. Later the Kremlin apparently retracted the assurance.

That week Kyiv was abuzz with rumours that Russia was

planning direct military intervention in Ukraine, and that Moscow had already secretly sent some Spetsnaz special forces. There was much speculation about their task. Some believed they would be used to open fire on demonstrators because Ukrainian troops from the army or MVS could not be relied upon to do so. The British journal, *Jane's Intelligence Digest*, said its sources 'confirmed five hundred members of Russian Spetsnaz forces from the Vityaz Special Forces division in Bryansk were deployed at a Ukrainian interior ministry military base in Irpin, near Kyiv. Two transports flew them into the Gostomel aerodrome near Irpin between 1 and 3am on 24 November and a third transport flew into the military aerodrome near Vasylkiv, Kyiv.' *Jane's* said the Russian forces were there to evacuate Kuchma and his immediate family if the 'Orange Revolution' turned violent. Some of the Spetsnaz troops, the magazine said, acted as Kuchma's and Medvedchuk's personal bodyguard, indicating the two men no longer trusted Ukrainian forces. The Spetsnaz troops were also detailed to remove secret documents from the presidential headquarters.

Tymoshenko told protestors after she came out of the presidential administration that she had seen Russian special forces inside, something she confirmed to me again months later. Tymoshenko had good reason to know what Russian uniforms looked like. In the run-up to the elections, the Russian prosecutor-general had demanded her extradition to Moscow to face charges of corrupting senior Russian army officers during her days as an energy magnate. The Russian military was entwined in the notorious barter deals her company used as a method to pay for Russian gas, and bringing the charges just before the election was an obvious Kremlin ploy to bolster their champion, Yanukovych. Tymoshenko, coming from East Ukraine, would easily be able to spot a

Russian accent and would also be able to identify a Russian uniform, as one of Moscow's corruption charges involved her supplying the Russian army with overpriced uniforms.

Another source with a Ukrainian intelligence background told me that the Russians were removed in a panic in December as conjecture about their presence mounted. They had been transported in civilian buses and in civilian dress to Odessa, where they were spirited out of the country but during the journey one of the buses had crashed on a highway about two hours' drive south of Kyiv near a small town called Kryve Ozero. Again I thought it would be wise to have witnesses on a story as sensitive as this one, and I travelled there with Volodymyr Ariev, whose investigative reports for Channel Five television were not only excellent journalism but had won him a well-deserved reputation for honesty and courage. When we reached Kryve Ozero, locals told us there had indeed been a ghastly accident where a bus had hit another vehicle making an illegal turn in the highway. We went to the hospital and were told that sixteen people, all Russians who said they were heading to a conference in Odessa, had been treated for light injuries. They had been swiftly removed by another bus. Only the bus driver, whose legs had to be amputated, remained in the hospital but was in no condition to speak. The hospital allowed us to see the register of names of the injured, and the local police confirmed they all carried Russian passports but refused to give further information. And that was where the intriguing trail ended.

As news of the MVS troops heading for Kyiv spread throughout the capital, the protestors braced themselves for a confrontation. They were by no means defenceless. Among them were hundreds of former soldiers who had donned new camouflage uniforms and boots, wore forage caps and orange armbands, and communicated with one another by walkie-talkie. These were the stewards who guarded the tented city against provocations by Yanukovych supporters, ensured that drugs and alcohol were not used by the demonstrators, and patrolled the city centre. Most of these men had themselves served in the army – as in Soviet times, there was still mandatory conscription for Ukrainians – and some of the older ones were veterans of the war in Afghanistan. They said they would resist any attempt by the authorities to break up the demonstrations. They were always courteous and I never saw any of them swagger, but they were impressive and it was obvious they took their responsibilities very seriously.

One of them was Leonid Shust, twenty-two, a tall, burly history student, who had spent two years doing national service and belonged to a group called Soldiers of Free Ukraine – one of three quasi-military formations in the Maidan. He said the groups were well disciplined and he was confident they could handle any attacks. 'If there is any attempt to cause trouble we are here to stop it. We are here to fight for democracy.' I asked him how they would resist armed soldiers without weapons. Shust just said: 'Everything that might be necessary is available.' The new justice minister, Roman Zvarych, told me in 2005 that another opposition member of parliament had control over a stockpile of weapons which had been cached a few minutes' walk away from the Maidan.

It was not just the groups in uniforms who were prepared to resist. Other demonstrators said they were ready to stand their ground even if that meant violence became unavoidable. One student called Andriy said: 'I don't know anybody here who wants a fight. But we are not scared and we know that we cannot remain silent. If we have to fight the police, or army, or government thugs to get democracy, then so be it.'

At the military intelligence headquarters, Tymoshenko said there was a feeling of foreboding as the night wore on. The army chief of staff, General Oleksandr Petruk, had finally managed to get through to the MVS and warned them that General Popkov's troops would not be facing helpless demonstrators, but would be confronted by army units and Spetsnaz detachments from the SBU's own armed forces.

As rival Ukrainian officers traded threats, demonstrators were facing down interior ministry troops outside the presidential administration as they had every evening since Tymoshenko had led them to the sprawling, white, five-floor complex, which took up most of one side of Bankova Street and had come to symbolise everything the opposition loathed. Both ends of Bankova Street were sealed off and the double row of security forces had erected a metal barricade in front of themselves. Beyond that, as a precaution against anyone who might be tempted to drive a vehicle into their ranks, were flatbed trucks carrying tons of sand to convert them into heavy and sturdy mobile barricades. The security services on and around Bankova Street were formidable. In the courtyards of nearby buildings were reinforcements from the notorious Berkut unit – the Ukrainian for 'Golden Eagle' – from the interior ministry special forces. Thousands of other special forces units had been deployed in different parts of the capital, some with armoured vehicles.

The protestors clambered atop the trucks and waved their flags and banners. Other Yushchenko supporters approached the metal barricades and stood inches from the police who viewed them warily through their plastic visors. And then the opposition deployed one of its most emotive tactics – their voices, raised not in angry chants but singing melodic, traditional Ukrainian folk songs, some of them lively, others filled with melancholy.

The troops were bewildered and glanced at one another. Expressions softened and smiles flickered across some of their faces. There was another surprise as women – young, middle-aged and elderly – all cheerful and smiling, strolled up to the police lines and placed orange chrysanthemums and roses in the perforations in the men's shields. Other bunches of orange flowers had been tied to the metal barrier. Some of the girls flirted with the police and the young men looked around awkwardly, not knowing how to react. The women gently chided them, asking: 'You're not going to shoot at us are you boys?'

Someone started to sing the Ukrainian national anthem. I knew the rather doleful words. Growing up in England, I had learned them at a time when singing them in Soviet Ukraine would earn the performer a long, possibly fatal, stretch in a hard-labour camp. Many people, on both sides of that barrier, would have had relatives who, during the wars, purges, massacres and other twentieth-century horrors inflicted on Ukraine, had suffered or had even been killed for standing up for their nation or simply for being Ukrainian. During Soviet times the government made it difficult and dangerous for Ukrainians to learn about their own history. Yet, many Ukrainians did know it, taught in hushed tones about past tragedies and glories; religious beliefs had been discreetly passed on; the forbidden words of the national anthem had not been forgotten.

Unspoken emotions rippled across the barricade. Many that evening and during the long, freezing days and nights of protest had thought about the courage of their ancestors. Some had felt their proximity, as an almost real part of the crowd urging on and emboldening them.

As people sang the anthem, one young policeman glanced behind him to ensure his superiors were not watching. Then a patch of mist appeared, alternately spreading and fading on his visor in time to the tune, as he silently mouthed the words of his national anthem.

In the early hours of 29 November, General Popkov said that he was going to withdraw his troops and for the moment the threat of bloodshed receded.

Immediately, a desperate scramble began to cover up the truth about who had ordered the deployment. The MVS said its troops had been involved in exercises to test the battle-readiness of its Kyiv garrison and that the manoeuvres had nothing to do with the political crisis. The obscure Popkov immediately claimed the entire idea for the deployment and withdrawal of troops had been his – something dismissed as absurd by those familiar with the strict chain of command procedures. In November 2005 Popkov gave a peculiar explanation of his actions in an interview in the *Kiyevskiy Telegraf* newspaper in which he said he had ordered the troop movements in order to provide a shock warning to both sides that the dangerous conflict was heading towards bloodshed. He said: 'I wanted to let those hot heads cool down by doing that, on both sides. It is one thing to talk and to call for specific actions and quite another to understand and see what you are pushing people into. It is better to take pictures of yourself against a background of troops in formation than to try to destroy the monolith of a well-organised special forces structure or use it against the people.'

Popkov confirms that the MVS special forces were issued live ammunition and contradicts himself during the interview by reiterating he acted alone but later admitting 'The command to hold a practice alert came by mobile phone'. A contact had told me in December 2004, a few days after the armed intervention scare, that intelligence forces had monitored instructions being given by mobile telephone and some of the communications were from a high-ranking Russian diplomat. Popkov refused my request for an interview, specifically to ask who had given the command by mobile telephone and why, if the whole exercise was a piece of theatre to bring people to their senses, was live ammunition issued?

Only a handful of people had the authority to issue such orders and they included President Kuchma, Prime Minister Yanukovych and the interior minister, Bilokon. Medvedchuk would have been heavily involved in any such decision. Popkov's explanation, assigning noble motives for his actions, sounds far-fetched and is similar to that of others in the military and security services who strove to depict themselves, after the outcome of the Orange Revolution, as unsung saviours and patriots who had been secretly working for the good of their country. That might indeed be the case for some, but Popkov's explanation sounds as if for one reason or another he is protecting those who issued the commands that brought Ukraine so close to civil warfare.

Tymoshenko was in no doubt who ordered the deployment: 'Yes of course it was the government who tried to bring in armed militia from the interior forces and distributed live ammunition to them. They gave them only oral commands, not written ones, because nobody had enough spirit left – not the president, not Medvedchuk, and not the interia minister – to issue written commands to take up arms against their own people.'

She said the events of that tense night were a watershed because both the opposition and the government understood henceforward that neither the army nor the bulk of the MVS forces were prepared to attack the demonstrators. 'They had reached the moral boundary where they no longer followed the commands of their superiors,' said Tymoshenko. 'You got the impression that Kuchma, Medvedchuk and their team were still at the steering wheel but it was no longer controlling the car.'

Fears remained, however, that the administration could still use mercenaries to attack demonstrators and disrupt the opposition's activities. A few days later there was a call for volunteers to join the groups already guarding the Maidan. More than three thousand people signed up immediately.

Chapter Twelve

PEERING OVER THE EDGE

The opposition was relieved that the immediate threat had receded, but calls in East Ukraine by Yanukovych supporters for autonomy or secession conjured up new fears of bloodshed. Kuchma and Yanukovych warned of civil war.

Nasha Ukrayina now pursued the battle for fresh elections on four overlapping fronts: the Maidan, parliament, the international arena and the supreme court. Their lawyers promised to present abundant evidence of mass falsification of the election results from around the country to back their plea for the supreme court to declare the 21 November vote invalid. In parliament a battle raged to secure three fundamental demands: the dismissal of the Yanukovych-led government, a change in the composition of the CEC, and amendments to election laws in order to curb the government's scope for fraud in any further round.

The opposition knew that international support was vital. The colourful demonstrations had gripped the world's attention and the international community had now become overtly involved because the implications of what was happening extended far beyond Ukraine's borders. Russia's open intrusion had jarred with world opinion, and while Putin was congratulating Yanukovych on victory, Europe and the US had refused to recognise the 21 November election. They were disturbed by clear indications that Putin's Russia was engaged in a risky game to install its own viceroy in Ukraine and wanted to turn back the clock to the time of empire.

The EU and the West were alarmed as soon as the dangers of violence or civil war, stoked by threats of separatism, surfaced. Conflicts, like forest fires, are stupidly easy to start and hideously unpredictable once they have flared, as the savage little wars in the former Yugoslavia had only recently demonstrated, and the West was at pains to prevent a conflict that might draw in neighbouring countries and send refugees streaming out of Ukraine into the EU. The West also wanted to show Moscow that its renewed imperial ambitions were simply unacceptable and did not tally with their vision for Europe's future. Ukraine presented, too, a good opportunity to buff up democracy's lately sullied image: imposing democracy on Iraq had descended into a bloody mess as thousands of Iraqi insurgents refused to be democratised. In Ukraine, however, the demarcation between the forces of good and evil was easily recognisable, and if the dogged struggle proved victorious, the Western democracies could chalk up a much-needed moral triumph. Ukraine now became the political battleground for a war of wills between Russia and the West.

Kuchma had kept out of public view for days as the crisis grew, and only broke his silence to suggest that Yanukovych and Yushchenko should meet for talks. Yanukovych said he was ready to talk but the opposition refused to participate unless government negotiators were headed by Kuchma. The president was adamant he would not be involved, and said it was up to the rival candidates to meet. Nasha Ukrayina member Roman Zvarych, the coalition's representative at the election commission and at the supreme court, told me at the time: 'If the other side thinks that we are ready to sit down around a table and discuss the possibility of Yanukovych remaining president, or to discuss any other compromises, they are mistaken. Such a possibility does not exist.'

As the situation seemed to drift again towards violence, the EU volunteered to break the deadlock and to mediate round-table talks involving all the Ukrainian parties. The team that arrived on 26 November with that purpose comprised EU foreign policy chief, Javier Solana, the Polish president, Aleksander Kwasniewski, and the Lithuanian president, Valdas Adamkus. It also included the secretary general of the Organisation for Security and Cooperation in Europe, Jan Kubis. Kwasniewski and Adamkus were leaders of two countries which had only recently become EU members and had experienced life under Moscow's rule. Whatever the diplomatically phrased reasons Poland, Lithuania and the other former Soviet bloc countries had given for wanting EU and NATO membership, the real reason, understood by all their people, was that membership of these two organisations dramatically reduced their chances of being occupied by Russia ever again. Cognisant of this, Adamkus and Kwasniewski were far blunter in dealing with Moscow and Putin than Western leaders; it was in their countries' interests to prise Ukraine away from Russia's ambit and they proved formidable allies of the opposition.

Moscow was represented by Putin envoy and Russian parliament speaker Boris Gryzlov who made no secret of his support for Yanukovych. Gryzlov apparently felt his job, in the Cold War tradition, was to challenge the points made by the EU mediators and to try to salvage Ukraine's crumbling pro-Moscow oligarchy.

Poland's president, Kwasniewski, who had maintained relations with Kuchma when most world leaders shunned him, was to emerge as the key figure in the discussions. After talks in the Mariyinsky presidential palace the parties agreed to a three-point plan proposed by Kwasniewski, which included verifying election results, potentially annulling those tainted by irregularities, and the renunciation of violence by all sides.

Before the second round of talks, Solana held a preliminary meeting with Kuchma on 30 November and then everyone met the following day. The opposition and the government agreed that they would take into account the supreme court's decision about the 21 November election. They also agreed to a political trade-off which would accede to the opposition's demands for a radical overhaul of the laws and regulations governing the conduct of elections before any next round, in return for introducing the constitutional changes that shifted presidential powers to parliament and would have the prime minister elected by that body. A critical behind-the-scenes contribution by Kwasniewski was eventually to convince Kuchma that if he wanted to salvage some credibility and respect for himself, he would have to agree only to a rerun of the second round of the election not to begin all over again. Initially Kuchma bucked against that counsel, which contradicted the advice of his presidential administration chief, Viktor Medvedchuk. Medvedchuk told Kuchma that if all else failed he should decree completely fresh elections to be held after a cooling-off period of several months, during which they could work out a new scheme for retaining power. Under Ukrainian regulations the two run-off candidates, Yanukovuch and Yushchenko, would be excluded from fresh elections. In the interval the regime calculated it would find a more palatable candidate than Yanukovych who could preserve the dominance of Kuchma's circle. Medvedchuk persuaded Kuchma that without Yushchenko as its presidential candidate, the opposition would fail.

The scheme appealed to Kuchma as it would buy time and even held out a dim hope that his own candidacy might prosper. He made known on 1 December that he was against a simple repeat of the 21 November vote and wanted an entirely new set of elections. The next day Kuchma flew to Moscow for an audience with Putin. Putin was on his way to India and met Kuchma – humiliatingly in the eyes of Ukrainians – at Moscow's Vnukovo airport where he also pronounced that he did not favour a repeat of the second round but preferred completely fresh elections.

On 2 December the European Parliament passed a resolution rejecting the result of the 21 November election and demanding a repeat round be held before the end of the year under conditions that would guarantee fairness. Putin was livid as he saw his plans unravelling. The next day the Duma, the Russian parliament, roundly condemned the European Parliament, the EU and the OSCE for their interference in Ukraine's internal affairs. The Duma warned that the meddling of these organisations could lead to 'massive disorder, chaos and a split of the country'. Putin's foreign minister joined the chorus repeatedly haranguing senior EU officials in Brussels by phone, accusing them of encouraging the Orange Revolution.

The supreme court did not enjoy a reputation for independence as most of its judges owed their positions to Kuchma, and initially the demonstrators at the Maidan thought that relying on a fair hearing from the supreme court was a forlorn hope. But soon encouraging indications emerged that the judges were not doing what the Kuchma regime expected of them. There were a variety of reasons why the judges chose to behave the way they did: many of them, despite their submissiveness over the years, retained a respect for the ideals of a society governed and protected by law; many could not bear the thought of a former convict becoming president; all had heard the secret recordings from

Kuchma's office, particularly one in which the presidential candidate had laughingly threatened to 'hang up for a night, by his balls' a recalcitrant judge from the Donetsk region.

But most of all they were impressed by what was happening at the Maidan, fifteen minutes' walk from the supreme court. Many had spouses and children who had joined the demonstrations, and many had been to see for themselves what was happening. What they saw were decent people chanting slogans about justice in society and the rule of law – concepts they had sworn to uphold. The case they were now hearing was probably the most important any of them would ever be involved in, and their decision would profoundly affect their country's destiny. The way they chose to act provided them with an opportunity to redeem their dignity.

In court, Yanukovych's lawyers found themselves receiving tough grillings from the judges who threw out many of their spurious arguments, prompting fury. Some judges were offered bribes while others received death threats against themselves and their families. The SBU assigned armed escorts to protect the judges and their families. Some of the family members were taken into hiding or sent abroad for safety. But the threats backfired and only served to consolidate the judges' resolve to act independently. Some of them even gave clandestine advice to opposition lawyers on the best way to pursue their case.

Ukrainian TV audiences were gripped when, for the first time ever, the proceedings of the country's supreme court were televised live: prominent government figures were reprimanded by the judges and sensational evidence about election fraud was given by dissident CEC members. On the evening of Friday 3 December, the chairman of the judges, Anatoly Yarema, standing in his burgundy robe and flanked by his colleagues, solemnly read out the decision in a voice that was cracking with emotion. He said: 'The conclusion of the court is that the rules of the electoral law were broken and the exact result of the voters' will across the territory of Ukraine cannot be ascertained.' Therefore, the judges ordered that a repeat of the second round take place on 26 December.

There was euphoria as Yushchenko went to the Maidan and declared victory. Hundreds of thousands of jubilant throats went hoarse through cheering and a party atmosphere prevailed throughout the weekend as the demonstrators saw for the first time that their protests had forced a concrete result.

The agenda for the third round-table talks involving the intermediaries was worked out in a telephone call between President Kwasniewski and President Kuchma on 4 December. The talks started on the evening of 6 December and carried over into the next morning, and helped weave together the strands from the supreme court's decision and the compromise proposals of both the government and opposition. On 8 December, at an extraordinary session of parliament, 402 of the 450 deputies voted for the compromise 'packet'. The CEC was summoned to parliament and then most of them, including chairman Serhiy Kivalov, were humiliatingly dismissed by an individual vote upon each one of them by the members of parliament. Then they watched as the MPs voted in their replacements.

The changes secured to the rules of the forthcoming election were sweeping:

- The number of absentee voter documents that could be issued was slashed from four per cent of Ukraine's thirty-six million electorate to half a per cent.

- People using absentee voter documents would have a stamp inserted in their identity document to prevent multiple voting.

- The Central Election Commission announced plans to use special numbered packets, printed at a secret location, and incorporating security elements to bring tallies of local results to the commission headquarters in Kyiv.

- Ballot papers were to be printed and distributed under greater scrutiny to prevent the use of excess ballots for various frauds.

- Changes were made to ensure that the work of the opposition's local election committee representatives would not be hampered.

- The scope for fraudulently exploiting home voting by the handicapped was severely curtailed.

In an emotional speech at the Maidan Yushchenko thanked the crowd: 'When it was cold, when it snowed, when there was rain, you remained here,' he said. 'You have ensured that we will not be ruled by bandits and their gangster rules any more. You demonstrated a confidence in what you were doing and have given the opportunity for tens of millions of other Ukrainians to see that another kind of Ukraine is possible.'

Referring to the security forces, Yushchenko said: 'I thank the people in uniform who, when there was a test before them, showed they were with the people.'

Many of the protestors decided to return to their homes

across Ukraine. But many others were determined to stay in Kyiv until Yushchenko became president. Natasha Dyonina, a student who had lived since the start of the protests in one of the tents, was optimistic after the events in parliament but expressed a view shared by many of her companions: 'I believe that we can only say we have achieved half the victory at the moment and there will only be a complete victory after the election. I will remain until that day of victory – 26 December.'

Some, like Yaroslav Kostyniuk, a middle-aged construction worker, believed the opposition had conceded too much. 'We should have been sterner with these bandits. Resignation is not enough. They should be held to account. I'm not for bloodshed. But you understand that you must punish bandits otherwise they will repeat their crime.'

The prime minister, who had already directed an outburst against Kuchma at the dramatic meeting discussing the use of force against the demonstrators, suspected more than ever that he was being abandoned by President Kuchma and his acolytes. A week after the parliamentary 'packet' of measures was adopted he accused Kuchma of working to defend his and his family's interests during the election and not the nation's. Yanukovych described his former patrons as traitors and cowards and had some particularly bitter words for Kuchma: 'Ukraine hasn't got a president. If you see one, show me where. Where was he during this Orange putsch? I'm very disappointed that I trusted cowards and traitors who I worked with for these past two years.' He called everything that had happened following the 21 November election illegal and said 'a coup d'état is happening in Ukraine. Lawlessness is getting an upper hand. Decisions are made only under the impact of force.'

His campaign manager, national bank chief Serhiy

Tyhypko threw in the towel, and Yanukovych in return reportedly threw a heavy crystal ashtray at the deserter. Putin's support for Yanukovych also became noticeably muted. On 15 December Medvedchuk travelled to St Petersburg to see the Russian president, but Putin would not admit him into his presence. The Russian spin doctors led by Gleb Pavlovsky were sent packing to Moscow where Pavlovsky tried to worm his way out of the public relations disaster he had helped to create by complaining he had done the best he could with a convict as a candidate.

Yanukovych was left in increasing isolation trying to recast himself as a regime opponent and someone whose reputation had been tarnished by the government's falsifying of results in the October and November votes. Without resigning as prime minister, he said he was taking a leave of absence from government to campaign full time.

The demonstrations in Kyiv and the rejection of the election results caused genuine indignation in some of Ukraine's eastern and southern areas where support for Yanukovych was strong, although not as strong as he claimed. Soon after 21 November there was angry talk of autonomy and separatism in Ukraine's eastern regions. Five days after the election a pro-Yanukovych meeting was held in Donetsk attended by seventy thousand people. Speaker after speaker called the events in Kyiv an 'orange putsch'. The incensed orators – governors, mayors and other senior regional leaders – called for a referendum to be held on the formation of a 'south-eastern republic' to include the cities of Donetsk, Luhansk and Kharkiv. Yanukovych was there, though he chose neither to speak about separatism nor to condemn it.

Senior Russian politicians also showed support for the separatist machinations, and it is unlikely they did so without the Kremlin's approval. The mayor of Moscow, Yuriy Luzhkov, one of his country's most powerful political figures and a vitriolic Russian nationalist, attended as did Parliament Speaker and Putin envoy Boris Gryzlov who said unless Yushchenko called off street protests, there would be 'a split of the country or bloodshed'. It was obvious they hoped in their hearts for both these calamities to befall Ukraine. The opposition believed Russia wanted to 'Moldovise' Ukraine. In Moldova in the early nineties, Moscow backed Russian-speaking separatists in a short but bloody conflict to break away from the Romanian-speaking majority, and ever since the country has remained split, dangerously unstable, with the Russian-controlled section regarded by the EU and the world generally as a wholly criminal state.

For a few days these local leaders, backed by members of parliament from their areas, discussed schemes that varied from autonomy to outright secession. They accrued to themselves powers over the police and army and announced they would no longer pay money into the national exchequer in Kyiv. However, polls showed that Ukrainian separatists and their Russian sympathisers lacked grass-roots support. There were no popular demonstrations backing autonomy, and many senior officials, by no means Yushchenko supporters, distanced themselves or opposed the separatist flirtation.

Soon the ringleaders were backtracking and claiming they had been misinterpreted. A conference of regional leaders, intended to galvanise separatist action, was half-hearted and inconclusive and their support melted away. The opposition demanded that those stirring up separatism should be prosecuted and promised they would be under a Yushchenko government. If anything, the threats of secession ultimately strengthened the Orange Revolution. But the political drama had yet again focused the spotlight on the real and perceived divisions in Ukrainian society that were ripe for exploitation. And one of the easiest places to stir up such passions was Yanukovych's stronghold of Donetsk.

Donetsk was founded in 1869 by Welsh metallurgist John Hughes after he was granted a concession to start an iron business by a Tsarist government eager to develop the farming area for industry. Originally called Yuzivka (Hughesivka) after the Welsh entrepreneur, the town grew rapidly and on the surface there seemed no rhyme or reason to the way its streets and suburbs sprung up. But they were charting a subterranean plan and following the latest discoveries of iron or coal ore as the miners built homes close to the new seams that provided them with work. People came from across the Russian Empire, drawn by the pay which, pitifully small as it was, still represented an improvement for many, and the city expanded exponentially during the Soviet period when Ukraine's Donetsk Basin – Donbas – with Donetsk at its centre, became the Soviet Union's coal and steel powerhouse. From the twenties until 1961, when it grew to a population of more than a million, it was called Stalino before acquiring its present name.

It is now a sprawling place of imposing buildings in the centre fringed by dilapidated high-rise apartments and tiny, squalid, disintegrating houses that have sunk into the earth. When the train draws into the main railway station it passes two gigantic slag heaps. A hundred or so other black man-made hills are scattered around Donetsk and on its outskirts. Fires smoulder for years within some of the slag heaps, exhaling smoke and investing the landscape with a brooding aspect. A faint chemical smell pervades the air.

During Soviet times coal miners were lauded as the elite vanguard of the workers' society and Soviet propagandists wove legends around miners' devotion to Communism. There were reports of miners performing Herculean tasks, most famously Alexei Stakahnov who in 1935 was showered with medals and was honoured with monuments commemorating his achievement in mining fourteen times the normal quota of coal in a single shift.

Donetsk miners were indeed rewarded lavishly by Soviet standards and the city bloomed. A massive planting campaign in the seventies covered the parks, gardens and boulevards with endless varieties of roses and Donetsk was dubbed 'the City of Roses'. Now most of the roses to be seen are the ones bought from flower-sellers and when the Soviet Union collapsed, the mining industry also fell into rapid decline. More than a third of Ukraine's mines have shut since independence in 1991 while three quarters of the remaining two hundred are deemed unprofitable. But successive governments feared the consequences of greater unemployment among the eight hundred thousand mineworkers, who still had enormous political clout. So unprofitable mines were subsidised to operate on paltry, frequently unpaid wages. The previously generous medical facilities mostly vanished and safety inspection became a bad joke: an average of three hundred miners die each year in mine collapses and explosions – the worst record for any mines in the world with the exception of China. Services are held in a tiny chapel in the city centre every time a miner dies. Often they are for several miners at a time. Thirty-five miners died in one accident in 2002 while the previous year fifty-four perished in a fire.

I was taken down the Chelyuskintsiv mine by its administrator, Alexander Potapenko, a former miner who said the conditions there were better than in most others because private investors had backed the operation. He was proud that he had tried to improve safety conditions and that only two people had died there in recent years.

Potapenko, a beefy, amiable man who exchanged curses affectionately with his employees, and I began our journey to the coalface in a lift that descended for seven minutes to a gallery 880 metres below ground. We walked deeper through tunnels supported by arched steel girders, many twisted and bulging from the weight they have borne in the ninety years since the mine was sunk. The final stretch led through a narrow opening into a claustrophobic shaft two feet high. It would have been impossible to escape in an emergency. Here was the mine's most prized possession – a huge machine that gouged out 1,500 tons of coal a day as it moved along a miniature rail track, attended by miners who looked as if they had stepped out of a Dickens novel as they followed the mechanical monster and scraped away at the seam with puny shovels.

The deeper we went, the hotter it became and at the coalface it was around forty degrees centigrade. Most of the miners were stripped to the waist and bathed in sweat. Some mines, in a desperate effort to be profitable, are working at depths of up to 1,300 metres where temperatures are hellish and the technology for minimising the hazard of explosions from methane and coal dust is only just being developed in the West. In Ukraine, the miners' work environment is a bomb waiting to be triggered.

Sashko Skyl, an engineer at the mine, and an Afghan War veteran, spent twenty-one years working in coal mines. He said: 'Before we could afford to eat whatever we wanted, we had holidays on the Black Sea or in rest homes run by our mines. Now people feel they are lucky if they get enough to pay for their rent, sausage to eat and vodka to get drunk on. There are no illusions or prestige any more about this job.

People do it because they have to. It's about survival. I don't want my son working in a mine.'

Cheap labour means cheap coal and iron ore which means cheap steel production. It is through control of the mining industries that Ukraine's richest oligarchs, such as Rinat Akhmetov who dominates Donetsk, have made fortunes. Akhmetov, the son of a coal miner and an ethnic Tartar, was born in Donetsk in 1966. He has used a combination of business savvy, political connections and robust methods to become Ukraine's richest man and, according to *Forbes* magazine in 2005, the world's 258th richest billionaire. Ukraine's miraculous economic growth in 2003 and 2004 was driven to a great extent by exports of that steel to China. Kuchma's son-in-law, Viktor Pinchuk, is also a steel magnate with businesses producing steel pipes for the world's oil and gas industries. Working together the two oligarchs bought Ukraine's largest and most lucrative Kryvorizhstal steel-producing company in a rigged privatisation auction that undervalued the complex by a staggering four billion dollars. Seizing back the plant from Akhmetov and Pinchuk to resell it at its true value became the centrepiece of Yushchenko's pledge to fight oligarchic corruption.

Everything surrounding Ukraine's mining business is seamy indeed. The state was not selling mines that operated and, in any case, no private entrepreneur wanted to take on such large numbers of employees. But many of the mines were acquired after they were allowed to flood so that, on paper, they were inoperable and all their miners and surface staff were made redundant. The new owner, who picked up the mine for a bargain price and pumped it out, was treated as a saviour by the grateful miners, a fraction of the original number, who he then re-hired to send back underground.

It was in the clan's interests to blame the collapse of living standards and decline of the mining industry on Kyiv and to portray Akhmetov and the other oligarchs as good Samaritans. The same individuals dictated what information the region's inhabitants received, because they own or control most of the important media outlets and Akhmetov owns the region's biggest TV station. In a place where only a small minority has access to the independent news available on the Internet, most believed the version served up by the oligarchs or by television beamed in from Russia. Before the elections started, Channel Five was switched off in the Donetsk region by the authorities. Transmission of Ukrainian WBC world heavyweight boxing champion Vitaliy Klychko successfully defending his title in December 2004 was blacked out because he wore an orange stripe on his shorts and after the bout spoke of his support for the Nasha Ukrayina demonstrators

The Donetsk population became used to accepting fanciful statistics showing their region produced an overwhelming percentage of Ukraine's total economic output and that the rest of the country was sponging off them. They had been taught nothing about the Soviet-era massacres of Ukrainians or about the artificially engineered famine, but they had been taught that West Ukraine was teeming with 'traitors' and 'Fascists' who had offered armed resistance to Soviet rule. With no countervailing view, it was easy to paint Yushchenko as an American agent working for NATO or as a Fascist bent on imposing the Ukrainian language and suppressing the Orthodox Church.

Donetsk had been developed as an industrial asset with workers from scores of ethnic backgrounds and a Ukrainian identity was not deeply rooted. For many of the inhabitants, whose parents hailed from distant lands, their own identity was obscure.

Ukraine was merely a geographical identity and it was this region of the USSR that witnessed the evolution of the closest thing to 'Homo Sovieticus' – a being eschewing traditions, culture, national identity and human spirit.

Others, who were aware they were Ukrainian, had been taught that to be proud of Ukraine or to use the Ukrainian language was tantamount to an admission of 'nationalism', the sin that West Ukrainians – baby-murderers and Fascists to a man – were guilty of. Ukrainian was rarely heard in Donetsk. Russian was the common language for the disparate peoples who had settled there but using it was also proof that one was not a Ukrainian nationalist. Much of that Soviet-era mentality has lingered and a visit to Donetsk, with its large Lenin statue and other grim Communist monuments, feels like a journey back in time.

During the elections, Yanukovych's allies in Donetsk promoted a degree of intolerance towards the opposition that had no mirror image in attitudes in the central and western parts of the country. It was at a rally in Donetsk that Yanukovych's wife, Lyudmylla, announced that the protestors in Kyiv were being fed narcotic-filled oranges that had turned them into zombies incapable of leaving the square, a revelation that was received in high seriousness. Her audience – all literate, numerate, adult Europeans – welcomed her explanation because it reinforced their prejudices and meant they did not have to give consideration to other political views.

Cynicism about the government in Kyiv was prevalent throughout the country, but in Donetsk there was a particular type of disdain for central authority and a respect, not merely born of fear, for the colourful characters who ran Donetsk.

During the election I met a young man in his twenties

called Kostya who once had a promising boxing career ahead of him until an injury ended his sporting hopes. Kostya still knew how to use his fists and worked as a security guard and mixed with criminals. He had been paid during the elections to do odd jobs for the pro-Yanukovych campaign. With his lean fighter's build wrapped in a leather jacket, Kostya was a member of one of the intimidating gangs that roamed around the polling stations and would deal with anyone who objected to ballot stuffing or other scams.

He was an engaging, friendly person who could be thoughtful and generous towards others. His very straightforward view was that the type of people he admired – the Akhmetovs and Yanukovychs – had simply grabbed what they wanted and crushed any enemies; this was something, he felt, worth emulating. If you live in Donetsk, Akhmetov is quite impressive: apart from his industrial interests and television station, he owns the finest hotels and restaurants in Donetsk and the city's Shakhtar – 'Miner' – football club, the country's second best after Dynamo Kyiv; he lives in a plush building that had been reserved for visiting members of the Soviet political elite and which he had refurbished opulently, defended by his private army. Working a scam came naturally to Kostya and interfering in the election process on behalf of the people he so admired did not trouble his conscience, especially as he believed most of the propaganda. 'Yushchenko is going to forbid people speaking Russian if he wins,' he said.

There were tens of thousands of young men like Kostya in Donetsk who had been brought up in a city governed for fifteen years by people whose leadership skills might have been gleaned from *Goodfellas*. And it was men like Kostya that the Yanukovych campaign hired by the train and busload to take part in the absentee voter scams, to bully people, and to attend his rallies in Kyiv. And it was to prevent the rest of the country becoming like Donetsk that many more thousands of people froze for weeks on end in the Maidan.

The Kuchma administration could not have carried on its vicious propaganda against the opposition and instilled such fear of civil conflict and separatism without the collaboration of a largely pliant press. But now this most valuable tool for deceiving their compatriots began to slip out of the government's control and its construction of lies, corruption and fear began to tumble down.

There had long been signs of growing discontent among journalists forced to distort their reports in line with the presidential administration's *temnyk* instructions. Some had left their jobs but there was not enough work on the small number of media outlets that refused to kowtow to the regime for all the disaffected journalists. Few wanted to make themselves unemployed so they stayed on, occasionally trying to slip some truth past the censor. Others, however, revelled in toeing the party line and accepting the pay and promotion that came with their spinelessly faithful service.

The opposition had seen that with all the big television stations under the government's control, the only way they could guarantee coverage for their point of view was by securing control of a channel themselves. To that end Petro Poroshenko, an oligarch member of Nasha Ukrayina, bought the Channel Five station in the summer of 2003 and employed some of Ukraine's best-known journalists with a proven record for honesty. But as the elections drew closer, the regime tried to take Channel Five off the air by challenging its licensing arrangements and by other methods; a week before the first round of the election it was still penetrating around half the country including, crucially, Kyiv. Channel Five enraged the regime by providing plentiful coverage for Yushchenko and focusing attention on the regime's shadier aspects. One of its signature programmes was a hard-hitting documentary series by journalist Volodymyr Ariev called 'Restricted Zone' which had exposed government corruption and revealed Yanukovych's criminal past. In Western countries the documentaries would have won awards; in Ukraine they brought governmental wrath.

On 21 October a pro-government member of parliament sued the station for defamation and won a court order to freeze Poroshenko's assets including funding for Channel Five, without which it seemed it would grind to a halt. The station's broadcast licence for Kyiv was also in jeopardy. But the next day Channel Five's reporters and staff appeared en masse live in place of a scheduled programme. One of the journalists, Roman Skrypin, said: 'Channel Five's audience has increased fivefold in a year because of the trust shown by our viewers. The attempt to try to close the channel ten days before the election is an attempt to deprive viewers of an objective view about what is happening in Ukraine.' The staff announced that they would work without pay to keep the station going and warned they would begin a hunger strike if the company's financial assets were not released by 25 October.

The assets were not released and so the hunger strike began. There were regular updates and viewers could see the faces of the presenters and to-camera journalists becoming gradually thinner.

The example of the Channel Five staff pricked the consciences of other journalists. Whilst other TV stations worked according to government instructions in the first round, as the run-off approached journalists became more vexed at the censorship and discussed what they could do. Many began sending open letters of support to their colleagues on Channel Five and petitioned their own employers to scrap the *temnyk* guidelines. Some refused to operate under censorship and resigned. The situation changed dramatically after the second round when the scale of the electoral fraud became known and huge numbers of people emerged for the demonstrations. The lie had simply become too big. Individually or collectively they found the courage to demand a change in policy from the station owners; some walked out, others launched protest actions.

One of the most remarkable protests was by Natalia Dmytruk who provided sign-language interpretations for deaf viewers on the nationwide state-owned UT-1 channel. UT-1 had broadcast only the Yanukovych camp's version of the news, which declared him the election winner. The channel kept silent about the international community's condemnation of the election and it did not show the scope of protests going on in the heart of the capital. Dmytruk later said that she visited the demonstrations with her children and felt uplifted by what she saw: 'I was observing it from both sides, and I had a very negative feeling. After every broadcast I had to render in sign language, I felt dirty. I wanted to wash my hands.'

On the Thursday morning following the election, Dmytruk walked into the studio with an orange ribbon hidden under her long sleeve. As the newsreader delivered the official version of the election results, Dmytruk ignored what he was saying and signed her own thoughts. The ribbon popped out from under her sleeve as her hands motioned to her deaf viewers: 'I am addressing everybody who is deaf in Ukraine. Our president is Viktor Yushchenko. Do not trust the results of the Central Election Commission. They are all lies . . . And I am very ashamed to translate such lies to you.'

As her broadcast finished she was expecting to be fired immediately. But her superiors said nothing although they quickly understood what she had done. When she told her colleagues they congratulated her. That same day more than two hundred journalists at UT-1 went on strike demanding that the station broadcast what was really happening. The action crippled the station and it had to use programming from a station still following the government script. But the next day it agreed to the demands of its staff.

The journalists' rebellion spread. Staff at the large private station, One Plus One, demanded the removal of their news director, the government's most toadying journalist, Vyacheslav Pikhovshek. The channel's co-owner, Oleksandr Rodnyansky, went on air to admit that his station had been distorting the news at the regime's command for the last two years: 'We understand our responsibility for the biased news that the channel has so far been broadcasting under pressure and on orders from various political forces.' Rodnyansky said the station would henceforward broadcast honest and impartial material.

Suddenly Yushchenko, Tymoshenko and the rest of the Nasha Ukrayina leadership, as well as Pora members and dozens of independent commentators, could not keep up with invitations to appear on TV stations that for years had ignored or vilified them. A Yanukovych press conference that only days before would have been covered ubiquitously and cravenly went largely unreported. The faces of the television journalists and presenters were animated. Every studio seemed to be decked out in orange and the presenters wore orange ties, scarves, jumpers, shirts, skirts and boots. As the Christmas season approached it was fitting that

Channel Five should have been the first station to show an orange Christmas tree in their studio.

The inspiring example of the demonstrators in Independence Square had affected the entire country and precipitated a dramatic cleansing process. Though some eastern areas, including Donetsk, still managed to censor news broadcasts, with much of the censorship gone, Nasha Ukrayina and Yushchenko now had a vastly improved ability to get their message across to voters.

The journalists' rebellion was only one of the dramatic ways the Orange Revolution was catalysing a transformation in the attitudes of those who manned the government's apparatus for securing control.

On the weekend that saw violence between interior ministry troops and demonstrators only narrowly averted, some forty men arrived in ten cars at the city of Uzhorod in the Transcarpathian Province that Medvedchuk's SDPU(U) party regarded as its fiefdom. The men refused to speak to townspeople and entered the grounds of a football club owned by one of the SDPU(U) chieftains. The local police and special MVS units, previously obedient to Medvedchuk's representatives, were, like the formerly obsequious journalists, impressed and inspired by the anti-government demonstrations in Kyiv and elsewhere, and suspected the visitors to their town were not soccer fans. They had also received information the men had arrived to stage an attack which was somehow to discredit the opposition. So they rounded them up. A search of the men and their vehicles revealed a large assortment of weapons including machine guns, pistols, knives and clubs. Within hours, Medvedchuk's handpicked governor of Transcarpathia, Ivan Rizak, and officials from Kyiv were applying immense pressure to the local police authorities to release the men.

The incident, along with warnings from Nasha Ukrayina sympathisers within the government, showed that the regime had by no means discarded violence as an option. A week before the 26 December election, Hryhoriy Omelchenko, an opposition MP, claimed to have evidence that up to three hundred AK-47 automatic rifles, as well as grenades and explosives, had been handed over to groups linked to separatist politicians in East Ukraine and that the weapons had come from the Russian Black Sea Fleet's arsenals. A spokesman for the Russian Black Sea Fleet, based in the Ukrainian Crimean peninsula port of Sevastopol, denied the allegations.

Omelchenko, a former Soviet-era KGB officer who also served as a colonel in the Ukrainian intelligence service after independence, said he received his information from serving officers. 'The intention is to use bloodshed to disrupt the election so badly that it is declared invalid. After the violence they will argue that any new election should have neither Yushchenko nor Yanukovych as candidates and fix it for one of their people to win.'

The plan, Omelchenko said, called for police officers from Donetsk loyal to Yanukovych to lead 'small groups of criminals' given guarantees of immunity to cause mayhem. 'I hope that if these people know their plans are no longer secret they will think twice about them and they will throw all these weapons down a well or an old mineshaft.'

On 15 December at a meeting in Mykolaiv, South Ukraine, Yanukovych conceded that he knew that volunteer units were being formed which were ready to come to Kyiv after 26 December to ensure there was no coup, by which he meant a Nasha Ukrayina victory. But he said he was not connected with the groups' organisers. Addressing a rally of his supporters in another southern city, Kirovohrad, a few days later, he again warned that tens of thousands of his supporters were prepared to converge on Kyiv if he did not win.

As part of the raft of compromises negotiated with the government, Kuchma was supposed to fire the interior minister Mykola Bilokon, accused of colluding in the electoral fraud and of abusing his powers on many other occasions. Instead Bilokon was allowed to take temporary leave but retain his title. Nasha Ukrayina member of parliament Yuriy Pavlenko said: 'General Bilokon has proved in the past that he is ruthless and he knows that if Yushchenko becomes president, he will be prosecuted. He has nothing to lose and the danger is that many of these people feel they have nothing to lose.'

Pavlenko said Kyiv police chiefs had successfully resisted a government attempt to replace their chief with a general from Donetsk who was ready to use violence against the demonstrators.

Intimidation and attacks continued against Nasha Ukrayina activists. In the southern port city of Mariupol attackers torched the Nasha Ukrayina HQ with Molotov cocktails. In Luhansk opposition supporters holding a meeting in the town centre were set upon by an organised group of around forty people who attacked them with batons and whips and stole mobile phones and video cameras.

In December information emerged about an alarming but strange incident when police had arrested two men on the morning of the first round of the election who were discovered in a car outside a Nasha Ukrayina office where Yushchenko was working at the time. Police claimed they came to the area because a burglar alarm had gone off nearby and they approached the men in the car, which had

Russian number plates, because they looked suspicious. Inside police found, they said, three kilograms of explosive. The driver and passenger were Russians from Moscow and they were held until released, for lack of evidence, by the new government. They apparently said they intended to use the explosives for fishing. In 'dynamite fishing' explosives are hurled into the water and the explosion stuns fish and brings them to the surface. Yushchenko initially talked about the incident as an assassination attempt but then kept silent about the matter, which raised more questions than it answered.

Furthermore, on 11 December doctors at the Vienna clinic where Yushchenko had been treated confirmed he had been poisoned with dioxin as he campaigned for the Ukrainian presidency.

It was in this climate of suspicion and danger that the presidential rivals clashed bitterly on live television on 20 December in their first face-to-face encounter since the massive street protests began.

Unlike their only previous television appearance together – a strictly choreographed affair at the insistence of the Yanukovych camp – the rematch was played out under Yushchenko's rules. Yushchenko, who at the outset of the election campaign had been mild-mannered, showed that the intervening months had taught him more strident language. He said: 'You viewers may be asking why we two guys are back here again. It's because Mr Yanukovych and his team tried to steal the election.'

Yanukovych spoke mostly in Russian, occasionally slipping into Ukrainian, while Yushchenko spoke Ukrainian throughout. Yanukovych's Ukrainian is less eloquent than his Russian. But in the first debate he had mostly spoken in

Ukrainian. It was plain that he was now staking all his hopes on the Russian-speaking voters and trying to emphasise the differences between East and West Ukraine. Several times he suggested the two presidential candidates should work out a power-sharing compromise. 'You think that you will win and become president of Ukraine. You are making a huge mistake. You will be president of part of Ukraine.'

Responding to the accusations that the protestors were sponsored by the West, Yushchenko said: 'Those people out on the streets are not being paid by anyone. You can see that by looking in their eyes.' He said their motivation was 'they don't want the president of Ukraine to be elected in Russia'. The Nasha Ukrayina leader also forced Yanukovych into a humbling apology for calling opposition supporters 'orange rats' and *kozli* – arseholes.

Yanukovych, meanwhile, said he understood why protestors were opposed to the regime and that he agreed with much of what they complained about. He portrayed himself as also a victim of government chicanery and said that Kuchma had now sided with Yushchenko. Yushchenko called the notion that his rival was separate from the regime ridiculous and referred to him as 'Kuchma Three' – a prolongation of Kuchma's two terms in office. He also mocked Yanukovych's public piety: 'You're a religious person, right? Remember, Thou shalt not steal . . . And then you stole three million votes.'

Journalist Dmytro Ponamarchuk, a political analyst working for the Yanukovych election team, said the government candidate's performance had been disastrous. 'None of those who were undecided, and we calculate that as up to ten per cent of the electorate, will have decided in favour of Yanukovych after that television debate. More likely they will have decided in favour of Yushchenko.' There was no word this time from the mysterious French pollsters who had awarded Yanukovych such high marks in the first debate.

In fact the government conducted its own polls and my contact from the administration showed me the results of two surveys carried out a week before the third and final election. One gave Yushchenko fifty-three per cent compared to Yanukovych's thirty-eight per cent, while the other forecast fifty-six per cent for Yushchenko and thirty-nine per cent for the government candidate. The sets of figures do not add up to one hundred because voters were allowed to register dissatisfaction with both candidates. 'Kuchma has resigned himself to the fact that Yanukovych is going to lose,' my contact told me. A last rally in Kyiv before the election brought only around two thousand Yanukovych supporters out on the streets, the majority having been transported from Donetsk.

Yushchenko looked supremely confident when he arrived in the centre of Kyiv on the morning of 26 December to cast his vote at a polling station on the edge of the Maidan. A little later a huge crowd mobbed him as he came out of the same polling station carrying his youngest child, while his wife held the hands of their other two children. His face, deeply marked by the poisoning, was creased with smiles, and dozens of people pressed forward to kiss him. He thanked his supporters for their courage and perseverance and said: 'I will win. I'm one hundred percent absolutely certain.'

Observers said that there were few disturbances and on the whole the vote passed peacefully. But this time it was the Yanukovych camp that loudly complained they had been the victims of electoral abuse. They claimed the change in election rules relating to voting at home for the handicapped had disenfranchised up to three million voters and suggested, without showing why, that most of these would have voted for Yanukovych. This was the beginning of a long, drawn-out procedure where the Yanukovych camp aped the opposition's recent techniques to challenge the result of the vote.

But during the early hours of 27 December, when three separate exit polls showed he had a big lead over his rival, Yushchenko went to the Maidan to address his supporters. For a month the chant of 'Yushchenko' had echoed around the centre of Kyiv. Now it was modified to a jubilant 'Pres-i-dent Yush-chen-ko'.

Flanked by his wife and his political comrades, Yushchenko bowed to his supporters and said: 'My first thanks are to you. The people proved their power. They rebelled against perhaps the most cynical regime in Eastern Europe. This is a victory for the Ukrainian people, for the Ukrainian nation. Perhaps we have been moving towards this for several centuries. For the past fourteen years we were independent but now we have become free. Today we are turning the page of disrespect for people, of lies, censorship and violence. The people who were dragging Ukraine into a hole are at this moment becoming the past. A new epoch is beginning of a new great democracy. Many tens of millions of Ukrainians have dreamed of this.'

By 28 December, with nearly all the votes counted, Yushchenko's share was fifty-two per cent to Yanukovych's forty-four per cent, according to the country's Central Election Commission. Nearly eighty per cent of the country's thirty-six million voters turned out.

International monitors were satisfied with the election's conduct. OSCE chief Bruce George said: 'The people of this great country made a great step forwards to free and fair elections by electing the next president of Ukraine.'

There were, however, some flagrant abuses observed by monitors at a few polling stations, though many believed the regime deliberately mounted displays of egregious ballot stuffing because it wanted international monitors to declare the election sub-standard. Some observers admitted they had overlooked questionable actions by the Yanukovych camp as long as Yushchenko won the election.

One crucial factor in ensuring fairer elections was the enormous number of election monitors. Yushchenko had called on his supporters to volunteer as 'an army of observers' for the vote and a remarkable three hundred thousand people answered the call, with twenty thousand travelling from West and Central Ukraine to bolster the opposition activists in eastern regions. Thousands of the foreign volunteers present were Westerners of Ukrainian origin. They came from all over Europe, America, Canada, Latin America and Australia, the children, grandchildren, or even great-grandchildren of Ukrainians. Many of them spoke Ukrainian – with an English, American or Canadian accent. Many did not know the language but perhaps could hum the melody of a half-remembered Ukrainian song taught by a grandparent. It is safe to say that most of them were not impartial, but they were fair.

The Ukrainian elections were also a proud moment for international bodies like the OSCE and the Council of Europe, often scorned for not being able to counter obvious electoral fraud when it is happening, and for publishing toothless condemnatory reports months after they can do any good. The OSCE published preliminary reports the day after both the first two election rounds in October and November, and the analyses were immediately used to good effect by the opposition and Western governments. The fact that the

Ukrainian government, however grudgingly, took note of the OSCE criticism showed that despite years of corruption and authoritarianism, Ukraine was not yet the black hole for democracy that Russia and Belarus were swiftly becoming, where OSCE reports were contemptuously ignored.

One of the Nasha Ukrayina monitors sent from West Ukraine to the village of Mospanovo in the eastern province of Kharkiv was a relative from Buchach, my aunt's grandson, Yaroslav Spachuk, who explained how their presence brought about dramatic changes in the third round. 'There were four observers from Nasha Ukrayina. The local Yanukovych people said that if we tried to stay in the area our car and the premises where we were staying would be set on fire. So we stayed about thirty kilometres away because we did not want to risk the safety of the Nasha Ukrayina organisers in the village. There was no doubt that the majority of people really were for Yanukovych but our presence meant that the ballot stuffing that had happened in the previous two rounds did not happen on this occasion. The result was seventy-two per cent voted for Yanukovych and twenty-eight per cent for Yushchenko. Previously only three per cent had voted for Yushchenko. If you allowed that there were thousands of Mospanovo-type frauds happening in the first two rounds, then you are talking about a huge number of stolen votes.'

The regime proceeded to use every legal device to challenge the results of the election and, as Nasha Ukrayina had done the previous month, took the matter to the supreme Court. The court threw out their case but the government managed to prolong its time in power by nearly a month. Yanukovych vowed never to acknowledge Yushchenko's victory and tried to cling on to his prime minister's post, but blockades composed of opposition protestors made it impossible for him to attend government meetings. They claimed his only purpose was to plunder Ukraine for as long as he could.

The Yanukovych campaign team also tried to mimic other techniques gleaned from Nasha Ukrayina. They organised demonstrations in Donetsk, announced their supporters were beginning hunger strikes and set up tented protest camps. They could organise rallies for a few hours but there was little spontaneity or vitality to the demonstrations, which were organised like old-style Communist Party events. The tented camps and hunger strikes fizzled out after an embarrassingly short time. Yanukovych and what he stood for could not inspire the same passion or commitment that permeated the Orange Revolution demonstrations.

The opposition accused the government of using its last moments in power for frenzied illicit distribution of billions of dollars in government assets – property, enterprises, and licences – to its favoured associates. The regime was also trying to hide the traces of a decade of murky dealings. Smoke was seen emerging from the presidential administration courtyards as documents were burned, and the shredder machines did sterling work.

Some of the loose ends were human. The transport minister, Heorhiy Kyrpa, was found in the sauna of his country house with a bullet in his head the day after the poll. It was an apparent suicide and police found a pistol next to his body. But the investigators said they were looking into the possibility of a 'forced suicide'. Kyrpa had been accused of funnelling hundreds of millions of dollars under his ministry's control to fund Yanukovych's election campaign. The railway system, also part of his remit, was used to transport thousands of pro-Yanukovych supporters both to government rallies and to take part in the multiple vote fraud which was one of the chief reasons why the supreme court ordered a repeat election.

The theft of funds had been carried out in the expectation that the government would remain in power and the huge fraud could be covered up. But with the opposition's victory Kyrpa knew he would inevitably be exposed. Rumours abounded that Kyrpa was considering naming his highly placed accomplices in the theft when his life was cut short. Parliament Speaker Volodymyr Lytvyn said he spoke to Kyrpa by phone a few hours before his death and the minister 'did not sound like a man preparing to kill himself'.

The minister's death was the second suspicious suicide of a prominent person linked to the government that month. On 3 December Yuriy Lyakh, the head of Credit Bank, was found with a suicide note beside him after apparently slashing his throat with a letter opener. Lyakh was one of the closest business partners of the presidential administration chief Viktor Medvedchuk, and had been accused of helping to channel the illicit funding of Yanukovych's election campaign.

Some of the regime's other luminaries fled to Moscow. These included Ihor Bakaj who had headed two of the most lucrative areas – the energy business and the vast empire of a department overseeing the state's assets and properties – and had been accused of relieving both of huge amounts of cash for his own benefit and that of his patrons. Ukraine issued an arrest warrant for him on charges of stealing three hundred million dollars but Russia refused to hand him over because he had suddenly become a Russian citizen. It emerged Bakaj had been awarded Russian citizenship by a special decree of Putin's for contributions 'on behalf of Russian culture and art'.

The former interior minister, Mykola Bilokon, one of the

most unsavoury characters in the Kuchma regime, who had boasted he would use force to crush any opposition, also fled to Moscow. He is wanted for questioning in Ukraine on suspicion of abuse of office.

Presidential administration staff made more than two hundred applications for diplomatic passports to the Ukrainian foreign ministry in their last days in power. Yushchenko said he had information that the government was involved in hasty privatisations and distributions of valuable rights and licences to its cronies. He said there had been a flurry of suspicious money transfers including one for seven hundred million dollars.

He promised his government would pursue high-level wrongdoers. He said: 'I do not like the words re-privatisation or nationalisation but where there has been blatant fraud there will be prosecutions.' Yushchenko denied any clandestine immunity deal had been made with Kuchma and said the former president could also find himself being investigated for corruption and taking part in the electoral fraud. 'He is responsible before the law the same as any ordinary person.' Tymoshenko hinted, though, that some sort of deal had been struck.

On 31 December, an embittered Yanukovych finally resigned the post of prime minister. His announcement added extra verve to the New Year's Eve celebrations as hundreds of thousands of Yushchenko's supporters gathered at the Maidan. As champagne corks popped around him, student Yaroslav Rivniy, said: 'This is a great New Year's gift for Ukraine and democracy. We hope this is the beginning of a new era of freedom for Ukraine but it won't really start until all this old guard has gone.' Nasha Ukrayina encouraged the inhabitants of the tent city to disperse but pro-democracy supporters were suspicious of last-minute government skullduggery. 'We will not be dismantling anything. We intend to stay here until Yushchenko is inaugurated,' said Oleksiy Lomtyev. 'Our worry is that if we go, Yanukovych's supporters could set up something in our place.'

After Yanukovych exhausted all the legal challenges, Yushchenko was declared winner on 10 January and was finally sworn in as his country's president on 23 January. It was a sunny day that felt almost like spring. The capital was decked out with orange banners as well as the blue and yellow of the national flag. Polish and Swedish museums lent seventeenth-century Ukrainian historical artefacts for the ceremony, including a mace – the traditional symbol of power of Ukrainian Cossack leaders – and a banner used by one of Ukraine's most famous Cossack chiefs, Bohdan Khmelnytsky.

Yushchenko first took the oath of office in the Ukrainian parliament. More than sixty representatives of foreign countries, among them presidents and prime ministers, attended the ceremonies. President Putin was absent and sent a low-ranking representative; he would not, in any case, have received a warm welcome from the Kyiv crowds. The guests, many of them wearing orange scarves and ties, looked happier than politicians usually look on these occasions and many of them later mingled with the sea of orange supporters who celebrated into the night.

After the ceremony in parliament, Yushchenko went to the Maidan to retake the pledge in front of hundreds of thousands of supporters. The new president said the Maidan would be inscribed in Ukrainian history as a symbol of the country's desire for democracy. He recalled the Orange Revolution 'when the heart of Ukraine was beating on this square'. Yushchenko added: 'Ukraine has opened a new page in its history, and Independence Square has a special place in it. It is a symbol of a free nation that believes in its future.'

Yushchenko told the rapturous crowd about his vision for Ukraine. He said: 'Our way to the future is the way of a united Europe. We, along with the people of Europe, belong to one civilisation. We share similar values. Our place is in the European Union. We are no longer on the edge of Europe. We are situated in the centre of Europe.'

Yushchenko had promised, weeks before the final round of the election, to make Moscow the destination for his first foreign visit as president. It was intended as a conciliatory gesture to mend relations after Putin's and the Kremlin's machinations to prevent him becoming president.

But Yushchenko emphasised that these relations would not be the old master–servant relationship where Kyiv was expected to follow Moscow's instructions. He pledged that Ukraine would only build relations with Russia on an equal basis and in a way that would not obstruct Kyiv's declared ambitions to join the EU and NATO. He was not going to Moscow, as his predecessors had done, in the role of a supplicant.

It must have been an uncomfortable meeting for Putin, whose neo-colonial tendencies had been exposed and who had just presided over the Kremlin's biggest foreign policy disaster since the break-up of the Soviet Union. He was also aware that Yushchenko knew Moscow had been ready to see bloodshed in Ukraine and that the Ukrainian president was not alone in suspecting Kremlin involvement in his poisoning. When he shook hands with Yushchenko, Putin was dealing not only with a new president but with a new country.

EPILOGUE

I visited Ukraine a year after the Orange Revolution to gather information for this epilogue. As I approached Independence Square a few days before the first anniversary I was startled to see tents set up near the Maidan and scores of demonstrators dressed in orange clothes, scarves and headdresses milling around Kyiv's main Khreschatyk Street. I wondered if this was the start of another revolution but discovered that the demonstrators were in fact extras in one of two films being shot about the dramatic events of the previous year. It seemed the myth of the Orange Revolution was going to be safely preserved, but I had come to Ukraine to find out what realities the revolution had yielded and why many Ukrainians were expressing disappointment at its results.

Two ministers told me that there was a lot of disappointment because many of the opposition supporters who froze and risked their safety on the Maidan had interpreted the statements made by the Orange Revolution leaders too subjectively and had heard in them what they wanted to hear – promises that reflected their own hopes and desires but which had not in fact been uttered. One year was not enough to undo the economic mess, crime, ignorance and moral bankruptcy spawned by the preceding fourteen years of corrupt governments since Ukrainian independence, and more than three hundred years of despotic and degrading rule by Communist and Tsarist dictators.

But some things were difficult to blame on misperception

or on the past. People were disappointed because of the acrimonious rupture between the revolution's two main heroes, Yushchenko and Yulia Tymoshenko, who had been appointed as the orange government's first prime minister. None of the major figures in the former government that Yushchenko and his comrades labelled as criminals and pledged to bring to justice had been brought to trial. Former President Leonid Kuchma, after some initial anxiety, was walking with a new spring in his step and with a smug smile on his face. Suspicion was rife that Yushchenko had secretly made a deal granting Kuchma immunity from prosecution for alleged involvement in the murder of journalist Georgiy Gongadze and corruption charges as the price for avoiding bloodshed when the authorities looked set to crack down on protesters.

Veterans of the demonstrations were appalled when Yushchenko signed a cooperation agreement with the former regime's presidential candidate, Viktor Yanukovych, and shook hands with the man he had accused of trying to steal the election. Yushchenko needed Yanukovych's support for the appointment of a new prime minister. He justified the move by saying he could not leave the country floundering chaotically without a government. The deal also let off the hook hundreds of minor bureaucrats implicated in fixing the election results.

Yushchenko said they were small fry and the true culprits were highly placed Kuchma regime members. He explained the absence of prosecutions by saying he did not want Ukraine to behave as a lawless state where people were condemned at a politician's whim. He believed they would be brought to justice once the judicial and law enforcement system became transparent and was shorn of corruption.

From the outset Tymoshenko's government had been beset

by quarrels as it divided into two camps – people loyal to the prime minister and those whose allegiance was to Petro Poroshenko, the oligarch businessman and politician who believed he should have been the prime minister. Instead he was made head of Ukraine's National Security Council, which he turned into a power base from which to undermine Tymoshenko's intitiatives. Sniping by the two sides turned into a bitter feud and as Poroshenko was known to be close to the president the fight was increasingly perceived as a struggle between Tymoshenko and Yushchenko.

Tymoshenko was accused of being a populist and pursuing her own presidential ambitions for 2009 by applying economic policies which the country could ill afford, and which scared off foreign investors, to boost her popularity. Yushchenko was clearly unhappy when her popularity ratings overtook his own.

The factional fighting became increasingly vicious and the government seemed to concentrate entirely on self-destruction and squandering the good will of millions who had voted for change rather than to embark on essential economic reforms. The crisis came to a head with mutual accusations of corruption. Yushchenko fired the entire government. Some members were reappointed but Tymoshenko and Poroshenko were out. The new prime minister, Yuriy Yekhanurov, an able loyal colleague of Yushchenko's, posed no challenge to the president.

Perhaps the corruption accusations were baseless but Yushchenko certainly showed bad judgment in selecting some of his closest advisers and colleagues – people who everyone believed were more interested in exploiting his favour for their own leeching ends than for Ukraine's good. They looked and behaved like the creeps who had gathered around Kuchma like flies to a pot of honey.

I met in Kharkiv with some of the police officers I had seen the previous year and who had told me about how they were being forced to help in the electoral fraud. Two, Lieutenant Colonel Serhiy Zadepriansky and Colonel Ihor Bohadytsia, had been forced out of their jobs before the election campaign started after they refused to take bribes to drop investigations involving criminals with political connections. Bohadytsia said: 'During his election campaign Yushchenko urged police and other security services not to obey illegal orders to help manipulate the election and promised to reinstate those removed for refusing to obey illegal orders.

'But it's been a year and people like us have not been reinstated and matters have got worse. There were only superficial changes and most of the corrupt senior police officials have remained in their posts. They have got back up on their hind legs and they mock us and ask what the revolution we believed in so much achieved.'

They said the new Interior Ministry had twice promised to take up their request for reinstatement and had done nothing. The two also sent a letter to the president but had not received a reply. They were not just disappointed – they were disillusioned and hurt.

Investigations into the killing of journalist Georgiy Gongadze and Yushchenko's poisoning proceeded slowly. Late in 2005 Major Mykola Melnychenko, the bodyguard who secretly recorded former President Kuchma's conversations, returned to Ukraine vowing to help bring Kuchma and his cronies to justice. Preliminary court hearings for three police officers accused of involvement in killing Gongadze began in December 2005. Everyone wondered whether Melnychenko's evidence and that of the accused policemen would lead to indictments against Kuchma and his associates.

One of those with a direct link to Kuchma, former Interior Minister Yuriy Kravchenko who was secretly recorded being ordered to take care of the journalist, was found dead with two bullet wounds in the head in March 2005. Another principal suspect, police General Oleksiy Pukach, fled the country. Other prominent members of Kuchma's regime also fled and were hiding in Russia. One, Ihor Bakaj, wanted for allegedly stealing hundreds of millions of dollars, swiftly received Russian citizenship for his supposed services to Russian culture.

At the Orange Revolution commemoration there was a huge crowd and it was obvious people wanted Yushchenko and Tymoshenko to renew their alliance ahead of the 2006 parliamentary election. Both made feeble attempts to hold out an olive branch and could not find the strength for reconciliation. The people's fervent hopes were once more deflated.

With their forces split, opinion polls showed that Yanukovych – leading the Party of the Regions, representing the former regime – was actually ahead of Yushchenko and Tymoshenko if they ran separately. Informal collaboration between the two and the Socialists before the election and in a coalition government afterwards was mooted. But tension remained high between Yushchenko and Tymoshenko and one presidential adviser even told me a coalition with the Party of the Regions but without Yanukovych was a possibility.

Yuschenko's supporters justified his flirtation with Yanukovych and other oligarchs as intended to heal the divisions within the country, especially with its eastern regions where there had been separatist threats. But as the campaign for the 2006 elections began, Yanukovych and his paymaster, Ukraine's richest billionaire oligarch, Rinat

Akhmetov, ratcheted up hostility to the president. Perhaps Yushchenko should have reached out to the people of eastern Ukraine instead of to the region's oligarchs.

One of the promises Yushchenko fulfilled was to renationalise the Kryvorizhstal steel plant sold to Akhtmetov and Pinchuk in Ukraine's most notorious fixed auction. The two had paid eight hundred million dollars. After fierce legal battles Tymoshenko clawed back the steelworks and at a transparent auction it fetched an astonishing five billion dollars. Tymoshenko advocated more such massive embezzlements should be investigated.

After losing that battle Akhmetov swore revenge. He and more than thirty of his associates and minions were standing for parliament in 2006. With the money he was throwing at the election, Akhmetov and his people were likely to win. Ukraine faced the unhealthy prospect of a segment of parliament working to support the power and avarice of one oligarch.

Russia's ruling party and Russian chauvinist politicians supported Yanukovych's and Akhmetov's party in its election bid. Russian President Vladimir Putin and the Kremlin, determined to avenge the Orange Revolution humiliation, were hostile to Kyiv and Moscow remained Ukraine's biggest problem. Russia decided to use its near monopoly on the supply of gas and oil in the region as an instrument for punishment and to reassert dominance in Eastern Europe. It threatened to quadruple gas prices for Ukraine to crippling rates in 2006. Because of the energy factor Ukraine did not dare to tear up Putin's plans for a Single Economic Zone – a new empire lead by Moscow.

Yushchenko did undoubtedly preside over some great achievements in 2004. He was spectacularly successful in winning Ukraine international goodwill. Complete freedom of speech and of the press became a reality. Corruption remained but was no longer organised and sanctioned from the very top.

But the greatest and most lasting legacy of the Orange Revolution is that it was a psychological watershed for the Ukrainian people where they learned that their voices counted and they could have a say in their country's destiny. The times are over when voters could be treated like a herd of dumb animals by a crooked political 'elite'. All politicians now have to explain themselves before the public. The rupture between Yushchenko and Tymoshenko was sad but not devastating because such things happen in real democracies.

Yushchenko is of a completely different moral calibre to Kuchma. Millions continued to adore him and he can claim to be the true 'father of the country' by giving it freedom. There was great support too for Tymoshenko. Both care for their country and its people and there are other honest and visionary potential leaders.

Yushchenko and Tymoshenko were wonderful symbols of the Orange Revolution but they alone did not make the revolution come about. It was millions of Ukrainians who did that by displaying their will in such a magnificent way. That proven strength is alive. It could lead to a further revolution but it can manifest itself in other ways. I believe it will eventually exert the political force needed to make Ukraine the kind of democratic, fair and above all decent place that my parents and so many millions of their compatriots dreamed about for generations.